THE TRIUMPH OF THE CRUCIFIED

The Triumph of the Crucified

A SURVEY OF HISTORICAL REVELATION IN THE NEW TESTAMENT

By

ERICH SAUER

Translated by

G. H. LANG

With a Foreword by A. RENDLE SHORT, M.D., B.Sc., F.R.C.S.

WM. B. EERDMANS PUBLISHING COMPANY

GRAND RAPIDS   MICHIGAN

ISBN 0-8028-1175-2

First Published, June 1951
Second printing, July 1960
Third printing, July 1963
Fourth printing, June 1966
Fifth printing, July 1968
Sixth printing, March 1972
Seventh printing, November 1973

This American Edition
Published by Special Arrangement
with
The Paternoster Press, London

PHOTOLITHOPRINTED BY GRAND RAPIDS BOOK MANUFACTURERS, INC.
GRAND RAPIDS, MICHIGAN, UNITED STATES OF AMERICA

TABLE OF CONTENTS

PART III

THE COMING KINGDOM OF GOD

Section I—The Antichristian World System

Section II—The Visible Kingdom of Christ

PART IV

WORLD CONSUMMATION AND THE HEAVENLY JERUSALEM

FOREWORD

by A. RENDLE SHORT, M.D., B.SC., F.R.C.S.

IF one reads a new book to obtain fresh light upon Christian truth, there is a special value if the author has been brought up in a school totally different from one's own, provided of course that it really is Christian truth which he sets forth. All this is eminently to be found in the volume before us. The writer is a well-known German expositor of the Scriptures, belonging to an independent group of churches, of strong evangelical traditions. He is principal of a Bible school in the Rhineland, and has for many years been in great request as a teacher all over Central Europe. He has visited Britain several times, and we can testify to his preaching ability.

The Germans have a reputation for unusual industry and thoroughness, and this book is characteristic. A vast body of Christian doctrine is included, arranged in historical order, beginning with the Incarnation, the Person of our Lord, His Death and Resurrection, the work of St. Paul, and the character of the church. The writer then passes to the signs of the Second Coming, and a very full description of Old and New Testament teaching about the reign of Christ on earth. The concluding chapters deal with the Last Judgment and the Eternal State.

The material of the book is summarized in about ninety sermon outlines, and no less than 3,700 Scripture references are given. The teaching might be described as utterly Scriptural. No speaker who is trying to expound a portion of the New Testament could fail to profit from looking up what Sauer has to say on that particular subject. That is the main value of the book. It is far more than a mere synopsis. The writer is always thoughtful, sane, and sound, and he has no one-sided theories to advocate. People who like to borrow a book, read it quickly to get the main idea, and then return it, will waste their time here. It is a book to buy, to keep, to refer to again and again when need arises. Nearly all the ninety sermons could well be preached again, and very profitably.

The translation runs very smoothly; indeed, almost the only indication that the original was German is that a good many Continental writers are quoted.

A. RENDLE SHORT
Professor of Surgery, University of Bristol.

7

TRANSLATOR'S PREFACE

THIS excellent work, and its equally excellent companion *The Dawn of World Redemption,* were written as one book. My esteemed friend, the author, gave me the privilege of reading the original manuscript. I know no English books that correspond to these and I felt that they ought to be made available to English readers. To this Herr Sauer gladly consented. The war greatly retarded the work, but at length, by the help of God, and the hearty co-operation of several friends, the books are now offered to all who search into the words and ways of God.

Of the friends mentioned my special thanks are due to Mr. R. C. Thomson, late Senior Translator at the Foreign Office, for carefully scrutinizing the translations of both books and making many valuable suggestions.

But I am especially happy that Herr Sauer and his wife were able to go through both translations with me in minute detail. Their competent knowledge of English has assured a degree of exactness in representing his meaning scarcely otherwise to have been attained.

I have added a few notes, marked [Trans.], and matter in square brackets is mine.

Quotations from Scripture are given in the English Revised Version or the American Standard Version, but frequently, where the writer's thought follows some particular turn of the German, a more literal rendering in English is given.

These works have had a quite remarkable circulation in German, before, during, and since the war. They have been translated into Swedish and Norwegian and one into Dutch. A Spanish translation is being prepared. May the illumination of the Spirit of truth attend them in English.

G. H. LANG

AUTHOR'S NOTE

IT is with gratitude to the Lord that I see my two books, *The Dawn of World Redemption* and *The Triumph of the Crucified,* published in English. I have read and approved this translation and have used the opportunity to make some improvements and changes from the German text. I am very much indebted to the translator of both books, Mr. G. H. Lang, for his very careful and most reliable work.

The text contains many Scripture references (in *Dawn of World Redemption* about 2,200, in *The Triumph of the Crucified* about 3,700). They are intended, not only to prove from the Word of God itself the statements given in the books, but also to help those readers who will use what is here offered for their private Bible study or in preparation for preaching the word. Not seldom they are at the same time an expansion of the line of thought.

In the German editions I have given theological literary references. But as these are not of great profit to the English reader, I have omitted them in the English edition. German-speaking English readers may find them in the German editions. Quotations are set everywhere in inverted commas.

It is my prayer that God will use this English edition to the blessing of readers and to the glory of His name.

Wiedenest. ERICH SAUER

AUTHOR'S PREFACE

THE Triumph of the Crucified—this is the import of the New Testament historical revelation. The winning of the church, the conversion of the nations, the transfiguring of the universe are the three chief stages in the triumphant course of His redemption. Christ Himself is the first-fruits, the beginning of a new humanity. In harmonious rhythm of ages and periods the Divine economy moves towards its eternal goal. The end of the whole, as its beginning, is God Himself (I Cor. 15: 28).

To show this connexion is the task of the present history of salvation. It is an attempt at an outline drawing of the Divine unfolding of the redemption of the world culminating in the heavenly Jerusalem.

At a time of great events in world history this book speaks of the greatest event which has taken place on earth and is still taking place, the redeeming work of the Son of God. It speaks of the people called His church, and of the carrying through of His plans for His kingdom, with Israel and the nations, with the individual as with the universe.

Out of all the darkness of time our gaze will be directed to the sunrise out of eternity, to the victory of the cause of Christ and the glorious future of His church. And our hearts shall rejoice over the plans of His love, and as we march on through this world, with its crises and catastrophes, we shall know that "light must ever arise to the righteous" (Psa. 97: 11), that "the path of the righteous is as the brilliant light of dawn, which shines ever clearer until the height of day" (Prov. 4: 18).

ERICH SAUER

Wiedenest, Rhineland, Germany.

PART I

THE DAYSPRING FROM ON HIGH

CHAPTER I

THE APPEARING OF THE WORLD'S REDEEMER

AMID the triumphant shouts of heavenly hosts the gospel entered the arena of the earthly world. "Glory to God in the highest, and on earth peace, good will toward men." This rang out at that hour of night in the fields of Bethlehem-Ephrathah (Luke 2: 14).

He, whose coming the fathers had so long awaited, entered into the midst of His people as the "hope" (Acts 26: 6) and the "consolation" of Israel (Luke 2: 25). "God manifest in the flesh." What a mystery of godliness! (I Tim. 3: 16). It is true that He came in the form of a servant (Phil. 2: 7) and in poverty-stricken lowliness (II Cor. 8: 9, Gk. *ptōchos*); but this exterior was only the "tabernacle" of His inherent divinity (John 1: 14, Gk. *eskēnōsen* = tabernacled). Even in the realm of death He remained the Prince of Life (Acts 3: 15); for "in him was life, and the life was the light of men" (John 1: 4).

I. THE DIVINE MESSAGES OF THE CHANGE OF EPOCH

1. *Christ—the Son of God.* The first announcement occurred in the temple to Zacharias the priest (Luke 1: 8–13). It was linked directly with the last and greatest of the Old Testament prophecies (Mal. 4: 5). It spoke first of the birth of the one who would prepare the way, the second "Elijah," and said that He, whose forerunner this "Elijah" was to be, would be no less a person than the Lord, the God of Israel Himself. "Many of the children of Israel shall he turn to the Lord their God. And he it is who shall go before his face in the spirit of and power of Elijah" (Luke 1: 16, 17). It was this coming Lord and God that Malachi had viewed in spirit and had named "the Lord of hosts (*Jehovah Zebaoth*), who shall come unawares to his temple" (Mal. 3: 1). How appropriate it was, therefore, that the imminent fulfilment of this prophetic message was announced in a temple and to a priest.

2. *Christ—the Son of David.* The second proclamation was made to Mary, the pious virgin of David's house (Luke 1: 26–38). Beginning with the Davidic promises and indeed with the earliest and first promise, which had been given to David himself

by Nathan the prophet and had described the Messiah as the Son of God and the Son of David (I Chron. 17: 11-14), the angel added these words: "He shall be great, and shall be called Son of the Highest; and the Lord God shall give unto him the throne of his father David" (Luke 1: 32). Thus here again the angel's message is most significantly suited to the person who receives it.

3. *Christ—the Saviour.* Finally, the third announcement was made to Joseph. Despite his Davidic descent he came into the story not as father, but only as foster-father, and thus merely as a believing, penitent Israelite appointed only to receive the Redeemer into his house. To him was therefore stated what the Messiah would be to believing Israel in need of redemption. He is the "Immanuel, God with us," predicted by Isaiah (Isa. 7: 14). "Thou shalt call his name Jesus, for it is he that shall save his people from their sins" (Matt. 1: 21-23). Here the office and the work of the Redeemer are spoken of as such. And this is the most important point; for Christ did not become Redeemer in order to be the Son of God and Son of David, but He appeared as the Son of God and the Son of David in order to be the Redeemer. Jesus—the Lord is salvation—is therefore His particular name, and the Redeemership is so entirely His very own and innermost being that He bears the name "Saviour" as a direct human and personal name.

All three angelic proclamations were, however, comprised in the message of the heavenly host that night above the shepherds' field of Bethlehem:

"Unto you is born this day a Saviour"—this is the fulfilment of Isaiah's prophecy and of the name "Jesus" committed to Joseph;

"Who is Christ the Lord"—this is the fulfilment of Malachi's message of the coming Lord and God as repeated to Zacharias;

"in the city of David"—this is the fulfilment of Nathan's message concerning the Son of David as given to Mary.

With this fourfold testimony of direct heavenly messages through mouths of angels there also sounded in harmony a sevenfold indirect witness of the Spirit through the mouths of believing men. Zacharias, the shepherds, Simeon, the wise men from the east, with Elisabeth, Mary, and Anna stand forth like flaming torches lighting the portal at the turning point of the ages, directing to Him, the Coming One, the Dayspring from on high (Luke 1: 78), the great Deliverer out of David.

Zacharias praised God that He had visited men (Luke 1: 68, 76-79);

the shepherds praised the Saviour (Luke 2: 20, comp. 11);

the wise men praised the King (Matt. 2: 11, comp. 2);

Simeon praised the Light of the world (Luke 2: 31, 32); and of the three women

Elisabeth celebrated the happiness (Luke 1: 41–45);
Mary celebrated the mercy (Luke 1: 54, 50, comp. 48); and
Anna celebrated the redemption (Luke 2: 38).

II. THE INCARNATION AS HISTORICAL FACT

Mighty movements in the world above must have preceded
the appearing of the Son of God on earth. Scripture lifts the
veil but slightly. But it informs us, as if out of a conversation
within the Godhead, of one word which the Son, at His entrance
into the world, spake to the Father: "Sacrifice and food-offering
hast thou not willed; but thou hast indeed prepared a body for
me: in burnt offering and sin offering thou hast found no pleasure.
Then said I, Behold, I come (in the roll of the book it is written
of me), that I may do, O God, thy will" (Heb. 10: 5–7).

And then the incomprehensible came to pass. The Son for-
sook the splendour of heaven and became as really a man as
ourselves. Surrendering the eternal form of God above all
worlds He voluntarily entered into human relationships within
the world.[1] Leaving the free, unconditioned, world-ruling
absoluteness of the Divine form the Son entered the limits of time
and space of the creature. The eternal Word became a human
soul and emptied Himself of His world-embracing power as
Ruler. The self-seeking mind may hold with tenacity even
strange and unjustly acquired possessions, as being welcome
"prey" (Phil. 2: 6); but He, the primary fount of love, did not
regard even His own original and legitimate possession, the
Divine form and Divine position, as something to be maintained
at all costs, but surrendered it in order to save us. He descended
"into the lower regions of the earth" (Eph. 4: 9), so as to take
us, the redeemed, with and in Himself up to the heights of
heaven. God became man that man might become godly. He
became poor for our sakes that we through His poverty might
become rich (II Cor. 8: 9).

The history of human salvation concentrates on the appearing
of Christ as its central point. What took place before Him
came to pass wholly in anticipation of Him; what took place after
Him was accomplished in His name. As the variegated colours
of a prism, in spite of all differences, are rays of one and the
same light, so is the history of revelation, with all its dispensations, the product of one uniform life principle. Christ the
Mediator is the corner stone of the whole. His work on earth
is the turning point of all development, and the history of His

---

[1] The fact of the personal, conscious, real pre-existence of Christ is taught
plainly in John 8: 58; 17: 5; Phil. 2: 6–8, where voluntary action is ascribed to the
Son of God as before the world was. This excludes a merely "ideal" pre-existence.
Compare further the passages which deal with the "sending" of the Son and
His "going out from" the Father. Further see Mic. 5: 2; John 1: 14, esp. 1–5;
Heb. 10: 5–7.

person is the essential content of all history. Therefore the incarnation of Christ is the coming out into view of the Divine basis of all that exists, the entrance of the Lord of history into the history itself; and the manger of Bethlehem, in conjunction with Golgotha, will for ever be

" of all times   the turning point,
  of all love   the highest point,
  of all salvation   the starting point,
  of all worship   the central point."

But *how* in Christ these two, His deity and His humanity, unite in one, no one is able to explain. The secret of His self-humbling is for ever unfathomable. Christ not only did wonders but was Himself a wonder, indeed, the wonder of all wonders, the original Wonder in person. We still do not comprehend time; to us it is a riddle. Still less do we comprehend eternity; truly much more is it to us a riddle. How then could we comprehend the riddle of riddles, the union of these opposed mysteries, the intersection in time of two parallels, the organic harmonious union of the infinite and the finite.[1] No, there remains for us here only the one confession:

When I this wonder contemplate
My spirit doth in reverence wait:
It worships, as it views this height—
The love of God is infinite (*Gellert*).

III. INCARNATION AND RESURRECTION

But to see and feel the saving significance of the Incarnation still more distinctly we must consider it in connexion with the resurrection of the Lord, and this under a threefold contrast:

1. Humiliation and Exaltation;
2. Obtaining salvation and Perfecting salvation;
3. Historical Form and Eternal Idea.

1. Yet in fact, in spite of all the descent from the height of heaven, it was not properly the incarnation in itself which meant for the Son of the Highest that infinite humiliation, but rather the taking the form of man standing dishonoured under the consequences of sin. Not indeed that He came in sinful flesh, yet truly "in the likeness of flesh of sin" (Rom. 8: 3). For if the becoming man *as such* had been a humiliating of the Son of God, then His exaltation could not have consisted at all in a glorifying of His entire human nature, but rather in a complete renunciation of it. Yet it is the clear teaching of Holy Scripture that Jesus in

[1] How insufficient here are all speculations, even the best intentioned, the Christological controversies of centuries four to seven have sufficiently proved, as have both the discussions of the "inter-*trinitarian*" relation of the eternal " Word" (*Logos*) to God (Arius), and the monophysite and monothelite contentions over the inner *human* relation of the divine and human "nature" of God's Son incarnate (Apollinaris, Nestorius, Eutychus).

His exaltation has retained the form of man,[1] and that thus His resurrection and ascension to heaven involved nothing less than the making of His humanity eternal in transfigured glorified form, even if in a manner wholly incomprehensible to us. He took indeed the "form of a slave" (Phil. 2: 7), which belongs to man in his present lowliness; yet through His redeeming work He so exalted and transfigured it that it can no longer even form a contradiction or antithesis to His own proper glory as the One sitting at the right hand of the Father. For the glory of the transfigured Man, Christ Jesus, in heaven is certainly no less than that which the eternal Word had before His incarnation. He said Himself: "Glorify me, Father, by thyself with the glory which I already possessed by thee before the world was" (John 17: 5).

2. But yet more. This eternal continuance of the manhood of the Son of God is an indispensable condition for the completion and preservation of His work. For only as glorified Man could He be the "last Adam" (Rom. 5: 12–21; I Cor. 15: 21, 22, 45), and the exalted Head of the "new man" (Eph. 4: 15; Col. 2: 19; Eph. 2: 15) and the redeemed human organism, His church. Only so could it become possible that the saved should be "in Christ," with organic life-fellowship as the "members" of His "body" with Himself, the "Head" (I Cor. 12: 12, 27; Eph. 1: 23). Therefore that Christ remains man is a necessary, an essential part of His exaltation, and only through the resurrection and ascension is the wonder of Bethlehem set in its proper Biblical light.

3. Christ became *man* that He might be the "last Adam." This is the eternal basic idea of His appearing in created form, and so far this is a glorifying of His person as the Redeemer. Yet He was a *humbled* man so that, by the way of substitution for the sinner, he should reach through suffering the glories of this last Adam. That was the historical form of His coming into the world; and in this respect it was a self-deprivation and self-emptying of His glory.

But the historical form was only the means to the realization of the eternal idea. He came to serve and to give His life a ransom for many (Matt. 20: 28), in order, through His "hour" on Golgotha, to save for eternity those who, called by Him to repentance, permit themselves to be sought and found (Luke 19: 10). And through our being incorporated into Him who is our life, the heavenly Christ gains in us an ever more victorious stature; and thus the process advances to a continuous incarnating of His holy nature in us, His redeemed (II Pet. 1: 4), and "the incarnation of the Son as the central point of universal history becomes at the same time the central point of our personal life history and the goal of our future."

[1] John 20: 15, 25; Luke 24: 13ff., 36–43; Acts 1: 11; Rev. 1: 13; Phil. 3: 21.

CHAPTER II

THE NAME JESUS CHRIST: THE THREEFOLD OFFICE

"THY name is an outpoured ointment."—*Song of Songs* 1: 3. "And in none other is there salvation: for neither is there any other name under heaven, that is given among men, wherein we must be saved" (Acts 4: 12). What is meant by this name? Why exactly is the Redeemer called Jesus Christ?

I. THE NAME JESUS

The name "Jesus" has a threefold meaning. First of all it is simply

1. *His Personal Name.* "Thou shalt call his name Jesus" (Matt. 1: 21). But "Christ" is not first of all a personal name. Therefore to suit the context in Eph. 2: 12 and Heb. 11: 26 not Jesus but only Christ could be used, as is in fact the case. But inasmuch as by the incarnation the name Jesus would be given to the Son of God it is at the same time

2. *His Name in Humiliation.* Indeed, so much is this name connected with the humiliation of the Lord that He has it in common with others; as with Joshua the son of Nun, the successor of Moses (Gk. *Iesous* Heb. 4: 8), and with Joshua the high priest of the time of Zechariah (Zech. 3: 1), with Jesus Sirach, Jesus Justus (Col. 4: 11), and even with Jesus the father of the Jewish-Arabian sorcerer Bar-Jesus (son of Jesus, Acts 13: 6).

From this it is clear why the Gospels speak mostly of "Jesus," while throughout the Epistles the title "Christ" stands in the foreground. For the Gospels deal with the time of His humiliation, while the Epistles testify of Him as the One exalted and glorified; and in the name Jesus the thought of salvation preponderates, but in the title Christ the glory. In the Epistles "Jesus" stands alone only where His former lowliness is to be stressed: II Cor. 4: 10; Phil. 2: 10; I Thess. 4: 14; Heb. 2: 9; 12: 2; 13: 12 (contrasted with ver. 8).

As Peter said on the day of Pentecost, only by resurrection and ascension did Jesus become properly Christ, in the full sense of the word: "Let all the house of Israel know assuredly that God hath made him both Lord and Christ, this Jesus whom ye crucified" (Acts 2: 36). Inasmuch, therefore, as the path of the Lord passed from self-emptying to glory the New Testament follows the same path, the path from "Jesus" to "Christ;" just as, conversely, the Old Testament had gone forward from the general idea of Messiah, that is, Christ, to the historical appearance of Jesus of Nazareth.

But the chief significance of the name Jesus lies in the proper meaning of the word: Jehoshua, the Lord is salvation. Therefore it is especially

3. *His Name as Saviour*, the world's Redeemer: "It is he who shall save his people from their sins" (Matt 1: 21). As such it makes a threefold revelation of

the *exclusiveness* of His salvation, for He, and He alone, can save (Acts 4: 12). Hence the emphasis in the Greek upon the "He" in Matt. 1: 21;

the *limit* of His salvation, for He will save only "His people," that is, the saved from all nations (comp. I Pet. 2: 9; Titus 2: 14; Acts 15: 14); and

the *depth* and *breadth* of His salvation; for not only does He redeem from the consequences of sin—condemnation and judgment, but from the sins themselves, from their bondage, lordship, and power. He is the source not only of justification but of sanctification also (I Cor. 1: 30).

All this lies in the name Jesus. In it is declared the purpose for which the world's Redeemer was sent. It is the "Contents Table," title, symbol, motto of His saving activity. It is therefore no wonder that this is the name that fills the praise of the redeemed to all eternity; no wonder that in it every knee shall bow, of all in heaven, on earth, and under the earth (Phil. 2: 10).

But what is the method and manner in which the Lord reveals the treasures of His name Jesus? The answer lies in the title Christ.

II. THE NAME CHRIST

Here there are four main threefold facts which unlock for us the inner meaning of this title:

1. The threefold official anointing in the Old Testament.
2. The threefold unfolding in the New Testament.
3. The threefold bondage of man through sin.
4. The threefold work of Christ as Redeemer.

1. In the time of the Old Testament salvation there were three chief theocratic anointings ordered by God: an anointing of the high priest (Lev. 8: 12; Psa. 133: 2), of the king (I Sam. 10: 1; 16: 13), and of the prophet (I Kings 19: 16). Therefore when the Mediator of salvation is described as Christ, Messiah, that is, Anointed, this means that the highest offices and dignities of the whole of the old covenant are united in His person, and that in Him all prophecies have reached eternal fulfilment. According to the prophecy of Jeremiah concerning the new covenant (Jer. 31: 31-34; comp. Heb. 8: 8-12), Messiah brings

B

an extension of His kingship over the inner life (Jer. 31: 33; II Cor. 3: 3);

a general grant of the gift of prophecy, and

an eternal consummation of priesthood (Jer. 31: 34).

He ,puts His nature into His own people and makes them likewise kings, priests, and witnesses of His prophetic truth (I Pet. 2: 9; Rev. 1: 6). And thus the Giver makes Himself to be the gift (II Cor. 9: 15), and makes His own splendour as Christ, the sun, to stream forth from Christians, His redeemed (Acts 11: 26).

2. Not all at once but in three great stages the Lord unfolds the glorious content of His title, Christ.

First He comes as *prophet* (Deut. 18: 15–19), as Son, in Whom "at the end of the days" God has spoken (Heb, 1: 1, 2), and Who, as "the effulgence of the glory" of God, makes known His Father's nature with incomparable clearness, beyond all the prophets of old (John 1: 18; 3: 13).

And then this Prophet goes to the cross. He permits Himself to be laden with the sins of the world (John 1: 29; I John 2: 2), becomes at the same time both the lamb of sacrifice and the *priest* (Heb. 9: 12, 14, 25, 26), and effects through Himself the purification of sins (Heb. 1: 3).

Finally He is exalted and seats Himself at the right hand of the Majesty in the height (Heb. 1: 3), and now we see Him who "was made a little lower than the angels" "crowned with glory and honour" as *King*, on the very ground that He suffered unto death (Heb. 2: 9).

3. But why precisely a *three*fold office? Why this *three*fold activity of the Redeemer? Because there exists a *three*fold necessity in the salvation of man; because Adam's fallen posterity is held in a threefold bondage and therefore must be redeemed in three respects.

God has created man to be a creaturely reflection of His spiritual, holy, and blessed nature. That they might be a mirror of His spirituality He gave them the *understanding*; that they might be a copy of His holiness and love, the *will*; and that they should be a vessel of His blessedness and happiness, the *feelings*.

But then came sin. The whole man fell. His understanding was darkened (Eph. 4: 18), his will became evil (John 3: 19), and his feelings became unhappy (Rom. 7: 24).

4. Out of this total ruin the work of Christ now saves him.

As *Prophet* He brings knowledge, i.e. light, delivers the understanding from sin's darkness, and establishes the kingdom of truth.

As *Priest* He brings the sacrifice, cancels the guilt and thereby the consciousness of guilt, thus delivering the feelings from the crippling pressure of misery and an accusing conscience, and establishes the kingdom of peace and joy.

As *King* He rules the will, guides it in paths of holiness, and establishes the kingdom of love and righteousness.

Thus does His title Christ, embracing a threefold salvation, become the unfolding and explanation of His name Jesus. It is because the Redeemer is the Christ, the thrice-anointed, that He is Jesus, the Saviour. His threefold office sets man free in the three powers of his soul, the understanding, the feelings, and the will. A full, free, and complete salvation is introduced, so that the redemption could not be more perfect than it is. The threefold wretchedness of darkness, unhappiness, and sinfulness is met by a threefold, yet organically single salvation of enlightenment, blessedness, and holiness, and the spirituality (Col. 3: 10), glorious happiness (II Cor. 3: 18), and holiness of God (Eph. 4: 24) shine anew out of the creature who is His image.

CHAPTER III

THE MESSAGE OF THE KINGDOM OF HEAVEN

Repent, for the kingdom of heaven has drawn near.
Matt. 3: 2; 4: 17.

I. THE HERALD

IN the wilderness, at Jordan, John preached the baptism of
repentance unto the forgiveness of sins (Mark 1: 4). The
new element in the baptism of John was not that he baptized,
for already the Jews practised the so-called proselyte's baptism
on the Gentiles who came to faith in Jehovah; but it was that
he baptized *Jews*, thereby placing them on the same level as the
nations.

John was the "Elijah" (Mal. 4: 5, 6; Luke 1: 17; Matt. 17:
10–13), the preparer of the way (Isa. 40: 3, 4; Matt. 3: 3), with
greater authority than all prophets (Matt. 11: 9, 10), the witness
to the Light and to the Lamb (John 1: 7, 8, 29, 36). He was the
herald of the King whose coming was now at hand (Mal. 3: 1;
John 1: 26), and was the greatest of all that had been born of
women (Matt. 11: 11). He was a burning and shining lamp
(John 5: 35), a voice of one calling in the desert (John 1: 23;
Isa. 40: 3), who pointed to the "Word" out of eternity.

What is a voice? A sound, a noise, an indistinct cry, unless
a *word* accompanies it. A beast (Rev. 9: 9), a blast (John 3: 8,
lit.), a thunder (Rev. 6: 1)—these may well have voice, but only
through the *word* does the voice receive plain content and meaning. So John the Baptist without Jesus was an empty sound, a
breath, a nothing.

But the word can very well exist without the voice. The
unspoken or unwritten word remains a word in the fullest
sense. Thus Jesus is all that which He is, even without the
Baptist. The voice needs the word, but the word does not need
the voice. John needed Jesus, but Jesus did not need John.

But if the word and the voice combine then, from the standpoint of the hearer, the voice precedes the word; for the voice is
the first to reach the ear of the listener, and only then does the
meaning—the word— reach his spirit. So the Baptist came into
the world first, and Christ, the Word, followed after.

But in speaking this is reversed: then the word precedes the
voice; for the word must be conceived inwardly before the voice
passes over the lips. So John said: "*After* me comes a man who
has been *before* me; for he was earlier than I" (John 1: 30).

Finally; if the word has been spoken then the voice ceases, dies away and exists no more. But the word abides, for it has been planted in the heart of the hearer. Thus also with Jesus and John. "He must increase: I must decrease" (John 3: 30). As soon as John had fulfilled his commission he was removed; but Jesus abides.[1]

II. THE KING

The King took up the message of the herald (Matt. 4: 17; comp. 3: 2). In His person the kingdom of God had come among men (Luke 17: 21; 10: 9, 11). He Himself was the personal present kingdom. This He expressed, both veiled and unveiled, by His designation of Himself as "Son of man."

1. *The Origin of the Title "Son of Man."* This title is found over eighty times in the Gospels. It has its root in the book of *Daniel.* There the Messianic kingdom, in contrast to the wild-beast nature of the world empires—lion, eagle, bear, panther, terrible beast—was described as the kingdom of the Son of man, that is, as being the first and only kingdom of history in which true humanity, in the sense of Holy Scripture, will rule on earth. "I saw in the night visions, and, behold, there came with the clouds of heaven one like unto a son of man, and he came even to the Ancient of Days . . . and to him was given dominion and glory and a kingdom" (Dan. 7: 13, 14). This prophecy of the Son of man on the clouds of heaven who as the Messiah King establishes the kingdom, Christ unmistakably applied to Himself, both as He discoursed to His disciples on the Mount of Olives (Matt. 24: 30) and in His oath before the High Council: "Henceforth ye shall see the Son of man sitting at the right hand of power, and coming on the clouds of heaven" (Matt. 26: 64).

2. *The Meaning of the Title Son of man.* Calling Himself Son of Man
Christ does not denote simply His lowliness and humiliation, in contrast to His heavenly *past*, that He, the Son of God, had now become man (comp. Phil. 2: 5-11);
nor, in the first instance, with reference to the *present*, does He mean that He, as the sinless and Holy One, is the only true man according to the mind of the Creator (Gen. 1: 27);
but rather, looking at the *future*, He declares His divine dignity as Messiah, that He, as the glorified Man, coming again on the clouds of heaven, will bring in the kingdom of God in the time of consummation, and thereby in His divine person will exalt the realized idea of true manhood on the throne of human history.

The expression "Son of man" is thus a divine Messianic and

[1] See Trench, *Synonyms of the New Testament*, 336, ed. 12.

royal title, even as David, the psalmist, had already said of the son of man: "With glory and splendour hast thou crowned him. Thou hast made him ruler over all the works of thy hands. All things hast thou set under his feet" (Psa. 8: 5, 6; Heb. 2: 6–9). And because in the veiled title Son of man there is contained the veiled mystery of His Sonship to God, therefore Christ, in answer to the high priest's question "Art thou the Son of *God?*" could say: "Henceforth ye shall see the Son of *man* sitting at the right hand of power and coming on the clouds of heaven," for the latter includes the former (Matt. 26: 63, 64).

Again and again this divine and royal connexion of the title Son of man comes to the fore. "The Son of man will come in the glory of his Father" (Matt. 16: 27), "with great power and glory" (Matt. 24: 30), and "all the holy angels with him" (Matt. 25: 31). The return of the Son of man will be "as the lightning goeth forth from the east and shineth even unto the west" (Matt. 24: 27). "The Son of man will sit on the throne of his glory" (Matt. 19:28), and as "King" will divide the peoples from one another as the Shepherd divides the sheep from the goats (Matt. 25: 32, 34, 40; comp. John 5: 27).

Of course, the title Son of man is a veiled description of the divine King (John 12: 15, 34; Matt. 16: 13, 16); for Christ, at His first appearing, desired that only by faith should He be recognized as the Messiah (Matt. 8: 4; 9: 30; 17: 9; John 6: 15). That He was the Messiah He made known publicly only immediately before His death on the cross, and even then only in the form of a symbolical act, the entry into Jerusalem (Luke 19: 29–40: Zech. 9: 9). It was in the circle of His own followers alone that, from the very beginning, but with ever increasing clarity, He had revealed Himself as Messiah (John 1: 41, 49; 4: 25, 26; 9: 35–38), till finally Peter, illuminated by revelation from the Father, uttered the victorious confession, "Thou art the Christ, the Son of the living God" (Matt. 16: 16).

III. THE KINGDOM

1. *The Term "Kingdom of heaven."* Before the time of John the Baptist the Jews had already spoken of the kingdom of heaven. They called it *malekut schamayim* (kingdom of the heavens), and understood by this the rule of God over all created things, especially His kingly rule over Israel, and particularly the glorious kingdom of Messiah at the end of history. As says the Talmud: "If any one as he prays places his hand before his face he takes upon himself the yoke of the kingdom of heaven." Again, the Targum of Jonathan on Micah 4: 7 reads: "When at Sinai Israel accepted the book of the law, it accepted with it the law of the kingdom of heaven." "The kingdom of heaven will

be manifested on Mount Zion." That the kingdom of God was called the kingdom of heaven was because the Jews, out of reverence for the holy name Jehovah, transcribed this by such expressions as "height," "name," "power," "heaven." Daniel had said: "the *heavens* rule" to indicate the sovereignty of *God* (Dan. 4: 26).

We may compare such Rabbinical expressions as "Ask heaven for pardon," "love heaven and fear it," "sanctify the name of heaven," "heaven does wonders." This circumlocution for God's name had nothing to do with the insipid conceptions of modern unbelief regarding "heaven" and "Providence." The former arose from an intense, the latter from an indistinct idea of God.

Thus John the Baptist and Christ were not the first who spake of the kingdom of heaven. Much rather they adopted the language of the Old Testament and of the Judaism around them, filling the same expression with new meaning; as Luke 15: 21: "Father, I have sinned against heaven (i.e. God), and before thee;" Matt. 21: 25: "The baptism of John, whence was it? from heaven (i.e. God), or from men?"; Matt. 26: 64: "Ye shall see the Son of man sitting at the right hand of power" (i.e. of God). Therefore with the Lord the prevailing description of the kingdom of God is the kingdom of heaven.[1]

God's kingdom is the kingdom of heaven because
> as to its *origin*—it comes from heaven (Rev. 1: 7; Matt. 26: 64);
> as to its *nature*—it carries heaven within itself (Phil. 3: 20; Eph. 1: 3; 2: 6; Col. 3: 1–4);
> as to its *centre*—it has the Lord as its King, through Whom alone heaven will be properly heaven (Psa. 73: 25).

2. *The Forms under which the Kingdom of Heaven appears.* The proclaiming, making possible, and bringing to completion this kingly rule of God was the entire purpose of the work of Christ; the proclaiming was His work as Prophet, the making it possible He effected as Priest, the completing will be His work as King. Therefore the proclamation of the kingdom of heaven was the

---

[1] On this account the expression "kingdom of heaven" comes only in Matthew (32 times), the Gospel originally intended for Jews: the other Gospels, having in view the understanding of their Gentile readers, translated it by "kingdom of God" (so for example, Luke, 32 times: Matt. 13: 31, 32, comp. Luke 13: 18–21; Matt. 19: 14, comp. Luke 18: 16, 17). As to the thing itself, the kingdom of heaven and the kingdom of God are exactly the same. This is proved by comparison of the following parallel passages: Matt. 4: 17=Mark 1: 15; Matt. 5: 3= Luke 6: 20; Matt. 11: 11= Luke 7: 28; Matt. 10: 7=Luke 10: 9; Matt. 13: 11= Luke 8: 10; Matt. 19: 14=Luke 18: 16; Matt. 19: 23=Luke 18: 24. In all of these places Mark and Luke give the same words of Jesus on the same occasions but reproduce Matthew's expression "kingdom of heaven" simply with "kingdom of God." Comp. further Matt. 19: 23 with 24.

distinctive theme of His earthly message, and all His parables
are parables of the kingdom, even those in which the words
"kingdom of heaven" are not expressly used (e.g. Matt. 13: 3;
21: 33). Nevertheless this omission is never without significance,
for the very silence of the Bible speaks (Heb. 7: 3). In consequence, the kingdom of heaven is not simply "heaven," the
heavenly kingdom, nor only the future kingdom of Messiah
(comp. II Tim. 4: 18), nor the church of the present age (comp.
Col. 1: 13; Rom. 14: 17), but quite generally and simply, it is the
kingly rule of God as it comes from heaven, by way of the
redemption, established on the old earth, and to be continued
eternally on the new earth.

Concerning all the periods, and all the forms of its appearing,
the King has testified as His own herald (*kēryssein*; Matt. 4: 17;
comp. *kēryx*, herald). He spoke

of the kingdom in *Israel*, the kingdom of the Old Testament,
which prepared the way for salvation, and which should be
"taken away" from the former possessors, the Jews (Matt. 21:
43):

of the kingdom in *Christ*, the kingdom personally present
in Himself, in the person (Luke 17: 21) and wonderful works
(Luke 11: 20) of the King Who had become flesh amongst Israel:

of the kingdom in the *church* (comp. Col. 1: 13), the present
hidden kingdom which in His own person had drawn near
(Matt. 4: 17), and which throughout the dispensation of the
church would endure (Matt. 13: 24–47; 18: 23; 20: 1; 22: 2)
in the "mystery" (Matt. 13: 11) until the consummation of the
age (Matt. 13: 39, 49). Finally He spoke

of the kingdom *in the consummation*, the Messianic kingdom
in glory, foretold by the prophets, which at last shall come in
power (Mark 9: 1), shall appear (Luke 19: 11), and will be given
by the Father to the "little flock" (Luke 12: 32), who will be
permitted to enter (Matt. 7: 21) as a reward (Matt. 5: 10–12) and
an inheritance (Matt. 25: 34; 8: 11; 13: 43).

3. *The Gospel of the Kingdom*. All the foregoing belongs to
the gospel of the kingdom (Mark 1: 14, 15; Luke 4: 43). It is
the true basic theme of the message of Christ. Only the context
can ever make plain the exact sense. Thus by "kingdom" Paul
also at times means something present (Rom. 14: 17; I Cor.
4: 20; Col. 1: 13; 4: 11), but often something future (I Cor.
6: 9, 10; Gal. 5: 21; Eph. 5: 5; I Thess. 2: 12; II Thess. 1: 5;
Acts 14: 22). So the message speaks now of the present, now
of the near, now of the distant, or of the most distant kingdom.

The kingdom is thus not something merely Israelitic and
future. Even Paul proclaimed the kingdom, and this to the
Gentiles, and *after* he had turned away from the Jews (Acts
20: 25; 28: 31). His activities during the "whole time" of his

stay in Ephesus (i.e. two and a quarter years, Acts 20: 18; 19:
8, 10) he describes by the two expressions: "to testify the gospel
of the grace of God" (Acts 20: 24) and to "proclaim as a herald
the kingdom of God" (Acts 20: 25). Both expressions belong
to the same time.

Thus it is always the same kingdom, which comes out of
heaven and eternity, continues through the ages, and runs again
into the eternity of God. One must also guard against a hasty
identification of "kingdom" and Millennial kingdom. The
kingdom is first of all wholly general, the rule of God, His
kingship as living and powerful, God's activity made known
throughout the different dispensations in ever new forms of
manifestation. As we have seen, even the Jews of pre-Christian
times denoted by "kingdom of heaven" not only the kingdom
of glory of Messiah, but very often the moral, spiritual, invisible
rule of God over Nature, the nations, and Israel (see p. 22).
Moreover, Christ stood in direct opposition to many conceptions of the kingdom of His Jewish contemporaries, who
limited it to affairs earthly (Luke 17: 20, 21; 19: 11 ff.). Therefore,
while we hold fast the expectation of a coming visible kingdom
(Matt. 19: 28; Acts 1: 6, 7), His idea of the kingdom certainly
cannot, without further ado, be explained by references to the
Jewish-Pharisaic conception of the kingdom.

So there is but *one* gospel (Gal. 1: 6–9), and this is
the gospel of *God*—for God is its source (Rom. 1: 1; 15: 16);
the gospel of *Christ*—for Christ is its Mediator (Rom. 15:
19; I Cor. 9: 12);
the gospel of *grace*—for grace is its very soul (Acts 20: 24);
the gospel of *salvation*—for salvation is its gift (Eph. 1: 13);
the gospel of the *kingdom*—for God's kingdom is its goal
(I Cor. 15: 28);
the gospel of *glory*—for glory is its whole effect (I Tim. 1: 11).
And Paul says of himself and his fellow-workers
"*my* gospel" (Rom. 16: 25; II Tim. 2: 8) or "*our*" gospel
(II Cor. 4: 3; I Thess. 1: 5)—for they were the messengers
(Gal. 1: 11; I Tim. 1: 11).

IV. THE WAY TO THE KINGDOM

But the way to the crown goes by the cross. Therefore
after the King had first placed at the centre of His message the
result of His work, the kingdom, He went on to bring more
and more to the front the *means* for reaching this goal, even
suffering.

He spoke of the *fact* of His death when He spoke of the taking
away of the Bridegroom (Matt. 9: 15), the drinking of the cup
and the being baptized with the baptism of suffering (Mark

10: 38, 39), but above all in the three chief announcements of
His sufferings, in Caesarea Philippi, in Galilee, and on the way
to Jerusalem (Matt. 16: 21-23; 17: 22, 23; 20: 17-19).

He spoke of the *necessity* of His death, of the divine "must"
of His being lifted up as the serpent in the wilderness (John 3:
14), and of His death as the corn of wheat to be glorified through
bearing fruit (John 12: 23, 24; comp. Luke 24: 26, 46).

He spoke of the *voluntariness* of His death: "No one takes
my life from me, but I lay it down of myself" (John 10: 18); and

He spoke of the *significance* of His death

as the foundation of full (John 19: 30), world-wide (John
12: 32; Luke 24: 46, 47) *salvation* (John 3: 14, 15), through
substitutionary death for lost sinners (Matt. 20: 28), for the
purpose of establishing a new covenant through forgiveness of
sins (Matt, 26: 28); and also

as the foundation for practical *holiness* in genuine discipleship, by self-denial and bearing one's cross after Him (Matt. 10:
38; Luke 14: 27; John 12: 24-26).

And in all things He always viewed His death in connexion
with His resurrection and glorification (John 10: 17). This is
shown by His words as to the destruction of the temple (John
2: 18-20), and the sign of Jonah (Matt. 12: 39, 40), and as to the
corner stone (Matt. 21: 42) and the corn of wheat (John 12: 23,
24). And on this ground of the resurrection, and the imparting
of His life to be the life of those believing, He saw the only
way for the sinner to share in the saving significance of His
work; and hence His words as to eating and drinking of His
flesh and blood, without which no one has life in himself (John
6: 53). "The bread which I will give is my flesh, which I will
give for the life of the world . . . he who eats this bread, he will
live for ever" (John 6: 51, 58).

V. The Message of the Kingdom

It is impossible to depict exhaustively the moral content of
the message of the kingdom of heaven: "the world would not
contain the books." The message is

1. *Sacred and sublime in its authority.* "He taught as one
having authority, and not as their scribes" (Matt. 7: 29; John 7:
46), which was confirmed. by signs and wonders (John 5: 36;
Heb. 2: 4). To confirm the message of the heavenly kingdom
was the principal purpose of the miracles of Jesus, as is shown
especially in the Gospel of John (2: 23; 3: 2; 6: 14; 9: 32, 33;
11: 47; 12: 37). In all this the miracles presuppose a longing
for salvation, and are intended chiefly for the receptive (Matt.
8: 8; 15: 28). Hence the refusal of signs where this readiness to
believe was not found (Matt. 12: 38, 39; Mark 6: 4, 5). And the

Lord's words were deeds; His deeds were wonders, and He Himself was the Divinely appointed Prince of life (Acts 3: 15). Further, the message of the kingdom was

2. *Marvellously wise in its instruction.* The old covenant Christ treated as preparatory to the new, as being proof of the truth (John 10: 34, 35; Luke 20: 41-44), as prophesying His own message (Matt. 5: 17; Luke 24: 27; John 5: 39). His teaching was therefore *explanatory.*

Nature He refined into pictures and parables of the kingdom of heaven (Matt. 13: 3, 31), and He did the same with human life (Matt. 13: 24, 33, 44, 45) and history (Luke 19: 12 ff.). Thus His teaching was a *transfiguring* message.

Questioning enemies He silenced by counter-questions (Matt. 15: 2, 3; 21: 23-25; 22: 17-22, 41-45). Thus the message was *defensive* and victorious.

Disciples eager to learn He initiated specially into His mysteries (Matt. 13: 18 ff.; Mark 4: 34). Thus it was *instructive.*

Therefore God said: "This is my beloved Son, in whom I am well pleased. Hear him!" (Matt. 17: 5). And He Himself testified, "Behold, a greater than Solomon is here" (Matt. 12: 42; I Kings 10: 1-10).

Of special significance here is the attitude of Jesus to the Old Testament. For Christ, the personal living Word (John 1: 14), the written word, the Old Testament, was an indissoluble unity, one organism, "the Scripture" (John 10: 35). And in particular it was for Him:

the Authority, under which He placed Himself (Gal. 4: 4);

the Food, upon which He nourished Himself (Matt. 4: 4);

The Weapon, with which He defended Himself (Matt. 4: 4, 7, 10; 12: 3);

the Text Book, which He explained (Luke 24: 27, 32, 44, 45);

the Prophecy, which He fulfilled (Matt. 5: 17, 18; John 5: 39);

the Preparatory Stage, which He surpassed (Matt. 5: 22, 28, 32; 12: 6, 41, 42);

His own word, which He interpreted and deepened (I Pet. 1: 11; Matt. 5: 28).

With all this His preaching was:

3. *Terribly severe in its judgment.* Man is by nature "wicked" (Matt. 7: 11), "an adulterous generation" (Mark 8: 38). All the treasures of the world are not worth *one* human soul (Matt. 16: 26); all fleshly piety is an "abomination before God" (Luke 16: 15). With consuming zeal (John 2: 17), Christ fought against the Pharisees, His enemies (Luke 19: 27), those chief representatives of feigned religion. He called them "whitewashed graves, full of dead men's bones" (Matt. 23: 27), fools (Luke 11: 40), and blind (Matt. 15: 14), liars (John 8: 55), and hypocrites (Matt. 23: 13-15), thieves (John 10: 8) and murderers (Matt. 22: 7),

ravening wolves (Matt. 7: 15), sons of the Devil (John 8: 44), a brood of serpents and adders (Matt. 23: 33).

The temple He called a "robber's hole" (Mark 11: 17), Herod a "fox" (Luke 13: 31, 32). Those who confessed Him falsely were "evil doers "(Matt. 7: 23), "sons of the wicked one" (Matt. 13: 38), and all who rejected Him are worse than Sodom and Gomorrah (Matt. 10: 15).

All who so continue are "lost" (Matt. 16: 25) and "accursed" (Matt. 25: 41); their lot is "howling and gnashing of teeth" (Matt. 24: 51; 25: 30), their place the "unquenchable fire" (Mark 9: 43; Matt. 25: 41).

And yet at the same time the message of the kingdom of heaven is

4. *Infinitely compassionate in its good news.* It shows
the Friend of sinners (Matt. 11: 19; 9: 13), and
the Physician of the sick (Mark 2: 17);[1]
the Refresher of the weary and heavy laden (Matt. 11: 28);
the Blesser of children (Matt. 19: 15);
the Proclaimer of good tidings to the poor (Luke 4: 18);
the Promiser of Paradise to the dying murderer (Luke 23: 43).

Thus the King became the Servant of His servants (John 13: 1-12), and, indeed, as the glorified One He is still ready for service: "Blessed are those servants whom the Lord when he cometh shall find watching: verily I say unto you, that he shall gird himself, and make them sit down to meat, and shall come and serve them" (Luke 12: 37).

And yet the message of the kingdom is:

5. *Unreserved in its demands.* It requires unlimited obedience. It both grants and commands, it is at once gift and task. If any kingdom has ever advanced totalitarian claims it is the kingdom of Christ and God. Authority and obedience, leading and following, command and subjection, this is its order. This is a totalitarian King, kingdom, and church. All half-heartedness and lukewarmness is an abomination to the King. The *whole man* belongs to Him, in spirit, soul, and body, in all relationships, heavenly and earthly. To renounce all (Luke 14: 33), to take up the cross (Matt. 16: 24), to love Jesus more than earth's dearest (Matt. 10: 37), to serve Him alone (Luke 16: 13), to hate his own self (Luke 14: 26), to lose his life, so as to gain it eternally (John 12: 25)—this is the *mind* which the King demands. And in *detail* He commands brotherly love and love to God (Mark 12: 28-31), truth and fidelity (Matt. 5: 33-37), lowliness and self-denial (John 13: 1 ff.; Matt. 16: 24), freedom from anxiety

[1] All the miracles of Jesus are miracles of help and thus at the same time deeds that symbolize the purpose of His mission. Even the single miracle of judgment—the cursing of the fig tree (Matt. 21: 19)—was in truth an act of His love, a symbolic warning to Israel.

with courageous faith (Matt. 6: 25; 21: 21), a prayerful spirit and a heavenly hope (Matt. 6: 6; Luke 12: 35–48).

But all this is to be born out of the life from above, out of the consciousness of the royal standing of the child nobly born out of divine seed. "Therefore ye shall be perfect as your Father in heaven is perfect" (Matt. 5: 48). "For I say unto you that if your righteousness is not superior to that of the scribes and Pharisees, you shall in no wise enter into the kingdom of heaven" (Matt. 5: 20). And yet! "When you have done *all* that is commanded you, say, We are unprofitable servants; we have only done our duty" (Luke 17: 10).

Finally, the End will come (Matt. 24: 14), and with it victory, for the message of the kingdom of heaven has

6. *World Deliverance as its goal.* "The field is the world" (Matt. 13: 38). "Preach the gospel to the whole creation" (Matt. 28: 19, 20). For "in his name repentance and forgiveness of sins must be preached to all peoples" (Luke 24: 47), for "a witness unto them" (Matt. 24: 14) in Jerusalem, in all Judea, Samaria, and unto the end of the earth (Acts 1: 8).

And then when the King appears His kingdom will be visible. The blessed of the Father will inherit the sovereignty (Matt. 25: 34), and the righteous will shine as the sun for ever and ever (Matt. 13: 43). This is the hope of the message of the kingdom.

VI. THE HEARERS

But all these words were spoken on Jewish national ground. In the days of His flesh the Lord was throughout a "minister of the circumcision" (Rom. 15: 8), and even He Himself was "under law" (Gal. 4: 4; comp. Luke 2: 22, 24, 41; Mark 1: 44). "I am not sent save to the lost sheep of the house of Israel" (Matt. 15: 24; 10: 5, 6). Those addressed in the sermon on the mount (Matt. 5–7), the talk by the sea (Matt. 13), the discourse on Olivet (Matt. 24: 25), and all the parables, were in the first instance sons of Israel. Only after the taking away of the "middle wall" through the Cross (Eph. 2: 13–16), and the opening of the kingdom of heaven to men wholly Gentile by the conversion of Cornelius (Acts 10; Matt. 16: 19), have the nations also had the right to take to themselves directly, in the same manner as Jews, the essential teaching in the Gospels. Only these two events, which came to pass *after* the earthly life of Jesus, opened later to non-Israelites the door to the lecture hall of the Lord.

But now no difference any longer exists (Acts 15: 8, 9); for both have the same salvation (Acts 28: 28; 11: 17). There are not two "good news"—a Jewish-Christian and a Gentile-Christian—but only one gospel and one church (Gal. 1: 6–9;

Eph. 2: 11–22; 3: 6). The assertion that, after the opening of the door of the kingdom through the cross and Acts 10, the doctrinal content of the gospel continued to be limited to Israel, and did not stand on the same dispensational ground as the message of Paul and the church, contradicts therefore the New Testament doctrine of salvation and that of Paul especially. Paul himself testifies of "his" gospel, as regards its area, that it had to pass through two periods—to the Jew first[1] and then (this *same* salvation, Acts 28: 28) to the Gentiles (Rom. 1: 16; Acts 13: 46).

Also, according to the writer of Hebrews, who was one of Paul's fellow-workers (Heb. 13: 23), the salvation of the church age "began" to be taught in the earthly message of Christ and not in that of Paul (Heb. 2: 3). And if Paul describes "his" gospel as "spirit" and "life" ("the spirit makes alive," II Cor. 3: 6), so also the character of the words of the Lord Jesus is on the same dispensational line: "The words which I have spoken to you are spirit and are life" (John 6: 63). So that which was proclaimed by Paul and his fellow-workers in the age of the church was not, as regards the message of the Gospels, a new dispensational message, but simply a continuation, widened and deepened by additional revelations of the Spirit (Gal. 1: 11, 12; Eph. 3: 3; I Cor. 11: 23; I Thess. 4: 15).

The words of the Lord were a message of joy, a pronouncing of blessing (Matt. 5: 3–12); they were "words of grace" (Luke 4: 22), revelations of the name of the Father (John 17: 6; Matt. 5: 45). According to Heb. 2: 3, "salvation" and "redemption" is the inspired superscription of His earthly preaching. His miracles were works of healing and help, and He was—not the "death" declared in the law—but the personal "grace of God" that had appeared (Tit. 2: 11; 3: 4), Himself the resurrection and the eternal life (John 11: 25; 14: 6; 17: 3).

Thus in the period of the Gospels the area, the surroundings, and often the form of the doctrine (Matt. 5: 21, 23–27, 31, 38, 43) of the kingdom of heaven had an Old Testament and national limit, but their essence and spirit were that of New Testament liberty. The dispensations of law and of grace are not to be sharply divided from each other by one single event, but they overlap, as the colours of the rainbow.

VII. The Glory of the Kingdom

A King Who dies for His subjects.[2]

A Judge Who is the Saviour of all.

---

[1] As Matt. 10: 5, 6, comp. 28: 19; and because of John 4: 22; Rom. 11: 18.
[2] Whereas usually subjects die for their king.

Aristocrats who were mere slaves (Luke 12: 32; Rom. 6: 20).
Judges who were sheer criminals (I Cor. 6: 2, 3).
Faithful who were once out-and-out rebels.

A law which is complete freedom (Rom. 8: 2; Jas. 1: 25).
A freedom which is wholly bound (Rom. 6: 18).

All in the kingdom were former enemies (Rom. 5: 10).
All rulers are at the same time servants (Rev. 1: 6).

Each born twice (earthly and heavenly, John 3: 3).
Many never die (I Cor. 15: 51).
All brought out of death into life (John 5: 24).

Defeated yet conquerors (II Cor. 6: 9, 10).
Heroes whose glory is their weakness (II Cor. 12: 9).
Despised whom the King of the universe exalts (Luke 12: 32).

A dominion on earth with its capital in heaven (Gal. 4: 26).
A little flock, yet innumerable as the sand of the sea (Gen.
    22: 17; Rev. 7: 9).
A kingdom without a country to which the whole world
    belongs (I Pet. 2: 11; Matt. 5: 5; I Cor. 6: 2).

And the secret of the whole?

A King of glory crowned with thorns!

This is the glory of the kingdom.

CHAPTER IV

THE DECISIVE BATTLE ON GOLGOTHA

"Theologia crucis—theologia lucis"
The theology of the cross is the theology of the light.
—Luther.

THE hatred of the Pharisees brought Christ to the cross. The execution of Jesus was the greatest judicial murder in the history of the world. "It was the most cowardly murder of an ambassador, the foulest outrage that rebels at any time committed against a kind father of their fatherland."

But what did God do?

"He has turned this devilishly mean rebellion against His person into the atonement for the salvation of these rebels! He has answered this blow on His holy face with the kiss of reconciling love! We wrought the extreme of wickedness against Him, but He has wrought the extreme of goodness toward us, and both at the same hour." Thus at the same moment the shameful deed at the cross became by redemption the turning point of human history and of the whole drama of universal super-history.

According to the latest reckoning the crucifixion of Jesus took place most probably on 7th April, A.D. 30. From every point of view the cross proves itself to be the victorious foundation of redemption.

I. THE SIGNIFICANCE OF THE CROSS FOR GOD

The cross is the greatest event in the history of salvation, greater even than the resurrection. The cross is the victory, the resurrection the triumph; but the victory is more important than the triumph, although the latter necessarily follows from it. The resurrection is the public display of the victory, the triumph of the Crucified One. But the victory itself was complete. "It is finished" (John 19: 30).

For God the cross is

1. *The supreme evidence of the LOVE of God.* For there the Lord of all life gave up unto death His most Beloved, His only begotten Son, the Mediator and Heir of creation (Col. 1: 16; Heb. 1: 2, 3). Christ the Lord died on the cross, He for Whom the stars circle in the ether and for Whom every gnat dances in the sunshine (Heb. 2: 10). Truly "in this God proves his love toward us, in that Christ died for us while we were still sinners" (Rom. 5: 8). At the same time the cross is

2. *The greatest evidence of the RIGHTEOUSNESS of God.*
For there the Judge of the world "as proof of his righteousness"
(Rom. 3: 25) did not spare even His own Son (Rom. 8: 3?). In
all the centuries before Golgotha, in spite of many individual
judgments (Rom. 1: 18 ff.), God had not at any time visited sin
with a hundred per cent punishment (Acts 17: 30); so that at
length, because of His patience, His holiness appeared to be
called in question "because of the passing over of sins done
aforetime, in the forbearance of God" (Rom. 3: 25). Therefore
only the atoning death of the Redeemer, as Divine self-justification for the past history of mankind, proves the irrefutable
righteousness of the supreme Judge of the world. All the
patience of the past was possible only in view of the cross (Rom.
3: 25), and all future forgiveness is righteous only through
looking back to the cross (Rom. 3: 26; I John 1: 9). Past
patience (Rom. 3: 25), present judgment (John 12: 31), and future
grace meet at the cross (Rom. 5: 8, 9). Therefore now for the
first time, in a unique manner, the righteousness of God is revealed in the gospel (Rom. 1: 17; II Cor. 3: 9), the righteousness
of God as both a Divine attribute and also a Divine gift which
comes from God and is valid before God (II Cor. 5: 21). Precisely
because of this the cross is

3. *The most marvellous augmentation of the RICHES of God.*
"Thou wast slain, and didst purchase *unto God* with thy blood
men of every tribe, and tongue, and people, and nation, and
madest them to be *unto our God* a kingdom and priests" (Rev.
5: 9). They are now acquired for God, a "people for His
possession" (I Pet. 2: 9), a people who are His own property
(Titus 2: 14). Yet it is not as if the wealth acquired by the cross
meant an augmentation of the Divine glory itself—for God in
Himself is infinite; yet it is true that in the church He has won
an instrument, an organ for the *revelation* of His glory. Even
now in the present the office of the church is not limited to the
earth. Even now "shall be made known to the principalities
and authorities in the heavenly world the manifold wisdom of
God" (Eph. 3: 10, 11). Brother or sister, let therefore thy
spirit raise itself up out of the everyday dust! In thee should
the principalities in the heavenly world learn something of the
wisdom of thy God! Upwards, to meet the stars! Yes, beyond,
above the stars! Let thy heart dwell by the throne of God, the
Almighty, thy and my Father!

II. THE SIGNIFICANCE OF THE CROSS FOR CHRIST

For Christ and *God* the cross is

1. The highest acknowledgment of the *authority* of God; for

c

the Son became obedient unto death, yea, the death of the cross
(Phil. 2: 8; Rom. 5: 19). It is

2. The highest perfection of *faith* in God; for He has
"learned obedience by the things which He suffered" (Heb.
5: 8, 9), and has thus become the "beginner" and "perfect
exhibiter" of faith (Heb. 12: 2; comp. 2: 13). It is

3. The most definite augmentation of the *good pleasure* of God;
for He gave Himself an offering "to be to God a sweet smelling
odour" (Eph. 5: 2); and it is

4. A ground of the eternal continuance of the *love* of the
Father to the Son: "Therefore the Father loves me, because I
lay down my life, that I may take it again" (John 10: 17).

As it concerns Christ *personally*, for Him the cross is

5. The way to the transfiguration of His position of love and
power into that of Victor, from His being "in the bosom of the
Father" (John 1: 18) unto the sitting "at the right hand of the
majesty in the heights" (Phil. 2: 9; Heb. 2: 9; 8: 1). And
further, it is

6. The way to the possession of His redeemed church, from
His being "alone" as the corn of wheat, passing through death,
unto victorious glorification and fruitfulness (John 12: 24).
Only so could the "Leader of salvation" be made perfect as
Leader (Heb. 2: 10), and win the joy that lay before Him (Heb.
12: 2). Only so could Christ become the Firstborn among many
brethren (Rom. 8: 29) and the Head of His members (Eph. 1: 22).
Only so could He acquire His "fulness," His "body," that
"church which is the fulness of him who fills all things in all"
(Eph. 1: 23). Certainly as a *Divine Person* Christ has won nothing
through the cross. The glorified Man in heaven possesses now
no more divinity and personal glory than as the eternal Word
He had before He became incarnate. He Himself said: "Glorify
me, Father, by thyself with the glory which I had by thee before
the world was" (John 17: 5). But as the *Redeemer* and "last
Adam" (Rom. 5: 12-21; I Cor. 15: 45) Christ has nevertheless
attained a fresh exaltation, even the name which is above every
name, in which every knee shall at last bow, in heaven and on
earth and under the earth (Phil. 2: 9, 10).

And finally, as regards Christ's relation *to us*, the cross is

7. The most wonderful expression of the love of the Son of
God. "Christ has loved the church and given Himself up for
her" (Eph. 5: 25; Gal. 2: 20). He has made His agonizing
death on the cross to be the source of our life, and thus has
answered our gainsaying and hatred with redeeming love.
Thereby Satan's apparent victory became his most mighty and
decisive overthrow, and the apparent overthrow of Jesus became
His most mighty and triumphant victory.

III. THE SIGNIFICANCE OF THE CROSS FOR US

A. THE INDIVIDUAL ASPECT

For the individual the cross has a double meaning: it is the basis of his *justification*, the putting his past in order legally; and the basis of his *sanctification*, the ruling of his present morally.

1. *The Ground of Justification.* Our sins must all be laid on the Surety (Isa. 53: 6); He must bear them as substitute for others (I Pet. 2: 24; Heb. 9: 28), so that they, having died to sin, shall now live unto righteousness (II Cor. 5: 21). And as the destruction of man was occasioned by the Fall, historically one single event (Gen. 3), so must he now, in the same manner, be raised from his fall, by the Surety through one single event, the "one act of righteousness" of Golgotha (Rom. 5: 18).[1]

As the nature of sin consists in the separation of the creature from the Creator, who is the Source of all life, it consists consequently in his death; and because of the necessity that sin and propitiation shall correspond; therefore must the Redeemer endure the sentence of this death, and thus through His death effect the restoration of life. "Without shedding of blood there is no forgiveness" (Heb. 9: 22). Only through death could He take away the strength of him who had the power of death, the Devil (Heb. 2: 14). The redemption must consist in this, that death, this great enemy of men (I Cor. 15: 56), must become the means of their salvation, and that which is the necessary continuance and punishment of sin must become the way of redemption from sin (Eph. 2: 16). But this means that the death of Christ is the death of death.[2] Compare the brazen serpent in the wilderness (Num. 21: 6, 8; John 3: 14), and how David slew Goliath with Goliath's own sword (I Sam. 17: 51).

This is the logic of salvation. It stands firmly rooted and unimpeachable in God's redeeming plan. On its compelling demonstration all proud attacks of unbelief are shattered. The hated "blood theology" of the Bible (Heb. 9: 22), with the crucified Christ as its centre (I Cor. 2: 2; Gal. 3: 1), remains

---

[1] The Greek word *dikaiōma* (righteous deed), which Paul uses here, in distinction from *dikaiosyne* (righteousness as an attribute), means a single right act. Not through the righteousness (*dikaiosyne*) of the holy *life* on earth of Jesus was salvation gained, but through the one act of righteousness, His obedience unto *death*. Of course, both belong together.

[2] "At CASTLE CAMPS the following quaint epitaph upon a former rector:
Mors mortis morti mortem nisi morte dedisset,
            Aeternae Vitae Janua clausa foret.
The translation is obviously:
Unless the Death of Death (Christ) had given death to death by His own death, the gate of eternal life had been closed."
            H. E. Norfolk's *Gleanings in Graveyards*, p. 11 (1861). [Trans.]

nevertheless the rock of salvation: to many, indeed, a stone of stumbling and a rock of offence (I Pet. 2: 8), a sign everywhere spoken against (Acts 28: 22; Luke 2: 34); but to the redeemed the living corner stone, chosen, costly, and most firmly grounded (I Pet. 2: 4, 6; Isa. 28: 16; Psa. 118: 22). It is appointed to be the falling and rising of many (Luke 2: 34); to the one a savour of death unto death, to the other a savour of life unto life (II Cor. 2: 15, 16); to the Jews a stumbling-block, to the Greeks folly (I Cor. 1: 23), but in either case the truth (Rom. 15: 8), the power (I Cor. 1: 18), and the wisdom of the Most High (I Cor. 1: 24).

Note on Substitution.

So deeply was the thought of substitution impressed in advance on the Old Testament that sometimes it uses one and the same word for *sin* and *sin offering* (Heb. *chata-ah*). In Exod. 34: 7 and I Sam. 2: 17 this word means *sin*; in Num. 32: 23 and Isa. 5: 18, the *punishment* of sin; and in Lev. 6: 18, 23 and Ezek. 40: 39 the *sin offering*. Thus also Christ, Who knew no sin, was "made sin for us," that is, was caused to be the sin *offering* (II Cor. 5: 21). Indeed, He Himself testified to this truth of substitution. It was not first taught by Paul, whom unbelief slanders as the "falsifier" of Christianity. For in Matt. 20: 28 Christ says Himself that He gives His life "a ransom price instead of many," where for "instead of" the original text uses *anti*. It cannot be denied that this word has here the sense of "in place of;" for when, for example, at Gen. 22: 13 the Greek Old Testament says that Abraham offered the ram "for" (Gk. *anti*) his son; or when in the catalogue of the kings it says that the son became king "for" (*anti*) his deceased father (Gen. 36: 33–35; etc.) it is plain that *anti* has the meaning "instead of." Thus Paul drew from Christ Himself his right to describe the self-offering of the Lord as a "ransom price instead of all" (*anti-lutron*, I Tim. 2: 6).

For the saved the cross is then

2. *The Basis of Sanctification.* Christ the Lord died on the cross that we might be saved from the cross. That for us is the *ex*cluding, judicial side of His death, the *release* provided by Golgotha. Nevertheless, in spite of this, Christ died there on the cross in order that we should come on the cross together with Him. This for us is the *in*cluding, moral side of His death, the *obligation* of Golgotha. We are "planted together" with the Crucified One and associated organically with "the likeness of his death" (Rom. 6: 5). We are followers, cross-bearers (Matt. 10: 38), corns of wheat as He was, who only through death

really live (John 12: 24, 25). We are called to share in the character of the indeed dark, but none the less precious foundation of our own redemption. We have been "crucified with Christ" (Gal. 2: 20). For us

(a) The world *around* is dead through the Crucified One. Through the cross it is "crucified" for us and we to the world (Gal. 6: 14).

(b) The world *within* us is likewise with us on the cross. "Knowing this, that our old man was crucified with Him . . . that we should no more serve sin" (Rom. 6: 6, 11).

(c) The world *beneath* us is completely conquered through the cross: for "after that Christ had disarmed the powers and authorities, he set them publicly in the pillory and through the cross triumphed over them" (Col. 2: 15; Gen. 3: 15). And finally through the cross

(d) The world *above* us is, for us, grace and blessing; for the curse of the law is done away (Gal. 3. 13). The indictment contained in its commandments, which testified against us, is cancelled and nailed to the cross (Col. 2: 14). God's glance can no longer fall on it without at the same time falling on the cross. It likewise has died together and been crucified with Him: "I through the law died to the law, that I might live unto God" (Gal. 2: 19).

The law of God had suspended death over the sinner (Gal. 3: 10), and Christ has borne this in his place. Thus Christ also has died "through" the law. But thereby the law has lost any further valid claim against Him, even as by means of the execution the man condemned to death passes out of the relation of a subject to the authority that executes him. Thus Christ also is now dead to the law. Now what Christ experienced the believer in Him experienced together with Him (Rom. 6: 5–11). Thus is he also dead as regards the law, and lives now in the liberty of the One raised from the dead (Rom. 7: 4).

B. THE CORPORATE ASPECT

For mankind corporately also there has been introduced through the cross a completely new order, in three respects:

inwardly — by removal of the law;
outwardly — by admission of all nations to salvation;
in general — by the universal triumph of the Crucified.

1. *The Removal of the Law.* As to the inner life the cross signifies the fulfilment and therefore the abolition of all Levitical sacrifices (Heb. 10: 10–14), and therewith the annulment of the Levitical law in general (Heb. 7: 18); for the sacrifices were the basis of the priesthood, and the priesthood was the foundation of that law (Heb. 7: 11). But thus Christ through the cross has become "the end of the law" (Rom. 10: 4), and also the

Surety of a better covenant (Heb. 7: 22), even the new covenant (Matt. 26: 28), through which "the called receive the promise of eternal inheritance" (Heb. 9: 15–17). But inasmuch as the Levitical priesthood is dissolved the "former tabernacle" is gone (Heb. 9: 8), the veil of the temple is rent (Matt. 27: 51), the way into the most holy place is free (Heb. 9: 8; 10: 19–22), and the whole people of God is now a kingdom of priests (I Pet. 2: 9; Rev. 1: 6).

2. *The Admission of all Nations to Salvation.* But as the law is done away inwardly it must also have been done away outwardly. Until the cross the law, as Israel's "tutor unto Christ" (Gal. 3: 24), was the "hedge" that separated the Jewish people from the peoples of the world (Eph. 2: 14). The nations were "without law" (Rom. 2: 12), and "aliens as regards the covenants of the promise" (Eph. 2: 12). There existed a tension between the two, a kind of "enmity" in the annals of salvation (Eph. 2: 15), which did not permit those "far off" and those "near" to come together. But now Christ is "our peace." By the fulfilment of the law He has removed "the middle wall of partition," and both, Jews and Gentiles, in the *one* body of His church, He has reconciled to one another, as well as to God, through the cross (Eph. 2: 13–16).

Therefore the fulfilment of the law through the death of Christ signified that "the promise to Abraham had broken through the bounds of the Mosaic law" (comp. Gen. 12: 3; Gal. 3: 13, 14). This further meant the enlargement of salvation beyond Israel to the peoples of the world, and the way, by the extreme straitness of the cross, out into all-embracing breadth, and so the passing from the nationalism of preparation into the universalism of fulfilment (John 11: 52). "And I, if I be lifted up from the earth, will draw all to me" (John 12: 32).

3. *The Universal Triumph of the Crucified.* "Now is the [or, as R.V. mgn, a] judgment of this world. Now shall the prince of this world be cast out" (John 12: 31). It was through the cross that the dying One triumphed (Rev. 5: 5, 6). It was through the cross that He robbed the principalities of their armour (Col. 2: 14, 15). It was through His death that He took away the might of him who had the power of death, the Devil (Heb. 2: 14). Hence His victorious cry "It is finished" (John 19: 30).

The casting out of Satan
as to its *power*—it is based on Golgotha (John 12: 31);
as to its *realization*—it comes about gradually (Matt. 12: 29);
as to its *final result*—it will in due time be complete (Rev. 20: 10).

Therefore the double sense in Scripture of the expression "uplifted" (John 3: 14; 8: 28; 12: 32; Phil. 2: 9). For the being "lifted up" on the cross and the being "exalted" to the throne of heaven belong together, and in Greek the one word is used for both events. The Crucified One is the Crowned One (Phil. 2: 8–11; Heb. 2: 9); and therefore must the old prince of this world be cast out, because the new, the rightful Prince will enter.

Therefore the earth shook at the death of the Lord (Matt. 27: 52), and the sun lost its light (Luke 23: 44, 45). For the cross of Christ is the great NO of God to every display of sin (John 12: 31). Therefore in the day of the world's destruction the earth will be convulsed (Hag. 2: 6; Heb. 12: 26, 27) and the sun be covered with shame (Isa. 24: 23); the moon will no more shine, the stars will grow pale, and heaven and earth will flee from before the great white throne (Rev. 20: 11). But then, indeed, out of the old world, by the transfiguration of its basic elements, which had been dissolved by fiery heat, there will emerge a new and glorious world; and as at the end of the time the universe must experience its death, its "Golgotha," so also, immediately after, on the basis of the cross, it will experience its resurrection and Easter morning through the transfiguring power of God. This is the prophetic meaning of the darkening of the sun and of the quaking of the earth in the moment of the death on Golgotha.

4. *Christ the Corn of Wheat.* Through all these experiences "Christ became

the corn of wheat whose world-redeeming love laid Him in the earth on Good Friday;

the corn of wheat which on Easter Sunday broke through the soil and began to grow towards heaven;

the corn of wheat whose golden stalk ascended to heaven on Ascension Day;

the corn of wheat whose ears, rich with myriads of grains, bent to the earth on Pentecost and scattered the seeds out of which the church should be born" (John 12: 24).

5. *The Cross from Eternity to Eternity.* Thus we see the cross everywhere:

the cross in eternity—the Lamb foreknown before the foundation of the world;

the cross in the past—Gethsemane, Gabbatha, Golgotha;

the cross in the present—the crucified Christ as the living foundation theme of our own proper proclamation (I Cor. 2: 2);

the cross in the future—the Saviour formerly humbled as then King of the manifested Messianic kingdom (Phil. 2: 8–11); and

the cross in the glory—the message that the Lamb is the precious stone which is the foundation of the heavenly city (Rev. 21: 14), and, in the midst of the throne, the Lamb Himself as the object of worship of the blessed spirits (Rev. 5: 6–10).

CHAPTER V

THE TRIUMPH OF THE RESURRECTION

CHRIST is risen! With this victorious cry the gospel has passed through the lands. The message of the cross is at the same time a message of the resurrection (Acts 1: 22; 2: 32). In this lies its invincibility.

In itself a return of the Redeemer to heaven without a bodily resurrection were conceivable. The Son of God would have remained the Living One had He, immediately after death, returned to the glory of the Father in spiritual nature. Before His incarnation He had existed eternally in heaven without a human body, and had nevertheless been the fountain and prince of all created life (Acts 3: 15; John 1: 4). No: continued existence after death and ascent to the heavenly throne were not of necessity the same as resurrection of the body.

And yet this last was precisely the prerequisite for the carrying through of the redemption, for it alone was:

I. The Full Outworking of the Redeemer's Victory over Death

By a return to heaven without resurrection of the body Christ would not have been displayed as the complete conqueror of death (Psa. 16: 10). He would have triumphed over death only spiritually and morally, but His victory over physical death would not have come to the front in a royal manner. His victory would have been, as it were, a "two-thirds" triumph but not a complete triumph; for of the threefold personality only two parts, spirit and soul, but not the body also, would have been included in the triumph of His resurrection.

But still more. Without bodily resurrection Christ would not have been revealed as *in any degree* the conqueror of death. For death is not the cessation of existence but is the dissolution of the human personality, it is not extinction of being but the tearing asunder of the connexion between spirit, soul, and body. Conquest of death must therefore be displayed in the restoration of this oneness, in the re-establishing of this organic connexion of spirit, soul, and body, which, from the point of view of the body, means the reuniting of the body with the soul and spirit. Therefore without bodily resurrection *no sort of* triumph of life (I Cor. 15: 54–57), without bodily resurrection *no* plain fruit of the victory. Only by resurrection of the body can it be shown that death has been conquered. And we must have so decided even did we not have in the four Gospels the testimony to the empty grave of Jesus (Matt. 28; Mark 16; Luke 24; John 20). Further, the resurrection was necessary as

II. THE PRESUPPOSITION FOR THE ARISING OF FAITH IN THE REDEEMED

"For faith comes through preaching" (Rom. 10: 14–17), and this goes back to the faith of the *first* period. The individual believes through the testimony of those who have believed before him, and their faith is unthinkable apart from the faith of the first generation (Eph. 2: 20). But it was precisely this faith that had collapsed after Christ's death on the cross (John 20: 19, 25; Luke 24: 21, 22; Mark 16: 14), and it was only re-established by the bodily resurrection of the Lord and His subsequent appearances as the Risen One (John 20: 8, 20; I Pet. 1: 21). Without the bodily resurrection no thinking man would ever have believed upon the Crucified One; for His end would have contradicted His own prior announcements of His resurrection and triumph (Matt. 16: 21; 17: 23; 20: 19; comp. 12: 40; John 2: 19).

The resurrection of the Lord is therefore the seal of the Father on the person and work of the Son (Acts 2: 32). By His resurrection Christ is demonstrated to be the Prophet and the Son of God (Rom. 1: 4). The resurrection is the seal on

1. the testimony of the prophets (Psa. 16: 10; Hos. 6: 2; the "sign of Jonah," Matt. 12: 39, 40; Isa. 53: 8–10);

2. the testimony of Jesus to Himself (Matt. 16: 21; John 2: 19–22);

3. the testimony of His apostles (I Cor. 15: 15);

4. the truth that Jesus is the Son of God (Rom. 1: 4; Acts 13: 33);

5. the Kingship of Jesus (Acts 13: 34);

6. the full authority of Jesus as universal Judge (Acts 17: 31); and it guarantees

7. our own future resurrection and glory (I Thess. 4: 14).

Therefore it is the most authentic and best attested event in the history of salvation. The first epistle to the Corinthians is acknowledged as genuine by the most radical critics of the Bible. It is in this epistle that Paul, appealing to *hundreds* of still living witnesses, sets before readers, some of whom were opposing and therefore critical (I Cor. 15: 6), the following four chief proofs:

i. *The proof of experience.* The Corinthians had themselves been saved through the message concerning the One who had experienced the resurrection of the body (I Cor. 15: 1, 2);

ii. *The proof from Scripture.* Christ had not only died but had also been raised "according to the Scriptures" (I Cor. 15: 3, 4);

iii. *The proof of witnesses.* More than half a thousand men, under the most diverse circumstances, had personally seen Him after His resurrection (I Cor. 15: 5–12);

iv. *The proof from the necessity of the event in the history of salvation.* "Is Christ not risen, then our preaching is vain, and your faith is vain; then those who have slept in Christ are lost; then we are the most wretched of all men" (I Cor. 15: 13–19).

Consequently the cross and the resurrection belong together. The Crucified One dies so as to rise (John 10: 17), the Risen One lives for ever as the Crucified One (I Cor. 2: 2; Rev. 5: 6).[1]

Therefore the saving effects of the redemption were always brought into connexion with both of these facts in unison, thus

the reconciliation of those to be led to faith in Christ (Rom. 5: 10);

the putting away of sin in believers (Rom. 6: 10, 11);

their living fellowship with the Redeemer (I Thess. 5: 10);

the lordship of Christ (Rom. 14: 9);

His heavenly priesthood (Rom. 8: 34);

His coming union with His glorified church (I Thess. 4: 14 ff.);

the perpetuation of the love of His heavenly Father (John 10: 17).

The foregoing shows that the resurrection, in connexion with the cross, is

III. The Foundation of New Life for Believers

That is to say, the sin offering of Christ can benefit the guilty sinner only when he believes on Him as the counterpart of the uplifted serpent (John 3: 14), as the Lamb of God Who has taken away the sin of the world (John 1: 29). But the resurrection was necessary to make this faith possible. For faith in the Lamb of God had not been possible apart from the display of the complete victory of Golgotha (John 19: 30) by the triumph of the resurrection.

Therefore only in the raised and exalted Mediator does the salvation won for us on the cross become available. Only in the Lamb exalted to glory does grace stand open to all. And because we have thus through faith received the forgiveness of sins, and thereby in the judgment of God have been made righteous and become His children, therefore God has sent the Spirit of His Son into our hearts (Gal. 4. 6). So the blessed fruit of that which took place in the sacrificial death of the Son of

---

[1] According to I Cor. 2: 2, Paul preached Christ as the "Crucified One," where the perfect participle (*estaurōmenon*) expresses continuance; that is, that Christ as the Risen One is viewed as eternally connected with the cross. Thus Thomas also sees the Risen One with His wound-marks (John 20: 27), and John sees the Lamb at the throne of glory "as if it had been slain" (Rev. 5: 6).

God, and in the reconciliation, is an organic union of the believer with Christ (Rom. 6: 5; Gal. 2: 19, 20; Col. 3: 3), a fellowship of the redeemed in the death and life of the Redeemer. It is, as it were, an eating and drinking of His flesh and His blood (John 6: 53, 32–35, 48–58), with which we may compare the Old Testament type of the eating of the sacrifice (Lev. 7: 32–34; Exod. 12: 3 ff.; I Cor. 5: 7; Heb. 13: 10); and so Christ *for* us becomes Christ *in* us the hope of glory (Col. 1: 27).

Thus in the doctrine of substitution the Scripture deals with something much higher than a merely intellectual process of subtraction and addition, a mechanical accounting and carrying forward of guilt and merit, a sort of mercantile matter-of-fact entering or not entering the items of debit and credit. It is concerned with the organic interweaving of a completely new life-principle, divine, personal, all-penetrating.

Christ the Giver can give the gifts only in Himself. Only thus does He become really the Giver (II Cor. 9: 15). He not only prepares the way and shows the way but is Himself the way (John 14: 6); for He is not only Propitiator but propitiation (I John 2: 2; 4: 10), not only Redeemer but redemption (I Cor. 1: 30). The personal is spoken of as the thing, that the thing may be shown to be personal. Therefore faith in Him is not only an external assent, but a faith that brings into union with Him personally, that is, *into*[1] His fellowship, and with Paul and all the redeemed the watchword "in Christ" is the word that describes the origin and essence of their experience of salvation.

With Paul the expression "in Christ" is found 164 times, as "justified *in* Christ" (Gal. 2: 17), "God's righteousness *in* him" (II Cor. 5: 21). Of this blessed, life-penetrating secret all his letters speak, each in its particular and specially prominent aspect. Thus:

in Romans	— justification in Christ;
in Corinthians	— sanctification in Christ;
in Galatians	— freedom in Christ;
in Ephesians	— oneness in Christ;
in Philippians	— joy in Christ;
in Colossians	— fulness in Christ;
in Thessalonians	— glorification in Christ.

Therefore the propitiatory sacrifice of Christ can only righteously benefit the guilty sinner if he is at the same time united to the holy Redeemer by the new birth. But the organic can only exist by the union formed by a head and members having the same nature (Heb. 2: 14–17), and therefore Christ must remain a man for ever. Only as man can He be the head of a human organism.

[1] Gk. *pisteuein eis* (e.g. Acts 10: 43; Phil. 1: 29; I Pet. 1: 8).

But the body is of the essence of man.   It is not "a prison of the soul," as Plato, Aristotle, and Origen thought, but it belongs to the very idea of manhood.   Without the body the man is "naked," unclothed (II Cor. 5: 3).   And therefore Christ also, since He is to remain a man, requires eternally a man's body. Without bodily resurrection Christ would, as it were, have left the human order, and could not be the completer and transfigurer of the work of redemption He wrought by His incarnation (Heb. 2: 14).

Therefore the bodily resurrection denoted the return of the Redeemer to full human nature, the immortalizing of His humanity in transfigured, glorified form.   It indicated that Christ is the "last Adam" (Rom. 5: 12–21), the "second man" from heaven (I Cor. 15: 45, 47), and that in heaven, at the right hand of God (Acts 1: 11; Dan. 7: 13; Rev. 1: 13; Phil. 3: 21), He is the creative Beginner and the organic "Head" (Eph. 1: 22) of a redeemed spiritual mankind.

At the same time we face here an immense strain upon our powers of thought.   For how can the Redeemer after His exaltation in glory be still "man," and, moreover, in the form of a transfigured body?   Did He not Himself say to His own, "Behold, I am with you all the days"? and above all, is He not the second Person in the Godhead?   Here appears anew the abyss of the eternal.   The super-spatial and the super-temporal are to us wholly beyond explanation.   When we here speak, as the Bible speaks, of the "material" and "corporeal," it all has for us a sense which is incomprehensible.   But the "eternal" is the very sphere into which Christ has gone.

Nevertheless the Holy Scripture teaches this eternal humanity of the Redeemer.   It is this very fact which guarantees the operation and permanence of His work.   His victory over death must include the endless continuance of His humanity. Only as the "Firstborn among many brethren" (Rom. 8: 29; Col. 1: 18 f.; Heb. 2: 11 f.) can He be the "cause of eternal salvation" (Heb. 2: 10; 5: 9; 6: 20).   Only so can become possible the renewing of the individual and that the redeemed shall exist "in Christ," only so are they "begotten again unto a living hope" (I Pet. 1: 3), and united to a church as its members (Eph. 4: 15, 16).   Thus they can now experience the "power of His resurrection" (Phil. 3: 10), and walk before Him in newness of life as risen with Him (Rom. 6: 5–11), and made alive with Him (Eph. 2: 5), and can in a living manner serve Him the living God (Heb. 9: 14; Rom. 7: 4–6).

This all shows that the bringing again to life of the Crucified One was not alone a work of the Father *on* the Son, not simply a sealing and ratifying of His person *after* His finished work (Acts 2: 32), and so "a resuscitation through the glory of the

Father" (Rom. 6: 4). At the same time, beyond all this, it was an indispensable element, in fact the most glorious wonder *in* the work of the Son Himself, as being, so to speak, a self-resuscitation[1] accomplished by the voluntary exercise of the power of His own life (John 2: 19). "Therefore doth my Father love me, because I lay down my life that *I* may take it again. I have power to lay it down and I have power to take it again" (John 10: 17, 18).

Finally the resurrection is:

IV. THE BASIS OF THE TRANSFIGURATION OF THE WORLD

As such it unfolds itself in three ever-widening circles. It guarantees:

in the life of the individual — the resurrection of the body;
in the life of the earth — the appearing of the kingdom of glory;
in the life of the universe — the transfigured new creation.

1. *The resurrection of the body* is possible solely through the resurrection of the Lord Jesus. His resurrection is the transfiguration of humanity in Him as its Firstfruits (I Cor. 15: 20, 23; Col. 1: 18). The resuscitation of many Old Testament saints at His resurrection shows that the way to the resurrection of the redeemed is open (Matt. 27: 52, 53). His triumph over death guarantees to us our own resurrection (Rom. 8: 11; I Thess. 4: 14). His body of glory is the pattern and type of our own future bodies (Phil. 3: 20, 21; I Cor. 15: 49). The resurrection of the "firstfruits" is the basis of all resurrection (John 5: 26–29).

Even the resurrection of judgment is committed to the Son for the very reason that "He is a Son of man" (John 5: 27, 29). So *all* resurrection, of both believers and unbelievers, is guaranteed by the resurrection of the last Adam. "Since through a man death came, so also through a man (the) resurrection of the dead. Even as in Adam all die, thus also in the Christ will all be made alive" (I Cor. 15: 21, 22). Further

2. *The Millennial Kingdom* is based entirely on the resurrection of the Lord Jesus. For the promise given to David spoke of an eternal transfigured human kingdom (II Sam. 7: 13). But for this purpose an eternal human King is required, even the Son of man, who will yet appear on the clouds of heaven (Dan. 7: 13; Matt. 26: 64; Rev. 1: 13). The continuing humanity of Christ in resurrection is thus the fulfilment in principle of the prophecy of the kingdom as given to David. The resurrection of the

[1] In the resuscitation Christ is passive, in the resurrection He is active. As resuscitation the Easter wonder is an act of the Father, as resurrection it is an act of the Son. In resuscitation the evidential preponderates, in resurrection the organic. But both are only different aspects of the same event.

King is the foundation for the "re-birth" (Matt. 19: 28) of the Messianic world, and that which will take place at the return of Christ will be only the historical manifestation of this "fulfilment" given long since at His first coming.

Therefore Paul says: "that God raised him (Jesus) from the dead . . . he declared thus: I will give you the inviolable blessings promised to David" (Acts 13: 34; Isa. 55: 3; comp. Acts 2: 30, 31). Spiritual resurrection of Israel (Ezek. 37: 1–14): spiritual re-birth of the nations (Psa. 87: 4–6; Isa. 25: 7, 8; 19: 21–25); renewing of nature (Isa. 41: 18; 55: 12, 13): elimination from the animal world of the destructive power of wild beasts (Isa. 11: 6, 7): increase of the life-energy and the age of mankind (Isa. 65: 20, 22)—in this manner in due time will the life-energy of the Risen One fill the whole earth, and the visible rule of Messiah will be re-birth and new life for the earthly creation (Matt. 19: 28).

But even the Millennial kingdom is only introduction and prelude. The final goal is

3. *The New Heaven and the New Earth* after the great white throne (Rev. 21: 1; comp. 20: 11–15). Then will not only soul and spirit but matter and nature be completely transfigured. In the heavenly Jerusalem there will be gold "transparent as glass" (Rev. 21: 18–21). Not simply spirit but spirit embodiment is the end of the ways of God with His creatures.

But there also the event of Easter is the creative basis. The resurrection of the Heir of all things is the guarantee of the new heaven and the new earth. In His risen body matter was for the first time transfigured (John 20: 27, and especially Luke 24: 39–43), and thereby the principle that matter is capable of transfiguration was revealed in the history of salvation and guaranteed. In this respect also Christ is the firstfruits (I Cor. 15: 20, 23). From that time all transfiguration of heaven and earth rests on the resurrection of the body of the Redeemer; and after the great white throne the living activity of the Risen One will be displayed in the most universal manner. Therefore the final and most inclusive import of the resurrection is this: "Behold, I create a new heaven and a new earth" (Isa. 65: 17; II Pet. 3: 13).[1]

---

[1] The significances of the resurrection given under I—IV above are as follows:
1. Christological-cosmical,
2. Subjective-apologetic,
3. Objective-organic,
4. Eschatological-universal.

CHAPTER VI

THE ASCENSION OF THE VICTOR

THE risen Victor has gone into heaven. He who by men was lifted up on a cross (John 12: 32, 33; 8: 28; 3: 14), by God was taken up into the glory (Phil. 2: 9; Acts 2: 33; 5: 31). "Sit thou at my right hand, until I lay thine enemies as the footstool of thy feet" (Psa. 110: 1).

For all three offices of the Redeemer the ascension to heaven has the most decided significance. It is

for the prophetic office—transition from the realm of immediate prophecy into that of spirit prophecy;

for the priestly office—transition to the high priesthood "after the order of Melchizedek;"

for the kingly office—extension of royal authority into royal rule.

I. THE PROPHETIC OFFICE

This was first of all and chiefly

1. *Testimony by Walk.* From the incarnation of the Redeemer until His public appearance the manifestation of God by Christ (John 1: 18) was throughout a prophesying by means of His personality. The life of the child, the boy, the growing man revealed the holiness of God. "He who sees me sees the Father" (John 14: 9). It displayed the divine ideal for the normal development of human life (comp. Luke 2: 40, 52). The theme of this prophecy was, so to speak, "The Man of God," and therefore that word of the Baptist, "I have need to be baptized by thee, and comest thou to me?" (Matt. 3: 14).

After the baptism there followed

2. *Prophecy by Word.* To prophesying by life was added that by teaching. Christ "taught as one having authority, and not as the scribes" (Matt. 7: 29; John 7: 46). His theme now was the kingdom of God (Matt. 4: 17). But His ascension to heaven indicated this transition of direct prophesying into indirect, and, connected with Pentecost, there commenced a prophesying which was effected from heaven, even

3. *Prophecy by the Spirit.* To us who are to be instructed there is now a "coming" of the exalted Prophet by word and in spirit (John 14: 18, 28). Not only do His messengers "come" —the apostles, prophets, shepherds and teachers (Eph. 4: 11), and His witnesses in general (Acts 1: 8), but in them and in their message Christ Himself comes (Matt. 10: 40), and from the

glory continues His prophesying through the Spirit.   Thus Paul says of the One crucified and risen, "He *came* and *proclaimed* peace to you who were far off (non-Jews) and peace to those 'near' (the Jews)" (Eph. 2: 17).   As the context shows, this does not speak of the coming and preaching of Christ in the days of His life on earth before Golgotha, but of the time after His finished peace-making work on the cross, and therefore of His "coming" in the present time, in word and spirit, to Israel and the peoples of the earth (comp. vv. 13–16).   His present theme is the completed redemption, with its peace and light (Acts 26: 23).

The ascension is of still greater significance for

II. The High Priestly Office

On earth Christ brought the essential fulfilment of the Aaronic priesthood (Heb. 5: 1–4; 9: 6–23; 10: 1; Col. 2: 16, 17), by the atoning sacrifice for the salvation of the sinner; yet as raised from the dead, and gone into the heavenly world (Heb. 9: 24; 4: 14), indeed, become higher than all heavens (Heb. 7: 26; Eph. 4: 10), He is now saluted by God as High Priest after the order of Melchizedek (Heb. 5: 10).   Therefore His ascension is not only the turning point between His humiliation and exaltation, but also between two forms of the exercise of His high priestly work.   At His ascension Christ entered the Most Holy place above "not with the blood of others," as the high priests of the Old Testament entered the most holy place on the great day of atonement (Lev. 16: 15–19), but "by virtue of His own blood," that is, on the ground of His personal merit through His self-offering on Golgotha; so as on this ground to appear now before the face of God for us (Heb. 9: 11–14, 24, 25; Rom. 8: 34).

On this account the ascension of Christ became at the same time the justifying of the Crucified One (John 16: 10; I Tim. 3: 16), see p. 41, showing the acceptance by the Father of the work of the Son.   The Highest Majesty in the heavenly world thus pronounced valid the earthly high priesthood of Christ (Acts 2: 34–36).   The ascension was the essential meaning and the central fulfilment of the most solemn high priestly act on the greatest of all Israel's festivals, the entrance into the most holy place (Heb. 9: 7), which took place on one single day of the year, the *yom kippur*, the great day of atonement (Lev. 16).

1. *Melchizedek and Christ.*   Who was Melchizedek?   He was king of the city of Salem (city of peace).   Where this city lay is not quite certain.   The church fathers thought it was the Salem by Aenon mentioned in John 3: 23 (Scythopolis on the Jordan). More probable is the assumption of Josephus and the rabbis

that it was the later Jerusalem, the Urusalim of the Tel el Amarna letters (about 1300 B.C.). Ir=Ur=city. Salem=shalom= peace (comp. Psa. 76: 2).

According to ancient Canaanite law [which was general in the ancient world] the king was at the same time chief priest of the city. And Melchizedek (as was Job in his day), in the midst of heathen surroundings, was a representative of the original revelation (Gen. 1 to 11) and therefore a priest of God Most High (Gen. 14: 18). Heb. 7: 3 does not mean that he was the Son of God Himself, for then there would have been an incarnation *before* the incarnation. Nor was he a kind of angelic appearing of the Son of God (comp. Gen. 18: 2), for as a lawful king of a city he had ruled an ancient Canaanite city State. He was a natural God-fearing man of the time of Abraham who in Heb. 7: 3 was simply compared to the Son of God.

His faith in God was rewarded in that he was ennobled by being made the highest of all types of the Redeemer. He is a type of Christ

by the union of his priesthood and kingship; he is at once priest and king;

by his personal name, Melchizedek, which means king of righteousness (Heb. 7: 2);

by the name of his city, Salem, that is, peace (Heb. 7: 2);

by his appearing in the life of Abraham (Gen. 14: 17–20). His significance here is treated only typically. Historically and in salvation's history, Abraham is the greater personality (Rom. 4: 11, 12, 16, 17); but typically Melchizedek is the greater. He is a type of Christ for he "tithed" the patriarch, and is therefore greater than the *law* (Heb. 7: 4–6); for under the law men who die received the tithes, but in Melchizedek they were taken by one of whom it is testified that he liveth. Moreover, as a consequence of the organic connexion of descendants and ancestors, in Abraham, Levi, the receiver of tithes under the law, was himself tithed (Heb. 7: 8–10). Then also, Melchizedek "blessed" the holder of the *promise* and so is greater than the promise (Heb. 7: 6, 7). He tithed and blessed in Abraham the tribe of Levi, and is therefore greater than the Levitical priesthood, the human ministers of the law and promise (Heb. 7: 9, 10). Thus he is greater than *all* that the old covenant included, for law and promise were the two pillars of and the summary of the whole Old Testament.

But above all Melchizedek is a type of Christ

by the silence of the Bible as to his ancestry, birth, and death (Heb. 7: 3). In this especially he is made completely like Him who is in truth without beginning of days, whose descent is eternal, and Who remains King and Priest eternally. In this eternity of the priesthood lies the express emphasis of the order

D

of Melchizedek. So also the priesthood of Christ is not something transferred, but is for ever His personally, and is therefore higher than the Levitical priesthood (Heb. 7: 16). It is not granted to mortal man, but to One to whom witness is borne that He lives.

Therefore He is the *only* High Priest and His office is for ever non-transferable (Heb. 7: 23, 24), founded on an oath of God the Lord. And because He, as the Son of David, is descended from the tribe of Judah and not that of Levi (Psa. 110: 1, 4; Matt. 22: 42–45; Heb. 7: 11–14), His priesthood intimates at the same time an eternal doing away of the Levitical order and therewith a definite annulling of the Levitical law based upon it[1] (Heb. 7: 12–18).

2. *The Priestly Order of Melchizedek.* This heavenly priesthood is the necessary complement of the earthly.

On earth Christ was at once priest and *sacrifice* (Heb. 9: 12–14): in heaven He is Priest and *King* (Heb. 7: 2; 8: 1);

On earth the centre of gravity was His *death,* the dissolution of His life on Golgotha (Heb. 9: 15–23): in heaven the centre of gravity is His *life,* the indissolubility of His life in the power of resurrection and ascension (Heb. 7: 16, 3, 24; Psa. 110: 1–4);

As the essential fulfilment of the Aaronic priesthood He *acquired* salvation, legally, through His sufferings, as Christ *for* us: as the Melchizedek Priest He *grants* salvation, as Christ *in* us, organically, through His victory (Col. 1: 27);

As priest on earth He laid once for all the basis (Heb. 10: 10, 14, 18); His work here below is historical and concluded (Heb. 9: 26): as Priest in heaven He works without intermission (Heb. 7: 25); His Melchizedek service is never concluded, is eternal.

As priest in lowliness He served for the redemption of the *whole* world, and without their co-operation He offered the reconciling sacrifice for *all*: as Priest on high He serves only His chosen; only for "us" His members, does He appear before the throne of God (Rom. 8: 34; Heb. 9: 24; John 17: 9).

Yet both belong together, eternally inseparable: the sacrifice and the intercession, the acquiring of salvation and the maintaining of salvation, the historical and the eternal, the suffering and the glory.

In all this His Melchizedek-priesthood is the perfecting of the Aaronic. As Priest in heaven He entered before the Father on our behalf, in the power of that which He won as priest on earth (Heb. 9: 24, 25); and so to the acquiring of salvation He adds the appropriation, preservation, and glorification; and

[1] [In Jer 31: 32 and Heb. 8: 9 it is stated distinctly that it was the covenant made at Sinai that was declared void. This leaves the prior and basic covenant with Abraham in force, which is the argument in Gal. 3: 15–17. By consequence, any provisions or features of the Abrahamic covenant which were incorporated in the Sinai covenant must also be still in force. Much follows from this. It calls for care in considering how much of the Mosaic economy has lapsed. Trans.]

the eternity of His eternal Melchizedekian dignity becomes therewith the earnest of the eternity of our own redemption. "Wherefore also He is able to save completely[1] those who draw near to
God through Him, seeing He ever liveth to make intercession
for them" (Heb. 7: 25).

But the chief significance of the ascension relates to

III. THE KINGLY OFFICE

It is the enthronement of the King of glory. He who
possesses

by birth kingly *right* (Matt. 2: 2; John 18: 37),

in His person kingly *dignity* (John 1: 49), and

in His kingly service full *authority* (Mark 1: 27; 4: 41; Matt.
7: 29), by His ascension took possession of kingly *rule*. In
heaven His hidden kingship became revealed (I Tim. 3: 16), and
His personal moral authority became world embracing, exalted
above all principalities, rule, and power (Eph. 1: 20, 21). Now
we see Jesus on the throne of God (Heb. 8: 1; Phil. 2: 9),
"exalted to the right hand of the Majesty" (Heb. 1: 3; Psa. 110:
1; Rom. 8: 34; I Pet. 3: 22), "crowned with glory and honour"
(Heb. 2: 9). In the ascension Jesus was properly made Christ
(Acts 2: 36), made Lord and Governor (Rom. 14: 9), made ruler
of all lands (Matt. 28: 18).

From heaven Christ displays His kingship in various ways:

in the founding of His church—by the outpouring of the
Spirit (Acts 2: 33; I Cor. 12: 3):

in the extension of His kingdom—by the confirming of the
message of salvation (Matt. 28: 18–20: Mark 16: 17–20):

in the control of His kingdom—by hearing prayer and by
authoritative command (I Cor. 9: 21):

in the defence of His kingdom—by overcoming hindrances
(Acts 5: 19; 12: 7, 23):

in the perfecting of His kingdom—by His coming in glory
(I Tim. 6: 14, 15).

Scripture distinguishes three "thrones," corresponding symbolically to the three chief periods of His heavenly sovereignty.

1. In the present time, between His ascension and His return,
Christ is on His *Father's* throne (Rev. 3: 21; Heb. 8: 1). "Sit
thou at my right hand, *until* I lay thine enemies as the footstool
of thy feet" (Psa. 110: 1). Throughout His "waiting" time
(Heb. 10: 13) His kingship is *super*-national, purely spiritual,
invisible, concerned with the course of salvation. This is the
kingdom of grace.

2. In the Millennial kingdom Christ is on *David's* throne

[1] ["completely" *eis to panteles*. See the only other occurrence in the New
Testament, Luke 13: 11. The woman bound by Satan was not bedridden, but
could not *completely* lift herself up; a picture of many believers. Trans.]

(Luke 1: 32; Acts 2: 30). The throne of this His earthly ancestor is then *His* throne (Rev. 3: 21; Matt. 19: 28; 25: 31), and He Himself, as the true perfect David, rules over Israel and the peoples of the world (Hos. 3: 5; Ezek. 37: 24, 25). His kingship is then visible, nationally universal from the point of view of both world history and salvation's history. This is the *kingdom of glory*.

3. The *throne of God and of the Lamb* belongs properly to the new world (Rev. 22: 1, 3). Then the kingship of the Son, under the kingship of the Father, is universal, eternal, super-historical. It is the *kingdom in consummation*.

Now a kingdom must have subjects, a king servants. But no one can own Christ as Lord except through the Holy Spirit alone (I Cor. 12: 3). For the law of His kingdom is a spiritual law (Rom. 8: 2), and the nature of His rule is righteousness, peace, and joy "in the Holy Spirit" (Rom. 14: 17). Therefore the outpouring of the Spirit was the prerequisite for the actual coming of His kingdom. Before that time the kingdom of heaven was not so real and open on earth. Pentecost was the outflow of His *kingly* office, and with the ascension there came by the Spirit a spiritual association of the subjects of the kingdom.

And the King must be on the throne before He can begin to rule. The ascension must precede Pentecost. Without the ascent of the Son there could be no descent of the Spirit: "It is good for you that I go away; for if I go not away the Comforter will not come to you; but if I go away, I will send Him to you" (John 16: 7; comp. 7: 39).

But when He sent the Spirit He thereby united Himself with His people. His person and His work are now for ever in them. Therefore everything which Christ experienced is also their portion. Crucified with Him, dead with Him, they are also made alive with Him, and with Him sit in the heavenly places (Eph. 2: 5, 6; 1: 3; comp. 1: 20). Their home country is now above, with Him in the height (John 14: 2, 3; Phil. 3: 20). Through the Spirit they have been associated with Christ in His ascension.

And at last their literal ascension to heaven will come, their rapture and exaltation to His presence (I Thess. 4: 13–18). The ascension of Christ was fundamentally the entrance of the Head of the new humanity into the heavenly glory. From then heaven —the heaven of our Lord Jesus Christ—is *our* heaven (Phil. 3: 20; Heb. 13: 14; Col. 3: 1–3). He, the Head, has gone in advance, as the Leader of His members to glory. For "does a head leave one of its members which it does not draw after it?" "I go to prepare a place for you" (John 14: 2, 3). For "where I am there shall also my servant be" (John 12: 26; 17: 24). The path to the glory is free.

CHAPTER VII

THE INAUGURATION OF THE KINGDOM OF GOD
(The Outpouring of the Holy Spirit)

"BECOME full in spirit" (Eph. 5: 18). With Pentecost a new era begins, the age of the Holy Spirit. The difference from the Old Testament period is threefold:

1. *The Extent.* Under the old covenant the Spirit came only on certain individuals (Num. 11: 29): under the new covenant He comes on all believers (Acts 2: 4, 17; Rom. 8: 9).[1]

2. *The Duration.* Under the old covenant the Spirit in each instance worked only for a time (Num. 11: 25): under the new covenant He *dwells* in believers (John 14: 17, 23; I Cor. 3: 16; II Cor. 6: 16; II Tim. 1: 14; Jas. 4: 5).

Only on this account can the church universal be described as a "temple" or "house" of God, and this as the whole church (Eph. 2: 21, 22; I Pet. 2: 4, 5), the local church (I Cor. 3: 17; I Tim. 3: 15), and the individual Christian (I Cor. 6: 19). Even of such believers as were at Corinth it is stated quite generally that "your body is a temple of the Holy Spirit, who dwells in you" (I Cor. 6: 19).

That the Holy Spirit is not merely a power, capacity, or attribute of God, but a conscious *Ego* with a will, a Divine *super*-personality, follows from this, that He speaks and calls (Acts 13:.2), commands, permits (Acts 16: 6, 7), leads (Rom. 8: 14), instructs (John 16: 13), comforts (John 14: 26), intercedes (Rom. 8: 26), bears witness (Rom. 8: 16), and can be grieved (Eph. 4: 30)—all expressions which can be used only of a living, personal being. Also in the baptismal command (Matt. 28: 19), and in the benediction in II Cor. 13: 14, He so plainly stands on the same level as the Father and the Son that He, exactly as They, is to be acknowledged as a Divine Person (*Ego*).

The third difference is

3. *The Content and Purpose* of the Spirit's work. Under the old covenant the Spirit worked only to educate and to capacitate for service: in the new He works in most manifold ways, namely, for the awakening of faith—

wooing unto salvation, as the Spirit of truth (John 15: 26);

---

[1] The difference is not expressed by the short "on" and "in," as if under the new covenant the Spirit of God is *in* believers whereas under the old covenant He came only *on* them. For not only the Old Testament working of the Spirit is described by *on*, but also that of the New Testament, indeed the event of Pentecost itself (Acts 2: 3, 17, 18; 10: 44; 11: 15; Luke 24: 49). Conversely, the Old Testament working of the Spirit is not only described by *on* but also *in* (I Pet. 1: 11).

for effecting the new birth—
  dispensing life, as the Spirit of sonship (Rom. 8: 15);
for leading in sanctification—
  educating, as the Spirit of holiness (I Cor. 6: 19, 20; I Thess. 4: 7, 8);
for stimulating service—
  equipping, as the Spirit of power (II Tim. 1: 7);
for bringing about the glorifying—
  transfiguring, as the Spirit of glory (I Pet. 4: 14).[1]

i. *Wooing unto Salvation.* The office of the Spirit is to glorify Christ (John 16: 14). As the Witness of the Lord to the world (John 15: 26; Rev. 19: 10) He is the great evangelist of the Son (Rev. 22: 17). He speaks to the world of sin, righteousness, and judgment; of the sin of the world, of the righteousness of Christ, and of the judgment upon Satan (John 16: 8–11).

The *sin of the world* He exposes by reference to their unbelief, by which they rejected the Lord, the only true good (John 16: 8, 9; Acts 2: 22, 23; 3: 13–15; 7: 52).

The *righteousness of Christ* He establishes by reference to the ascension to heaven; for by that exaltation He Who had been rejected by sinners as being unrighteous had been acknowledged by God as the holy and righteous One (John 16: 10; Acts 2: 25, comp. 34, 35; I Tim. 3: 16).

"Good Friday appeared to have adjudged Jesus to be a sinner and His judges to be righteous; but the ascension and Pentecost reversed this sentence; they awarded the righteousness to the condemned One of Golgotha and the sin to His judges." This is the meaning of the Lord's words, that the Spirit will convict the world of righteousness "*because* I go to my Father, and ye see me no more" (John 16: 10).

The judgment upon Satan the Spirit makes clear by reference to the Redeemer's victory by the cross (John 19: 30); for it is by the very cross itself that the prince of this world has been judged (John 12: 31; Col. 2: 15); and on that account the world can now be required to do homage to another, its proper Prince.

Thus through the witness of the Spirit the world, which is righteous in its own eyes, is declared *sinful*; He Who was crucified by the world is proved to be holy and *righteous*; and Satan, the instigator of the murder of Golgotha, is exposed as the one conquered and *judged*. This is the threefold witness of the Spirit to the world as the Lord Himself had described it. In all this the Spirit associates Himself with the word (I Cor. 2: 2–4). He puts the words in the mouths of His witnesses (Matt. 10: 20; Acts 1: 8), and makes the spoken and written word effectual and living (I Thess. 1: 5; Heb. 4: 12) unto salvation.

---

[1] Thus His activity is: 1. Evangelistic; 2. Organic; 3. Pedagogic; 4. Charismatic (*charisma*=gift of grace); 5. Eschatological (final history).

ii. *Dispensing Life.* Those who are won He transforms. To the winning of the soul He adds the renewing of the soul (Titus 3: 5). "It is the Spirit that makes alive" (John 6: 63; II Cor. 3: 6; Gal. 5: 25), who sets the captive free (II Cor. 3: 17; Rom. 8: 2), and makes slaves to be sons (Rom. 8: 14; Gal. 4: 6). They not only receive something new but *become* something new, recreated in the very essence of their nature (II Cor. 5: 17). They are men "in the Spirit" (Rom. 8: 9), the Spirit of Jesus Christ (Rom. 8: 9), and are therefore men "in Christ," united with Him as members.

The Old Testament had only an educative activity of the Holy Spirit (Psa. 51: 11), a preparing for service. He gave ability to prophesy (I Sam. 10: 6; I Pet. 1: 11; II Pet. 1: 21), to fight (Judges 6: 34; 14: 19), and for all kinds of handiwork (Exod. 28: 3; 31: 3-5). The significance of Pentecost consists in this, that to this pedagogic and charismatic activity of the Holy Spirit there was added the *organic*, and thenceforward the Holy Spirit works not only as the Spirit of God but especially as the Spirit of the *Son*. It is in this sense that the Spirit "was not there" before Pentecost (John 7: 39), and therefore in the Old Testament was foretold as still to come (Joel 2: 28, 29; Ezek. 36: 27; Zech. 12: 10). For this reason in Eph. 1: 13 He is spoken of as "the Holy Spirit of promise," that is, the promised Holy Spirit.

Thus the proper significance of Pentecost is that the Spirit of the Son (Gal. 4: 6) sent down from heaven, unites the redeemed with the Redeemer, carries through their incorporation as members (I Cor. 12: 13), and enables believers to appropriate personally the full fruit of the sacrifice of Christ.

Therefore to the phrase "in Christ" (used by Paul 164 times) there corresponds the phrase "in the Spirit" (19 times) and in reference to the same benefits, for example:

justification in Christ (Gal. 2: 17)
    and in the Spirit (I Cor. 6: 11);
peace in Christ (Phil. 4: 7)
    and in the Spirit (Rom. 14: 17);
sanctification in Christ (I Cor. 1: 2)
    and in the Spirit (Rom. 15: 16);
sealed in Christ (Eph. 1: 13)
    and in the Spirit (Eph. 4: 30);
indwelling of Christ (Gal. 2: 20)
    and of the Spirit (Rom. 8: 9).

Thus the relation which first, from the Divine side, was founded upon the incarnation and resurrection of Christ (that is, upon His continuing humanity), now, through the outpouring of the Holy Spirit, became also on the human side an experienced reality. "The Lord is the Spirit" (II Cor. 3: 17; I Cor. 15: 45), and he who is joined to the Lord is one spirit with Him (I Cor.

6: 17). He is a member in His body and therefore a sharer of His work. Thus Pentecost became the beginning of the period of full salvation, and the "day of the opening of the will and testament of Jesus Christ as the last Adam."

But inasmuch as they are all members in *Him* they are also *mutually* one body, members of one another (Rom. 12: 5). Through the birth of the Spirit they have become sons of the *one* kingdom of God (John 3: 3, 5; Matt. 13: 38), and "in one Spirit were all baptized into one body" (I Cor. 12: 13). This means that Pentecost was the birthday of the church and the inaugural day of the kingdom of God in the full New Testament sense. Thenceforth, alongside of the body corporate of the first Adam (I Cor. 15: 22), there exists the organism of the last Adam; alongside of lost men, the saved; alongside of Israel and the nations, the church, the "people" of God, the "new man" (Eph. 2: 15), "the Christ" (I Cor. 12: 12; 1: 13), that is, the mystical Christ, the Head of which is the glorified personal Christ.

And in the church the Spirit of God works as the Spirit of holiness,

iii. *Educating*. The Spirit glorifies the Head to the members, by showing them His glory (John 16: 14).

He *leads* the redeemed in paths of righteousness (Rom. 8: 14; Gal. 5: 25), and effects their sanctification (I Pet. 1: 2; II Thess. 2: 13).

He *comforts* them as an advocate (Gk. *parakletos*) (John 14: 16–18), and gives to them His witness (Rom. 8: 16).

He *convicts* them when unfaithful and leads them to repentance (II Cor. 2: 5–11).

He *teaches* them the words of Jesus (John 14: 26), and guides them into all the truth (John 16: 13; I John 2: 20).

iv. *Equipping for Service*. Then He prepares and uses them as His instruments. He orders their gifts and divides them according to His own will (I Cor. 12: 4–11).

He appoints their service in the church and in its gatherings (Acts 13: 4; 16: 6, 7; 20: 28; I Cor. 12: 28–30).

He animates their prayers (Jude 20; Eph. 6: 18) and grants to these authority (Rom. 8: 26).

He leads their witness (Matt. 10: 20; I Pet. 1: 12), fills it with the power of God (I Cor. 2: 4; Rom. 15: 19; I Thess. 1: 5; Acts 4: 31; 7: 55–57; 13: 9), and if they are reproached He rests upon them as the Spirit of glory (I Pet. 4: 14).

In all this He is the "power from on high" (Luke 24: 49; Acts 1: 8):

1. as a tree which brings forth its fruit (Gal. 5: 22);
2. as oil which anoints and shines (Acts 10: 38);
3. as fire which blazes (Acts 2: 3, 4; II Tim. 1: 6);
4. as water which cleanses (Ezek. 36: 25, 26);

5. as the early rain which refreshes (Joel 2: 23, 28);[1]
6. as a quiet, soft rustling (Zech. 4: 6; I Kings 19: 12, 13);
7. as a rushing wind, mysterious yet mighty (Acts 2: 2; John 3: 8).

v. *Transfiguring.* As to the future, the Spirit is the guarantee of our deliverance, the "seal" of our salvation (Eph. 1: 13; 4: 30; II Cor. 1: 22), the earnest of our inheritance (Eph. 1: 14; II Cor. 5: 5), the interest on the coming glorious estate, the first-fruits of the coming eternal harvest (Rom. 8: 23). And because our body is a temple of His Spirit God will not leave it a wilderness: "If the Spirit of him who raised Jesus from the dead dwells in you, he who raised Christ from the dead will make your mortal bodies to live, because his Spirit dwells in you" (Rom. 8: 11).

Thus the significance of Pentecost reaches on into eternity. Through the Spirit we are sons (Rom. 8: 14; Gal. 4: 6, 7), as sons we are heirs (Rom. 8: 14, 17; Gal. 4: 7), and as heirs we are sharers of His coming glory (Rom. 8: 17).

---

[1] From this picture comes the expression "the outpouring of the Holy Spirit." It is found at Joel 2: 28, and forms the contrasted spiritual counterpart to the outward dryness and inward sterility of the people of Israel in Joel's time (Joel 1: 10-12, 17-20, comp. 2: 23; Acts 2: 16, 17).

Part II

THE CHURCH OF THE FIRSTBORN ONES

Section I—The Call of the Church

CHAPTER I

THE NEW PEOPLE OF GOD

*"Evangelizing·is the greatest thing now going on in the world.
It is a great power in servant's form."*

THE message of the cross advances through the world. The present age is of especial significance. Its purpose is the calling out of the church. Everything in it is directed to this end.

I. THE GOAL OF THE CALL

The programme for the present time is not the transforming of mankind and the creating of Christian nations. This will not take place before the coming visible kingdom of God (Isa. 2: 3, 4; 19; 21–25). But the present work of God is "to take *out* of the nations a people for His name" (Acts 15: 14), that is, not Christianizing the races but evangelizing the races, for the purpose of calling out a *super*-national people of God (Matt. 28: 19; Mark 16: 15). "There is neither Jew nor Greek, neither slave nor freeman . . . but ye are altogether one in Christ" (Gal. 3: 28; Col. 3: 11).

In place of the former twofold division of mankind there thus arises a threefold division (I Cor. 10: 32), and to Israel and the peoples of the world there is added the church as a "third race." Thenceforth each who is not a Christian in the New Testament sense (Acts 11: 26), is either a Jew or a Gentile. A fourth possibility does not exist.

A general nominal Christen*dom* has no justification in the New Testament. It is apostasy from Christian*ity* and is after all only a "monstrous mental delusion" (Kierkegaard).

This people of God to be newly won the Scripture names *ecclesia* (Matt. 16: 18; Eph. 1: 22). It is the company of the redeemed who, by means of the proclamation of the gospel (I Tim. 2: 7), have been called out of Jews and Gentiles (Eph. 2: 11–22), who, in the enjoyment of the heavenly citizenship (Phil. 3: 20) and possession of the divine ennoblement (John 1:

12, 13), will become the future "legal administrative assembly" of the kingdom of heaven (I Cor. 6: 2, 3). They are to be exalted and glorified with Christ. They are "from heaven, in heaven, for heaven. Their nature is eternal. The church originates in eternity and is for eternity, taken out of time."

Under the old covenant Israel had already been called an *ecclesia*. This word occurs about 100 times in the Septuagint (the Greek translation of the Old Testament), which is almost as often as in the New Testament. In the latter it is used ten times of the whole church (especially Matt. 16: 18; Eph. 1: 22; 3: 10, 21; 5: 23–32; Col. 1: 18, 24), and over 90 times of the local church (e.g. Matt. 18: 17). Almost everywhere in the Septuagint it is the rendering of the Hebrew *kahal*. This comes from the verb *khl* "to assemble together" (Joshua 18: 1; 22: 12; etc.), or "to assemble" (Deut. 4: 10; 31: 12; etc.). Thus the word applies to almost every kind of gathering, as, e.g., I Sam. 17: 47; Jer. 26: 17; but it had acquired a special meaning by association with Jehovah the God of Israel. As the called and assembled people of God Israel is *kahal Jehovah*, *ecclesia* of God (Deut. 23: 2; 3: 8; Psa. 22: 25; etc.). Its visible presentation in this its character is found in the wilderness. "The tents of the twelve-tribed people lie in regular order around the Tabernacle. At the summons of the herald the people gather together in the space before the Tent, and stand there as the *people* of God, to receive his commands and blessing." In the New Testament also Israel is described as an *ecclesia* (Acts 7: 38). It is the word for the ideal oneness of Israel as the chosen people, even when as to locality it was not gathered as a religious fellowship (Exod. 16: 3; Num. 15: 15).

But Israel as a national unity too soon trod the path of apostasy. It lost in practice its character as the "people of God." It became *Lo ammi*, "not my people" (Hos. 1: 9). Only a fragment, the little company of the faithful, remained devoted to their God. Therefore in the history of salvation they became the kernel of the race, who carried forward its calling, the real Israel, the true people of God, the actual and essential embodiment of the Old Testament idea of the *ecclesia*. To them therefore attached all the promises of the kingdom of God. While unbelieving Israel, as a whole, fell under the judgment of the law, the company of the faithful were, as a remnant, saved out of the judgments (Isa. 6: 13; Mal. 4: 1, 2; Hos. 1: 10). At the same time they became the basis for the carrying through and completing of the plan that there shall be a people of God (Mic. 2: 12; 4: 7). "Therefore with the prophets 'remnant' became the direct and special description of the people of God, the *ecclesia* of the End time." As such it is the surviving "root-stock", the "holy seed" out of which new life shall sprout (Isa. 6: 13), the "little flock" which at last receives the great kingdom (Mic. 2: 12). The existence and history of this essential kernel of the Old Testament *ecclesia* is therefore the presupposition and preparation for a people of God at the End time.

The first Christians declared themselves to be this people of God of the End time. They are the goal of Old Testament history (I Cor. 10: 11), the Messianic church, the saved of the "last days." Upon us who live in the Messianic (Christian) age the "end points"[1] of the pre-Messianic (pre-Christian) ages are come (I Cor. 10: 11), that is, the time of the Messianic perfecting. (Upon the New Testament sense of the term "last days" see pp. 102, 103).

This is the reason why they do not apply to themselves any of the other descriptions of religious fellowship which were ready to hand, such as *koinos, syllogos, thiasos, synodos*. In the world surrounding early Christianity these were the terms for describing religious unions, even as today in Christian spheres we speak of Churches, Free Churches, Fellowships, Unions. But none of these terms was chosen by the Christians as their chief description. They much rather used the familiar word *ecclesia* taken from the Greek Old Testament, the name of the ancient believing community of which the "remnant" of the faithful were historically the kernel, the continuance, and the embodiment.

By this the early Christians "did no more and no less than Paul, who said of the Christians that they are Israel after the Spirit, the Israel of God (Gal. 6: 16; comp. I Cor. 10: 18; Gal. 4: 29), the (true) descendants of Abraham (Gal. 3: 29); or than Peter did when he brought over to the Christian community the titles of honour of Exod. 19: 6 and Isa. 43: 21, and called them 'chosen race, royal priesthood, holy nation, people for possession' (I Pet. 2: 9). The act of the Lord Himself must have brought His disciples near to this conception. For the choice of exactly twelve disciples to be apostles must have meant to them nothing else than that these, as formerly the twelve patriarchs, should be ancestors of a new people. . . . As the Passover in Israel, so the Lord's Supper was the great repast of this new people, and baptism was the parallel to the passage through the Red Sea" (I Cor. 10: 1).

The gathering out of this church, the church of the firstborn ones, is the proper, the chief object of this age. Its meaning is nothing less than the creating of a royal family, the ruling aristocracy of the coming kingdom of the ages (I Cor. 6: 2, 3). "Fear not, little flock, for it is your Father's good pleasure to give you the kingdom" (Luke 12: 32).

[1] The "goal points" (Gk. *ta telē*).

NOTE on the word *ecclesia*.

Who first applied the Greek word *ecclesia* to the New Testament church cannot now be settled. On the one hand Jesus spoke Aramaic, including originally the words in Matt. 16: 18; 18: 17. On the other hand Paul, applies the Greek word *ecclesia* in such a way as presupposes its use before the period of his activities (Gal. 1: 22), indeed, before the time of his conversion (Gal. 1: 13; Phil. 3: 6; I Cor. 15: 9). So most probably it was Greek-speaking Jewish Christians before Paul's conversion who first called the Christian community an *ecclesia*. Luke also calls the pre-Pauline Christian community an *ecclesia*. From Acts 6: 1, 9, we know that in the time of the very first church in Jerusalem there were Hellenistic, that is, Greek-speaking synagogues, of whose members a number had become Christians.

The Greek word *ecclesia* is derived from *ek* out of and *kaleo* I call. But too much stress is not to be laid on this derivation, as if the word had on this account been chosen as the new description of the fellowship of believers, so as to call them "the called out (company) of the Lord." Here and there this may indeed have had a sympathetic ring and have been found specially suitable and acceptable; but in principle the derivation of a word (etymology) and its meaning (definition) are not always or of necessity the same. It is indeed true that through the gospel the church is a company that is called out from sin, the world, death, and judgment, but this fact is expressed in another form and manner, not in the first place through the choice of the word *ecclesia*. Otherwise the verb which lies at its root, *ekkaleo*, must have been used at least once in the New Testament. And yet not in a single passage in the whole New Testament is this the case, although such application in certain passages would have been quite ready to hand (I Pet. 2: 9; 1: 15; II Thess. 2: 14; Rom. 8: 28 f.).

In Greek the work *ecclesia* was first of all the description of any occasional gathering of a people. It is used in this sense in Acts 19: 32, 41. But in political life in the Greek free States the word denoted the regular legislative assembly *called out* by a *herald* from the populace, composed of all free, irreproachable citizens entitled to vote. The points of agreement between the "*ecclesia* of God" and this Hellenistic political *ecclesia* are chiefly four, as follows:

1. The *summons* through the message of the herald of the gospel (Phil. 3: 14; II Tim. 1: 9). Preach=Gk. *kēryssein*, to herald; comp. *kēryx* herald).

2. The call *out of* the world (Rom. 11: 7; II Pet. 1: 10).

3. *Three conditions* of admission attached to the *ecclesia*:
   citizenship: "our citizenship is in heaven" (Phil. 3: 20);
   freedom: slaves were not admitted to the Greek *ecclesia*:

"ye were slaves of sin" (Rom. 6: 20): "Ye have been called to freedom" (Gal. 5: 13);

irreproachableness: no criminal had access to the Greek *ecclesia*: "justified freely through His grace" (Rom. 3: 24).

4. *The purpose* of the *ecclesia*: the ordering of public affairs of State, that is, government business : "Know ye not that the saints shall judge the world?" (I Cor. 6: 3; comp. 5).

Nevertheless, however well these parallels fit one another, and even though they might perhaps be sometimes yet closer, the New Testament use of the word is not derived from the Greek State life. As we saw, its root lies much rather in the Septuagint. For there, in this Greek (Old Testament) Bible of the early Christians, this word was already the designation of the people of Israel (Deut. 4: 10; Psa. 22: 22, 25; comp. Acts 7: 38). So in the time of Jesus and His apostles the word *kahal* (=*ecclesia*) was already in use as the Biblico-theocratical description of the conception "people of God." Consequently they did not need first to create it but could quite naturally take it over from the Septuagint and apply it to the New Testament people of God.

The word *ecclesia* is itself untranslatable. Contention as to the translation is idle. The chief matter is to attach to the word the right meaning.

II. THE BEGINNING OF THE CALL

In the early days of the Lord Jesus the church, in the full New Testament sense, did not exist. Therefore Christ spoke of it as still future: "I *will* build my church" (Matt. 16: 18). It was at Pentecost first that the believers "were in one Spirit baptized into one body" (I Cor. 12: 13). Therefore Pentecost is the birthday of the church.

Nevertheless the new beginning took place entirely on Jewish national ground. Only Israelites were recipients of the Spirit and only Jews and Jewish associates (proselytes) were hearers of the preaching (Acts 2: 5–11). Also in the period that followed it was only those who belonged to the nation of Israel, and such others as wholly or in part had gone over to Judaism, who were received into the church (Acts 3: 12, 26; 6: 1; 8: 26–40; 11: 19).

Thus the Samaritans (Acts 8: 4–25), although hated by national Judaism, were at least half-Jews (II Kings 17: 24–41), with circumcision and a so-called Five Books of the Law of their own (the Samaritan Pentateuch), and the pretension, in opposition to Jerusalem, the "false" place, to possess in and near Sichem the true chief place of worship of Jehovah (John 4: 20). The eunuch of Acts 8: 26–40, was a proselyte, who, as far as was possible to a eunuch, had already acceded to the Jewish faith and worship of God. Thus the oldest form of Christianity was the Israelitic.

No mission, properly so-called, to the Gentiles, where as wholly Gentile they could be baptized, yet existed. Everything took place by accession to and co-ordination with Israel. Therefore Pentecost is not yet in all respects the beginning of the present age. Indeed, even after Pentecost Peter made an offer of salvation expressly on the ground of Israel as a nation. "Repent ye, therefore, and turn again, that your sins may be blotted out, that so there may come seasons of refreshing from the presence of the Lord, and that he may send the Christ who hath been appointed for you, even Jesus, whom indeed heaven must receive until the times of restoration of all things, whereof God spake by the mouth of His holy prophets from of old" (Acts 3: 19-21).

Thus even later than Pentecost the New Testament message of salvation is still on Israelitic ground, and the setting aside of Israel which followed did not really occur because of their rejection of the Messiah while He lived on earth (comp. Acts 3: 17), but in final and decisive manner only because of their rejection of the Holy Spirit, who had glorified before them the Messiah as having gone to heaven and been exalted. Finally Israel had even murdered Stephen who, filled with the Holy Spirit, had testified to the resurrection, and thereby had confirmed this martyr's words: "Ye stiffnecked and uncircumcised in heart and ears, ye do always resist the Holy Spirit: as your fathers did so do ye" (Acts 7: 51).

But inasmuch as in Caesarea Peter had opened the gate of the kingdom of heaven to the uncircumcised Cornelius (Acts 10; 11: 3; comp. Matt. 16: 19), and the Spirit of God, as the "like gift" (Acts 11: 17) and in the "same manner" (Acts 15: 11), without distinction (Acts 15: 9), had come upon the Gentiles who believed (Acts 10: 44), God had annulled the Old Testament dispensational distinction between clean and unclean (Acts 10: 11-16), and the "middle wall of partition," which separated Jew and Gentile, was done away, not only in principle, but also historically. From that time the Gentile, without membership in the national Israel, partook fully in the same salvation (Acts 28: 28).

And precisely because the call of the Gentiles belonged to the essential nature of the church (Eph. 2: 11-22; 3: 6; Rom. 15: 9-12) it must be said that the church did not find its all-embracing full beginning in Jerusalem (Acts 2) but in Caesarea (Acts 10). This process was completed through the revelations to Paul, to whom in especial manner was entrusted the doctrinal unfolding of this mystery (Eph. 3: 1-7) and the evangelistic proclaiming of the saving message among the nations (Eph. 3: 8, 9). To the Jew first and then to the Greek also—this was the practice of

Paul in particular and also the course of salvation's history in general (Rom. 1: 16; Acts 13: 46).

The giving to the Gentiles an equal standing with the covenant people of the Old Testament signifies at the same time the annulment of the privileged standing of the Jew and the setting aside of Israel as a nation (Rom. 11: 25). Viewed from the standpoint of Israel's *national* place in the history of salvation the present age is thus a parenthesis. The Gentile can now drink from the public well of salvation without having first obtained the Jewish permit to draw (Rom. 10: 12, 13). A partial hardening has overtaken Israel, but its "fall" is the riches of the world (Rom. 11: 25, 11, 12). Those far off have become nigh (Eph. 2: 11-13): believing Gentiles have equal title with believing Jews. They are *fellow*-heirs, and *fellow*-members of the body, *fellow*-sharers of the promise, and *fellow*-citizens with the saints (Eph. 3: 6; 2: 19). They are sharers of their spiritual possessions (Rom. 15: 27), and are together with them "one new man," the body of Christ (Eph. 2: 15, 16). So in the church distinction no more rules. "It is as if someone made two pillars, the one of silver and the other of lead, then melted them together, and by a miracle they came out *one golden* pillar" (Chrysostom).

III. The Mystery of the Call

No Old Testament prophet had seen clearly this wondrous building (I Pet. 1: 10-12; Matt. 13: 17). Although determined from eternity in God (Eph. 3: 9), its structure was hidden by silence from the ages as a secret, a "mystery" (Rom. 16: 25; Eph. 3: 5; I Cor. 2: 7). The church in its New Testament character is therefore nowhere directly to be found in the Old Testament, but only indirectly, in types, as Eve, Rebecca, the Song of Songs, and the Tabernacle. Only since Pentecost, and the sending of Peter to Caesarea, and, above all, since the revelation of it given independently to Paul (Gal. 1: 11, 12; Eph. 3: 3), was made known to the sons of men the New Testament secret of the composition of the church, its call, standing, and hope. From that time it was made known through "prophetic writings,"[1] and the proclaimers of the gospel are "stewards of the mysteries of God" (I Cor. 4: 1).

Its *foundation* is the work of Christ—the mystery of godliness (I Tim. 3: 16);

Its *building*—the church, the mystery of the Christ (Eph. 3: 3, 4, 9; 2: 11-22);

Its *pleasure*—His fellowship, the *great* mystery of love (Eph. 5: 31, 32);

---

[1] Which means *New* Testament prophets (Rom. 16: 26; comp. Eph. 2: 20; 4: 11; Acts 13: 1; 15: 32; 21: 10).

Its *strength*—His indwelling, the mystery of "Christ in you" (Col. 1: 26, 27);

Its *expectation*—the transformation, the mystery of the rapture (I Cor. 15: 51).

And even if in Israel the mystery of hardening goes on (Rom. 11: 25), and if in the present age the nations of the world rage, and among them the mystery of lawlessness works (II Thess. 2: 7; Rev. 17: 5), yet the goal is certain: God will at last bring all together under one Head (I Cor. 15: 28). This is the "mystery of His will," His final goal and eternal triumph (Eph. 1: 9, 10; Phil. 2: 10, 11).

Until then we preach the crucified Christ and make known everywhere "the savour of the knowledge of Him" (II Cor. 2: 14).   Our message

as to its *origin*, is the mystery of *God* (Col. 2: 2):
as to its *mediation*, it is the mystery of *Christ* (Col. 4: 3):
as to its *proclamation*, it is the mystery of the *gospel* (Eph. 6: 19):
as to its *experience*, it is the mystery of *faith* (I Tim. 3: 9).

And faith is the key to all of these mysteries of God. For faith the mysteries are no longer merely things hidden, "for the Spirit searches all things, even the deep things of God" (I Cor. 2: 10).

NOTE on the "mystery of Christ."

Taken strictly the "mystery of Christ" in Eph. 3 is not the church itself, but the equality of title of believing Gentiles *within* the church: "that those of the nations are *fellow*-heirs [with the believing from Israel], and *fellow*-members of the body, and *fellow*-partakers of His promise in Christ Jesus" (ver. 6). Paul says that he has just written of the mystery, and thereby looks back to ch. 2: 13–19. There also he had spoken of the absence of difference between Jew and Gentile as regards admission to salvation and of the equal rights of both as an unity in the "one body" of Christ, the one "new man," so that since the breaking down of the law, as the "middle wall of partition," the once "far off" Gentiles are brought nigh, and together with those "near," the Israelites who believe on Christ, they form an organic unity with one another and with Christ.

Thus the "mystery of Christ" here is not the existence of the mystical Christ in itself, that is, the existence of the church as an organism, nor is it at all the organic oneness of the members with each other and with the Head, but it is the undifferentiated share of the Gentiles in this *ecclesia*, and their equal title to partake with Israelites who believe in Christ in the relationship to the risen and exalted One. It thus relates less to believing Jews than to the portion of the church formed of believing Gentiles.

E

It deals less with the *ecclesia* as the body than with the matter of believing Gentiles being fellow-members of the body *within* the *ecclesia*, and thus with the conditions of reception of believers from the peoples of the world and their enjoyment of blessings in the fellowship of salvation.

Christ Himself had already said that Christians would come into living organic relation to Himself, though He did not use the figure of the body but that of the vine (John 15). But the chief matter here is not the figure, but the spiritual reality, and this had been declared plainly by Christ.

Consequently in the expression "mystery of Christ" the genitive "of" cannot be taken as the genitive of explanation (*genitivus explicativus*), as if the "mystical Christ" were the "mystery of Christ" (comp. I Cor. 1: 13; 12: 12), but as the genitive of mystical relationship (*genitivus mysticus*): it is a mystery which is connected organically with the person and work of Christ, and exists only through Him, with Him, and in Him.

From Eph. 5: 32 it has been taught that Paul describes the church itself as "the great mystery." Taken strictly this is nevertheless not here the case. The "secret" of which the apostle speaks here is not the *church* but the relationship of love between the church *and Christ*, which has its human counterpart in the marriage relationship. "For this cause shall a man leave his father and his mother, and shall cleave to his wife; and the two shall become one flesh. This mystery is great: but I speak in regard of Christ *and* of the church." Thus the word "mystery" refers here not to the church alone, as if to its existence in itself, but to the church *and Christ*, that is, to the heavenly relationship, the unity in love, between the Redeemer and the redeemed. On the question of how far the plan for the existence of a church composed of Christians from both Jews and Gentiles was hidden in the Old Testament the apostle says nothing in this place.

IV. Entrance to the Calling

Wondrous is the redemption; wondrous also the entrance into salvation. The sinner experiences all three offices of the Redeemer in their proper historical sequence:

that of the Prophet—in his call and enlightenment;

that of the Priest—in his conversion and justification;

that of the Priest and King—in his sanctification and glorification.

He experiences first the prophetic service of Christ.

1. *The Leading to salvation*: the call through His word and enlightenment through His Spirit. The awakening: "faith comes through the preaching" (Rom. 10: 17). Alarmed by the

accusations of an awakened conscience, broken down under the word of God, self-condemned, the man is allowed to recognize in the gospel of Christ the offer of salvation. Then comes the priestly service, the experience of Golgotha.

2. *The Entrance into salvation* through conversion and regeneration. The sinner receives the pardon of his guilt on the ground of the priestly sacrifice, is renewed (Titus 3: 5), transformed (I Cor. 6: 11), made alive (Eph. 2: 5), and born of God (I John 3: 9; 4: 7; 5: 1, 4; John 3: 5).

Regeneration is therefore the real entrance into redemption (Titus 3: 5). It is the counterpart to Christ having become man, the imparting of His life to us, the dead (Col. 1: 27). Only by it do we become "new" men (Eph. 4: 24; Col. 3: 10) and members of the "last Adam."

But this new birth is connected inseparably with conversion, that is, a turning round (Acts 3: 19; 15: 19; 26: 18). Regeneration is the Divine side, conversion the human side of the same experience. Man experiences both simultaneously, but conversion is the *condition* for regeneration, and regeneration is the Divine *answer* to conversion. Man is responsible for conversion, for turning to God: regeneration is the work of God. In conversion the man is active; "turn yourselves"—imperative! (Acts 3: 19): in regeneration he is passive; he "becomes" regenerate.

Conversion itself (I Thess. 1: 9) is twofold: turning from and turning to, repentance and faith (Mark 1: 15). Repentance is denying (negative), faith is affirming (positive), repentance looks within, faith looks above; repentance sees our misery, faith our Deliverer.

But with all this the initial turning of a sinner to God is an act done once and for all. All New Testament conversions were sudden and basic. The man has "passed over" (John 5: 24) out of death into life. Thus he knows a "once" and a "now" (Eph. 2: 2, 11, 13). This break is set forth symbolically in the original Christian baptism, the confession of the believer that he has died with Christ and risen again with Him (Rom. 6. 1–11).

Repentance (Matt. 3: 2; Acts 17: 30) is one threefold action: in the *understanding*—knowledge of sin; in the *feelings*—pain and grief; in the *will*—a change of mind (Gk. *metanoia*) and a turning around. In general it is a gaining of insight, a despair as to oneself, a renouncing of all self-redemption (Rom. 7: 24).

Faith also is one threefold action: in the *understanding*—a being convinced of the completed redemption; in the *feelings*—restful reliance on the saving love; in the *will*—devotion to the personal Saviour. Thus faith is the hand of man that clasps the hand of God. It is no working up of the feelings, no tormenting of self, no expiating of guilt, but a personal relationship to Christ, a conscious acceptance of His grace, and a blessed "life in the Head" (Zwingli). "Repentance is hunger, faith is the open mouth, Christ the living food" (John 6: 54, 55). Faith experiences the present Christ now and here: it is even today a firm foothold in eternity, and therefore becames a "self-demonstration of invisible realities" (Heb. 11: 1).

Only when all this is present can experience of Christ's *royal* office begin.

3. *Preservation and Advance in Salvation,* that is, in sanctification. He who is "declared righteous" (justified) is not yet in practice "perfect in righteousness." The "holy ones" (saints) must become "holy" (sanctified, I Thess. 5: 23). Grace will "rule royally" (Rom. 5: 21). The new nature, implanted *in* the believer by the new birth, shall be a starting point from which the new life shall conquer the whole man. Only so can the Redeemer perfect the transfiguration.

The names of all souls who experience this saving process stand in "the Lamb's book of life." They are

before-known men—for the book of life exists since the foundation of the world (Rev. 13: 8; 17: 8);

blood-bought men—for it is the book of life of the *Lamb* (Rev. 21: 27);

new-born men—for it is the book of *life* (Rev. 20: 15);

happy men—for their names stand in heaven (Luke 10: 20);

holy men—for all there inscribed shall be called "holy" (Isa. 4: 3);

joyful witnesses—for they defy even the Antichrist (Rev. 13: 8; 17: 8; Phil. 4: 3);

victorious men—for they are overcomers (Rev. 3: 5; Dan. 12: 1);

glorified men—for they enter the heavenly city (Rev. 21: 27).

THE APOSTLE TO THE NATIONS

PAUL was of special significance for the call of the church. Granting fully the work of the others, from the point of view of the general history of the church he was "the first after the One." Jesus was "the One," He who laid the foundation, incomparable, unsurpassable. Paul was "the first," the herald (I Tim. 2: 7), the chief pioneer of the gospel in the world of the nations, the first in eminence in the great, far-reaching area of the peoples.

I. His Commission as a Preacher of the Gospel

Four external marks are the special characteristics of his apostolic activity.

1. Paul was a herald to the *Gentiles*. This he was in harmonious distinction from the apostles to the circumcision (Gal. 2: 7-10; Acts 15). To him in an especial manner it had been given "to proclaim the unsearchable riches of Christ among the nations" (Eph. 3: 8, 1; Col. 1: 25, 27; I Tim. 2: 7; II Tim. 1: 11). Therefore the "to me" (Gk. *emoi*) in Eph. 3: 8: "*to me* was this favour given to preach unto the Gentiles," stressed and made emphatic by being placed at the beginning of the sentence.

2. Paul was a *pioneer*. As such it was his to introduce the message of salvation into ever new lands. Therefore he went principally to regions where the gospel had not before been made known (Rom. 15: 20). The further carrying of the gospel in the regions where he had worked he left to the newly-won believers. His own task was to form centres of light, that is, missionary-minded local churches, mostly in the chief cities. Thus Philippi was the "chief city" in Macedonia (Acts 16: 12), Corinth that of Achaia, Athens the chief intellectual centre of Greece, Ephesus the chief city of western Asia Minor, Rome that of the whole world.

From these centres, the light of the gospel was to shine forth in the surrounding districts (I Thess. 1: 8). When such a centre had been formed Paul went further. In such a land Paul had "no more room" (Rom. 15: 23), though hundreds of thousands of heathen dwelled around, but there he had "fully proclaimed the gospel of Christ" (Rom. 15: 19). For him anything else would be "building on another man's foundation" (Rom. 15: 20). Paul travelled some 15,000 miles at least.

3. Paul was a messenger to *great cities*. The centres of his activities were the great centres of Greek culture. This is

sufficiently proved by the names Antioch, Troas, Philippi, Thessalonica, Athens, Corinth, Ephesus. Therefore also his endeavour to reach Rome, "the gathering of the whole earth," the metropolis of the world (Rom. 1: 11, 13; 15: 23).

This also accounts for his use of figures of speech from the civilized life of great cities. Jesus preached mostly in the open air, to peasants and villagers, and used figures of speech from the countryside; but Paul, teaching mostly in great cities, used in decided measure figures of speech from the culture of cities. Not only will he be in general "to the Jews a Jew and to the Greeks a Greek" (I Cor. 9: 20, 21), but also quite specially will he be to the city dwellers a city man. Jesus speaks more of the birds of the heaven, the lilies of the field, of shepherds, sowers, and the harvest field, but Paul more of the acquittal by the judge, the remitting of the debtor's debt, the armour of the soldier (Eph. 6: 13–17), the order of the commanding officer (I Thess. 4: 10), indeed, he draws his comparisons from even the world of sport and the theatre (Phil. 3: 14). Everything shall help him to make the gospel clear to the people of the cities and to reach their hearts.

Most of his pictures he draws from the law court, the barracks, and the sports' ground, and so employs technical legal, military, and sporting terms. His central and chief figurative expressions are drawn from the courtroom and the house of business. He had also an open eye for the world outlook, the poetry and philosophy of his non-Christian surroundings, and for the local details of religion and culture (Acts 17: 16–29). To the Athenians he spoke of "their" altar, to the Corinthians of the Isthmian games held near their city (I Cor. 9: 24–27). Paul was no unpractical student of books, a stranger to the world, an abstract "theologian," who spoke to his hearers in incomprehensible scholastic jargon or unctious pulpit tones and thereby spoke over their heads: but he was for his age a thoroughly modern man, a man of a great city (Tarsus, Acts 21: 39), for the great city, a practical man, who united in himself these two features—he was sanctified yet open to the world, joined to eternity yet near to the present.

4. Paul was a messenger to *seaports*. If one looks more narrowly at these large cities, and especially at their geographical situation and significance, one perceives that "the world of the apostle is to be sought chiefly where the sea wind blows." His gospel activity embraced particularly the Aegean Sea with the seaports which lie around it. There, or at least in the neighbourhood, lay the great commercial harbours of Troas, Thessalonica, Athens, Corinth, and Ephesus. Moreover, Antioch and Rome were ports, through their harbours Seleucia and Ostia. The reason for this method was obvious in a threefold advantage.

Seaports could be reached more easily than the provincial cities far inland. By sea one made swifter and safer progress than by the roads, which were indeed well-built, but where travel was slower and often not free from danger, as is indicated in Paul's own words, "in perils from rivers, in perils from robbers" (II Cor. 11: 26). Whereas, according to Pliny, one came from Spain to Ostia in four days, and from Africa in two days. There was a *daily* service between Alexandria and Asia Minor.

Then Greek was the language of world intercourse and had spread far more widely in harbour cities than in the rest of the world. For the pioneer preacher the time-consuming hindrance of learning languages was thereby eliminated and the conquering march of the gospel could advance with more than double speed.

Also, later, when the apostle had moved on, the gospel could spread more quickly from seaport churches than those lying more inland. Travelling merchants, visitors to harbours, seamen, and other travellers, who during a sojourn in a seaport were laid hold of by the gospel could on their own account, as they journeyed further or on their return home, always be fresh pioneers of the saving message in ever new lands and regions of the world. By this means the number of "missionaries," and the lands reached by them, increased, and were added to the workers and lands reached by the gigantic efforts of the apostle and the systematic sending out of the narrower circle of his fellow-labourers.

5. Paul's missionary *strategy*. Thus Paul's activities in the gospel could not have been planned in a more practical manner than they were. It is therefore just to speak of Paul's "missionary strategy." All is so systematic, so based on the principle of serving an end, so planned in advance for the swiftest and most extensive spreading of the gospel, that one cannot fail to see a deliberate plan which must have lain at the base of all the apostle's movements.

But with all this it was not Paul who planned but the Lord he served. Significant at once of this is the dream vision at Troas, through which the apostle, without personal impulse or self-dependent pondering, was called to Macedonia and Greece (Acts 16: 8-11), so that now, on the ground of Divine direction, not the East but the West—Japhetic Europe and the Western peoples in general—should be made the chief theatre of the wonders of the gospel. Indeed, it could have come to pass, and did come to pass, that Paul had planned certain journeys, but "the Spirit of Jesus suffered it not" (Acts 16: 6, 7, twice), and Paul followed the Divine initiative. So that it is very just to speak of a missionary strategy in the life of Paul, but the strategy was not

Paul's but Christ's, not of the ambassador[1] but of the Sender, not of the herald but of the Lord of the enterprise. Christ was the Leader, Paul the agent; Christ was the Director, Paul the traveller; Christ was the Commander, Paul the soldier (II Tim. 2: 3; 4: 2; II Cor. 6: 7; Eph. 6: 10–20).

To these more outward marks of his gospel activities must be added the more inward characteristics of his *teaching* ministry.

II. HIS COMMISSION AS A TEACHER OF THE CHURCH

1. *The starting point* of his systematic instruction lay in the chief event of the history of salvation. At the centre of this history stands Jesus Christ. Born in Israel (Rom. 1: 3; 9: 5) He was yet the Saviour of the world. In Him the promise to Abraham of blessing to all peoples reached fulfilment (Gal. 3: 8, 9). The preceding and intervening nationalism of the Old Testament revelation was broadened out through Christ and His work into the New Testament universal message of salvation. As the fulfilment of Old Testament sacrifices the cross is at once the abolition of the Levitical priesthood and law (Heb. 10: 10–14; 7: 11–18) and thereby the demolition of the wall of separation between Israel and the Gentiles (Eph. 2: 13–16). Salvation is now open to all.

Historically this world-embracing significance of the cross first came to light after Pentecost. The chief epoch-making event in this unfolding of Golgotha is the sending of Peter to Cornelius in Caesarea (Acts 10). For this reason it is given in the Biblical history the most detailed account of any event in the whole apostolic era. Here, for the first time a full Gentile is made to partake of the Holy Spirit, is baptized, and received into the church without any question of law or circumcision, that is, without connexion with national Israel, but on the sole ground of his faith in the finished work of Christ.

This is so vital that it must be further considered.

The vision of Cornelius is narrated no less than three times (Acts 10: 3–6, 30–32; 11: 13, 14), and the vision of Peter also is narrated twice (Acts 10: 10–16; 11: 5–10) and mentioned a third time (Acts 10: 28). The events themselves show a striking array of supernatural happenings: the vision of Cornelius, the triple vision of Peter, the Spirit's encouragement of Peter after the vision (ver. 19), the outpouring of the Spirit (ver. 44), and the effect of the reception of the Spirit in the accompanying speaking with tongues (ver. 46). This all shows what great weight attaches to this event; and the high significance the historian ascribes to it is shown by his detailed account.

[1] Acts 22: 21; 13: 4; I Cor. 1: 17. Compare the word "apostle," from the Greek *apostello* I send, dispatch. II Cor. 5: 20.

It was in this way that what had been introduced in principle at Golgotha became for the first time historical reality (John 12: 32; 11: 52; Eph. 2: 15, 16). It was thereby declared that before God there is no difference between Jew and Gentile. The separate standing of Israel was thus set aside, and the church, as consisting of former Jews and Gentiles, was established. The vision of Peter in Joppa and his being sent to Cornelius in Caesarea are therefore the beginning of a new type of Christianity, namely, the type of Christianity for all peoples, free from the law, which type was now added to the original Jewish-Christian type as being of equal birth.

Thereby and at the same time there first appeared in its full extent the new fellowship in salvation, which is super-national, historical, universal, and inwardly and outwardly world-embracing. Here for the first time was manifested historically the principle that God makes no difference between Jew and Gentile (Acts 15: 9), and grants to all believers, from both groups, "the same gift" (Acts 11: 17), in the "same manner" (Acts 15: 11); or, to express it in Pauline language, that "the middle wall of partition," which separated the two, God had now broken down (Eph. 2: 14). Thus the "mystery" which Paul discussed in Eph. 2 and 3 (especially 2: 13–3: 6) was not first revealed to him but to Peter. As in Jerusalem Peter had opened the door of the heavenly kingdom to Jews (Acts 2), so had he at Caesarea to Gentiles (Acts 10; comp. Matt. 16: 19).[1]

[1] The "church" had definite existence *before* Paul. Only so could Luke apply the term to the pre-Pauline Christian community (Acts 8: 1–3) or Paul himself confess that he had persecuted "the church" (Phil. 3: 6; Gal. 1: 13; comp. I Cor. 15: 9). In Eph. 3: 3, Paul does not assert that he was the first to whom the mystery of the church had been made known. He says only that the secret counsel that there is no difference in the church between Jew and Gentile, and the equal rights of believing Gentiles and believing Jews had not been made known in the time (not before him personally, but in general) before his generation, as it had now been revealed to "the holy apostles and prophets through the Spirit." The plural "apostles and prophets" is to be noted as implying that the revelation was not to Paul alone, and it was made to them "through the Spirit," not first by the agency of Paul (ver. 5). The "*as* it has *now* been revealed" may indeed suggest that this mystery had been hinted at in the Old Testament, but under veiled forms or types, and only now was properly revealed.

What Paul does declare is that he had received this mystery by "revelation" (ver. 3). But he says no word as to the sequence of these Divine revelations or the question of priority of reception. The emphasis of ver. 3 does not lie on "me" but on "revelation." He does not use here the emphatic Greek *emoi*, but the unemphatic *moi*, and he places it (in the original text), not at the head of the sentence, but appends it as unaccented. On the contrary, to stress the word "revelation" he places it early in the sentence: "according to revelation was made known to me the mystery." Here (as in Gal. 1: 12) he does not wish to declare any priority of time for himself or that the revelation was given to him exclusively, but only that he stood alone in the matter independently of man. Not till Eph. 3: 8, does he use the emphatic *emoi* and place it at the head of the sentence. But there he is not dealing with the first *reception* of the mystery but with his *proclamation* of it among the nations. This, of course, was then in fact the special task of Paul. He was the chief herald of the gospel to the peoples of the world.

[If one says: "I received this information from Mr. Jones himself," this does not assert that Mr. Jones had not formerly mentioned the matter to others. Trans.]

The setting forth and expanding of this mystery, together with the dependent and newly arisen basic questions connected with its place in salvation's history, was the special task of Paul as a teacher. In addition to this there were given to him further detail revelations as to the nature and completion of this church. Almost the whole of what is peculiar to the doctrine Paul proclaimed is derived from this source.

So, then, Paul was not indeed the first to whom this mystery of the church, in its New Testament composition and structure, was made known. Nevertheless, later, independently of men and of all that preceded, it was imparted to him, by the Lord Himself, by special revelation (Gal. 1: 11, 12; Eph. 3: 3 ff.). This was necessary for the sake of the independence of his service and the authenticity of his apostleship to the Gentiles (comp. Gal. 1: 11–24). As a result, under the leading of the Spirit, he has described this new and great truth, and its essential implications, with a width and depth beyond all others before, with, or after him, and in this sense he is not only the chief herald of Jesus Christ to the peoples, but the chief teacher and prophet for the church.

But this does not mean that Paul stood on different dispensational ground from the other apostles. There are not in the church two messages of salvation and doctrine, one a Jewish-Christian to be distinguished in content from another, a Gentile-Christian (comp. Gal. 1: 9, 10; Acts 15: 9; 11: 17), but all the apostles set forth *the same* New Testament truth. The distinctions lie only in their fields of work (Gal. 2: 7–10), in the form and manner in which they deliver their message, conditioned by their personalities (causing, for example, a difference in outlook, style, and use of Biblical figures of speech), and in the depth and breadth divided to each according to the measure of the gift of Christ. It was in precisely the last matter that Paul was specially graced.

The high significance of Paul in proclaiming the New Testament teaching is shown also by the great space which his and his fellow-workers' writings have in the New Testament. Paul's circle—that is, in this case, Paul, Luke, and the writer to the *Hebrews*—wrote rather more than half the New Testament, and Paul himself a quarter.[1]

2. *The Central Truths of Paul's Letters.* In the centre of the Pauline message stands Jesus Christ, and He as the Saviour crucified and risen. His atoning work on the cross extinguished

[1] More exactly 56 per cent, Paul 24 per cent. Luke, who was at the same time the author of the Acts (Acts 1: 1; comp. Luke 1: 1–4), was a close and long-standing fellow-worker and fellow-traveller of Paul (Col. 4; 14: comp. further the "we" accounts in Acts 16: 10, 13, 16; 20: 7; etc.). Style and contents show that *Hebrews* was not written by Paul personally, but it may well have been the work of one of his fellow-workers. Heb. 13: 23.

our sins (Rom. 3: 25). His life in the glory is the spring of strength for our sanctification. His coming (*parousia*) and appearing (outshining, *epiphany*) is the goal of our expectation. Through repentance (Acts 17: 30) and faith (Rom. 1: 16, 17) the sinner enters His fellowship (Eph. 3: 17), is spiritually raised from the dead and made alive (Eph. 2: 5, 6). The history of his Saviour is now his own history. He is crucified, buried, raised with Him, and is "set with Him in heavenly places" (Rom. 6; Eph. 2: 6). Thus the redeemed man of the earth is "in heaven" (Phil. 3: 20). A Christian is a "man in Christ" (II Cor. 12: 2).

The reverse also is true. Through the Spirit the Exalted One is present on earth in His own people (Gal. 2: 20). "Christ *for* us" is "Christ *in* us" (Col. 1: 27). The juristic is at the same time organic. The One crucified is the One crowned in us. The Substitute is the Ruler. Jesus Christ is the LORD (*kurios*) (Rom. 14: 9).

Thus for Paul the cross is no bare fact of past history, but he always looks on the cross together with the resurrection. Without the resurrection the cross is for him powerless and empty, yea, collapse and overthrow; indeed, most catastrophic tragedy (I Cor. 15: 14–19). He never asserted that he preached only the cross, not even in I Cor. 2: 2 (as to which passage see p 42, *n*.), but that he brought to men the Crucified One. But he brought Him, indeed, as his sole theme; not an event, but a Person; not a point but an endless line; not purely as past but as One ever present, even Christ the Exalted, who even in the glory must be viewed in connexion with His experience of the cross (comp. Rev. 5: 6).

This is the Pauline theology of the cross. It moves on the plane of resurrection. The darkness of death is seen in the sunlight of Easter morning.

Then this Sun streams out over all the world. Christ Himself had said: "If I am lifted up I will draw all to me" (John 12: 32), that is, Jew and Gentile, without any distinction of nation. By this the door was opened for the world-wide mission of the gospel. Historically this took place publicly in the house of the wholly Gentile Cornelius (Acts. 10). The law which divided was set aside as fulfilled.

Thus the setting aside of circumcision and the law was involved in principle in the redemptive work of Christ and in the revelation to Peter which led to the events in the house of Cornelius. But if since the time of Acts 10 the law and circumcision were no longer a condition for entering into salvation and its fellowship, then there arises of itself the great question:

To what purpose is the law? Here it is Paul—and among all apostles and New Testament writers principally Paul—who has dealt with and explained doctrinally this practical problem created by Acts 10. The law as discloser of sin is a "tutor unto Christ" (Rom. 3: 20; 7: 7; Gal. 3: 24), because it shows to the sinner his wickedness and helplessness and therefore the necessity of a Divine Redeemer. Therefore with His appearing it can dis-appear, and thus from the Old Testament purpose of the law follows the New Testament freedom from the law. Christ as the goal of the law is at the same time its end (Rom. 10: 4). This is the basic theme of the central passages in *Romans* and *Galatians*, especially *Romans* 1 to 8 (notably ch. 7) and *Galatians* 2 to 4 (especially ch. 3).

In the justification of Gentiles as practised since Acts 10, there lay further the actual setting aside of Israel as a nation. From now on in the history of salvation the Jew had no further precedence, and of necessity the question presents itself:

Has, then, God now repudiated His people? This also is dealt with by Paul and by him alone of New Testament writers; and he deals with it in precisely that central passage of Romans (at once history and prophecy, chs. 9 to 11), which in such unique manner enables us to look into God's plans of world rule. God's action is *free*; therefore Israel has no right to extort any-thing from Him (Rom. 9). God's action is *just*: therefore Israel, on account of its guilt, must bow to His judgment (Rom. 10). God's action brings *blessing*: therefore He turns Israel's fall into salvation for the world, and at last into full salvation for Israel itself. He will receive back His people (Rom. 11). See pp. 148 f.

And if further, in principle through Golgotha and in practice by Acts 10, all human religious performances, as prerequisite to experiencing salvation, are done away, so that without any pre-ceding worship of God ordered according to revelation, one completely heathen, solely through faith in Christ, can attain to salvation and the church, then at the same time the further question was broached as to:

The value of all human religious deeds in general. And here also it was Paul, and again he in the first instance, who gave the answer. This consisted in his teaching of the freeness of grace, of justification without works of law, on the sole ground of the sacrifice of Christ, and through faith alone. This is the heart and centre of the whole Pauline message, the great general theme of *Romans* and *Galatians*. "We therefore now hold that a man becomes justified without works of law, through faith alone" (Rom. 3: 28).

The manner in which Paul handles this question is deter-mined for him by his fundamental attitude to religious Judaism. From this arises the seeming contradiction to James (Rom. 3: 28; comp. Jas. 2: 24). In reality it is not a case of contradiction but of harmonious contrast. This is to be explained by the differing development and leading of the lives of the two apostles. Paul, the former Pharisee, seeking then to be justified by works, looks on the work and teaching of Christ in their great contrast to Phariseeism, that is, to *false* Judaism. James, on the other hand, the brother of the Lord (Gal. 1: 19), having grown up in the narrower circle of the family of Jesus, that is, in an environment of true Israelites without falsity, in the circle of the faithful remnant believing in the Messiah, sets forth the work and teaching of Christ as the perfecting of the *true* Judaism.

Hence, as to the doctrine of justification, Paul stresses its freedom from all dead, legalistic works. James, on the contrary, lifts into relief that, at the same time, true justification is a new life and therefore reveals itself in living works. Paul looks at the contrast to the false Judaism which he denies; James stresses the connexion with the true Judaism which he accepts. Therefore Paul speaks of freedom from the law but James of the law of freedom (Jas. 1: 25; 2: 12). But at bottom both emphasize the same truth; for Paul also speaks of the necessity of works of faith (Gal. 5: 6; Titus 2: 7; 3: 1, 8, 14; I Cor. 7: 19).

In general, what Paul contrasts is not so much the carrying out of Old Testament legal regulations in themselves, but much rather the false motive for doing so. He contends against circumcision, sabbath observance, and the like, only if they are regarded as means of justification or sanctification, and so fall under the *Pharisaic misuse* of the law (Gal. 5: 12; Col. 2: 16 ff.; comp. I Tim. 1: 8). Otherwise the apostle left sabbath observance free (Rom. 14: 5), indeed himself circumcised Timothy (as being a national Jewish custom, Acts 16: 3), and took upon himself certain sacrifices of the Levitical law (Acts 21: 26; 18: 18), when his doing so had value as a means of winning souls ("on account of the Jews," Acts 16: 3; 21: 24; I Cor. 9: 20).

Finally: If both of these, Jew and Gentile, by indistinguishable equality of title, were established in sharing the same redemption, there arose of necessity the question of

The nature of the new fellowship of salvation, especially of
    the fellowship of the redeemed to one another and
    the common relationship of the redeemed to their common
Redeemer.

And in this also Paul again is the chief teacher of the church. He describes this fellowship under the figure of a "body": Christ is the "Head," the redeemed are His "members." Paul is the only New Testament writer who uses this picture of the "body of Christ." He does this in *Ephesians* and *Colossians,* also in *I Corinthians* (especially ch. 12), as well as in individual passages elsewhere (e.g. Rom. 12: 4).

Thus in the history of salvation there arise out of Golgotha and the revelation to Peter at Joppa four great new fundamental questions—

the purpose of the law,
the setting aside and the hope of Israel,
justification apart from works of law, and
the organic oneness of the new fellowship in salvation;
and in all of these questions Paul—and he quite alone of all New
Testament writers—has become the chief teacher of the church.
From which we perceive that all great basic questions in Paul's
letters, as outworkings of the cross of Christ, are rooted in the
revelation given to Peter at Joppa. The revelations given to
Paul are the explanation and the deepening of the revelation
given to Peter on the basis of Golgotha.

The coronation of this comes at the end. To the man to
whom especially it was given to explain the beginning of the
New Testament church it was now granted to foresee its completion. That belongs to Divine logic. Thus Paul becomes the
prophet of the *hope of the church*. The resurrection of believers,
the rapture of saints, the judgment seat of Christ, the transfiguration of His people, their coming spiritual body—these
matters are all basic to the Christian hope, and concerning them
we receive from no other New Testament writer such clear and
detailed instruction as from Paul. This is the chief subject of
both the epistles to the *Thessalonians* and the resurrection chapter,
I Corinthians 15.

By all this Paul becomes the prophet of salvation's history.
With a vision that includes millenniums and embraces peoples
and times he surveys aeons and dispensations. He speaks of the
beginnings of sacred history, of Adam the ancestral father of
mankind, the counterpart of Christ (Rom. 5). He speaks of
the patriarchal age, of Abraham, the father and type of believers
(Rom. 4). He indicates the meaning of the Mosaic economy,
the millennium and a half of the Old Testament law (Rom. 7;
Gal. 3). He speaks of "the fulness of the season" in which
Christ appeared (Gal. 4: 4), of His cross, His resurrection, His
ascension to heaven, and His exaltation (Eph. 1: 20, 21). He
teaches the principles of the church, its call and standing, with
the glorifying of the redeemed and their being made manifest
before Christ (II Cor. 5: 10). He foretells the coming of the
Antichrist, his nature and his power, his victory and his overthrow (II Thess. 2). And he awaits the appearing of the Lord
and the setting up of His kingdom (II Thess. 2: 8; I Thess. 2: 12).
But beyond all this his glance passes finally into eternity, to
Jerusalem above (Gal. 4: 26), on to the consummation, to the
dawn of the day of God, when "the Son Himself shall be subject
to Him who has subjected all things to him, so that God may be
all in all" (I Cor. 15: 28).

But Christ is the radiant central Sun of the whole. Only in
Him, the Living One, are all living springs open. The short

phrase "in Christ," which comes in his letters over 160 times, is the key and kernel of his whole experience of salvation and of his public teaching.   For Him alone will he live.   To Him alone he will testify, Him only he will proclaim as God's greatest gift to the peoples of the world.   That is his commission.   As such he is the teacher of the nations, the chief apostle to the church, the prophet of salvation's history, the herald of Jesus Christ, the standard bearer of the coming King.

CHAPTER I

THE DISPENSATION OF THE GRACE OF GOD

Wᴇ will speak of the lofty position of the church. Called "through glory and perfection" she possesses the greatest promises (II Pet. 1: 3, 4). It is in this present age that the unsearchable riches of Christ are made known (Eph. 3: 8).

The heavenly blessings of the church are too manifold to be expressed by a single description. Therefore the Spirit of God employs the most varied pictures and comparisons so as to divide, as by a prism, the brilliance of its eternal light into its separate rays.

The church stands in relationship to all three Persons of the Divine Essence, to the Father, to the Son, to the Holy Spirit. In its relations to God it is a "household." God is the "Father" (Rom. 8: 15; Gal. 4: 6; John 20: 17), and the redeemed are the members of His household (Eph. 2: 19; Gal. 6: 10). As to duty they are His slaves (I Pet. 2: 16), as to privilege they are His sons (Rom. 8: 14).

I. THE STANDING OF THE REDEEMED AS SLAVES

Purchased for God through the blood of Jesus Christ (Rev. 5: 9), not with silver and gold (I Pet: 1: 18), but at the price of His life (I Cor. 6: 20; 7: 23), the "ransom money" of Golgotha (Matt. 20: 28; I Tim. 2: 6), the redeemed are no more their own (I Cor. 6: 19), but are slaves of God (Rom. 6: 22) and of Christ (Rom. 1: 1; Eph. 6: 6). They are for ever His possession (Titus 2: 14), His tools which He uses,[1] His slaves who, as a sign that they never can be sold,[2] He "has sealed" with His Spirit (Eph. 1: 13; 4: 30; II Cor. 1: 22). Their redemption is at the same time a purchase, their emancipation imposes obligation, and their position as slaves is at once and the same time a condition of

personal ownership (I Pet. 2: 9),
obedience (Rom. 6: 17, 18) and
protection (Gal. 6: 17; John 10: 28, 29).

[1] A slave is an animated tool, a tool an inanimate slave (Aristotle).

[2] As far back as the Babylonian legal code of Hammurabi, the contemporary of Abraham (=Amraphel, Gen. 14: 1), a master, by branding a slave with a mark, declared that he would never part with him.

The Greek word *doulos* does not mean servant but slave. A servant belongs to himself and consequently receives his own wage; a slave belongs to his owner and has no right to a wage (Luke 17: 9, 10). A servant sells to his master only his labour, and mostly for only a time; a slave belongs to him as a person and perpetually. Paul looked upon it as his "glory" to be, not merely a servant, but a slave of Christ (I Cor. 9: 15-18). In translating, this word should be rendered more exactly.

II. The Standing of the Redeemed as Sons

But God's counsel of salvation rises higher. Those freed from the slavery of sin are not only His servants, who, redeemed from destruction, are doers of His good pleasure, but He will bring them to be partakers of Himself, to become partakers of His divine nature (II Pet. 1: 4). They shall be children (Rom. 8: 21), sons (Rom. 8: 14), indeed, firstborn sons (Heb. 12: 23).

1. *Children.* This and nothing less is the meaning of Holy Scripture when it speaks of the redeemed as those who have been born of (out of) God; for the raising of the subjects of grace into the standing of sons is not merely a formal *declaration* of sonship, a legal exaltation and appointment, a, so to say, juridical adoption, but is an actual *begetting* (Jas. 1: 18), a being really born again, an organic birth from God (John 3: 3, 5; I Pet. 1: 23; 2: 2; I John 2: 29; 3: 9). "Behold, what a love the Father has shown to us, that we should be called children of God. *And such we are!*" (I John 3: 1).

2. *Sons.* But as such we have at the same time come of age. This is precisely the chief difference from the Old Testament era. For sonship was indeed already a possession of Israel (Rom. 9: 4; Deut. 14: 1). As shown in the revealed history Israel was God's firstborn son among the peoples (Exod. 4: 22). The Old Testament had already taught a fatherhood of God (Deut. 32: 6; Isa. 63: 16; 64: 8; Mal. 1: 6; comp. Isa. 1: 2; 30: 1-9). But the Old Testament sonship was based on the act of creation (Isa. 64: 8; Deut. 32: 6) and the national redemption of Israel out of Egypt (Isa. 63: 16); the New Testament sonship is based on the personal birth of the individual from God and the reception of the spirit of sonship (Gal. 4: 5, 6).

Therefore also Israel stood as yet under a "tutor," a trainer of boys (Gk. *paidagōgos*), even the law (Gal. 3: 24). "But now that faith is come, we are no longer under a tutor" (Gal. 3: 25). For an Israelite to become a believer signifies his coming of age, his independence of a tutor, that is, his freedom from the law (Gal. 4: 1-5); and since now in the church there no more exists a difference between Jew and Gentile, therefore believers rom the nations share the same freedom. So then compared

F

with the past we are of age, while as regards the future we still await the adoption (Rom. 8: 23).

But we are not only children and sons but also

3. *Firstborn Sons.* The redeemed of this age are "a kind of firstfruits of his creatures" (Jas. 1: 18), the "church of the first-born ones who are enrolled in heaven" (Heb. 12: 23). That men, not angels, are meant by the term "firstborn" is shown by the added expression "who are enrolled in heaven" (comp. Luke 10: 20; Phil. 4: 3).

As the firstborn they have:

priestly standing (Exod. 13: 2, 15; Num. 8: 16–18; I Pet. 2: 5);

kingly dignity (I Chron. 5: 1, 2; Rev. 1: 6);

a double portion[1] of the inheritance (Deut. 21: 15–17; Eph. 1: 3).

Thus their standing as sons is completed in the birthright of the firstborn: as children they have God's life, as sons position and dignity, as firstborn His glory.

The conceptions of childhood and sonship are thus not exactly the same, but are the necessary complement of each other. "Childhood" emphasizes more the mystic, organic, metaphysical; "sonship" (= acceptance as sons, adoption) emphasizes the juridical declarative. The idea of sonship prevails with Paul (Gal. 3: 26; 4: 7; Rom. 8: 14, 19), that of childhood with John (I John 3: 1, 2, 10; 5: 2); even as Paul is the principal juridical writer of the New Testament and John the mystic-metaphysical writer. Translations should keep distinct these two different terms (*tekna,* children, *huioi,* sons).

But with all this there remains for ever the infinite distance between the Son and the sons, the Firstborn and the firstborn ones. He is the *one* Son of the Most High within the Deity (Mark 14: 61, 62), and they are the *many* sons of the heavenly Father within the created universe. He is Himself the only-begotten (John 1: 14, 18; 3: 16), the heir of all things (Heb. 1: 2), "God over all, blessed for ever" (Rom. 9: 5); they are the objects of grace, rescued out of sin and misery. And therefore the Lord never used the expression "our Father" as joining together Himself and His people, but only "My Father and your Father" (John 20: 17). Yet He is not ashamed to call them His "brethren," for both He who sanctifies as well as those who are being sanctified are all of One (the Father) (Heb. 2: 11, 12). The members of the church are firstborn ones only in relation to the rest of redeemed creation; as regards eternity and the totality of the universe Christ is the Firstborn.

[1] On the death of the father, if there were, say, *six* children, the property was divided into *seven* portions, of which the firstborn took two. [Trans.]

THE UNSEARCHABLE RICHES OF CHRIST

THE relations between Christ and His church are exceedingly manifold, especially
   I. Teaching and learning (discipleship, school);
   II. Leading and following (flock, army);
   III. Ruling and obeying (commonwealth, people);
   IV. Loving and responsive loving (bride, wife);
   V. Quickening and being quickened (vine, body);
   VI. Founding and building up (spiritual house);
   VII. Blessing and being a blessing (priesthood, temple).

I. TEACHING AND LEARNING

Christ is the Teacher and we are the scholars (Matt. 23: 8). He is the pattern (John 13: 14, 15; I Pet. 2: 21). He says: "Learn of Me" (Matt. 11: 29; Eph. 4: 20). Our task is to "adorn" the teaching of our Saviour God in all things (Titus 2: 10). The church is a school, a discipleship. The Greek word for disciple, *mathētēs*, means a scholar.

II. LEADING AND FOLLOWING

Christ is the Shepherd and we are the flock. Out of the fold of Israel (John 10: 1-5) and the folds of the world civilization He has gathered together His own into one flock (John 10: 16).
   As the good Shepherd He laid down His life for His sheep (John 10: 11, 15; comp. Psa. 22);
   as the great Shepherd He is the One risen from the dead in the power of the blood of the eternal covenant (Heb. 13: 20, 21; comp. Psa. 23);
   as the chief Shepherd He will come again and give His undershepherds the crown of honour (I Pet. 5: 4, 2, 3; comp. Psa. 24).
   But in the present age He carries out a sevenfold service as Shepherd:

   He calls us (John 10: 3),
   He leads us (Psa. 23: 3),
   He nourishes us (Psa. 23: 2),
   He knows us (John 10: 14, 15, 27),
   He guards us (John 10: 28-30),
   He heals us (I Pet. 2: 24, 25),
   He carries us home (Luke 15: 5, 6; Isa. 40: 11).

III. Ruling and Obeying

Christ is the Lord and we are His servants (I Cor. 4: 1).
Christ is the Governor and we are His subjects (Jude 4). Christ
is the commander-in-chief and we are His warriors (II Tim. 2:
3, 4: see also Eph. 6: 10–17: I Thess. 5: 8, 9; II Cor. 6: 7). The
redeemed are a people (Acts 15: 14, and II Cor. 6: 16; I Pet.
2: 9; Titus 2: 14); they are fellow-citizens with the saints (Eph.
2: 19), a kingdom of priests (Rev. 1: 6; I Pet. 2: 9). The church
has the nature of a State. Her commonwealth is in heaven
(Phil. 3: 20). Its citizens are in the kingdom of the Son (Col. 1:
13). They should make manifest the kingdom of God (Rom. 14:
17; I Cor. 4: 20). Therefore they preach the kingdom (Acts 20:
25, 28, 31; Col. 4: 11).

A law appertains to the kingdom; to the kingdom of the Son
it is the law of Christ (Gal. 6: 2). Therefore to believe is at the
same time to obey. Therefore to trust is to be trustworthy.
For these two expressions the Greek language has one and the
same word, *pistis*. It is Paul, the apostle of freedom, who
speaks of "keeping the commandments" (I Cor. 7: 19). He
himself *commanded* (II Thess. 3: 6). Unbelief is to him the same
as disobedience (Rom. 10. 3). Conversion is to him an act of
obedience and subjection (Acts 26: 19), and the gospel message
is a *command* to repent (Acts 17. 30). Redeemed from "the law
of sin and death" (Rom. 8: 1, 2) and also free from the law of
Moses (Rom. 3: 21; 7: 1–6; 10: 4), the believer is by no means
without law (I Cor. 9: 21; Gal. 5: 13), but is now "under law to
Christ" (I Cor. 9: 21). He has to fulfil "the law of Christ"
(Gal. 6: 2) and to walk in the "obedience of faith" (Rom. 1: 5;
15: 18; 16: 26). Grace will "rule royally" (Rom. 5: 21). This
New Testament law is

as to its origin — the law of Christ (Gal. 6: 2);
as to its nature — the law of freedom (Jas. 1: 25; 2: 12);
as to its content — the law of love (Rom. 13: 8–10, comp.
　　　　　　　　　　Jas. 2: 8; I Tim. 1: 5; Gal. 6: 2);
as to its strength — the law of the Spirit (Rom. 8: 2);
as to its effect — the law of the Spirit *of life* (Rom. 8: 2);
as to its worth — the perfect law (Jas. 1: 25);
as to its dignity — the royal law (Jas. 2: 8).

In the Old Testament man stood under the law of God as a
natural man; he was "in the flesh;" hence the powerlessness of
the law (Rom. 8: 3). But in the new covenant he is a *new* man
(II Cor. 5: 17); he is "in the Spirit;" hence his victory (Rom. 8:
1–4).

In the old covenant the law approached the man from without,
on tables of stone, as letters which killed (II Cor. 3: 3, 6); in the
new covenant it is put into his *mind* (Heb. 8: 10; Rom. 6: 17),

written on "fleshly tables of the heart and with the Spirit of
the living God" (II Cor. 3: 3).

Thus the church is a wonderful people a "holy nation"
(I Pet. 2: 9):

its Governor	— the Lord Christ (Jude 4);
its law	— His will (Gal. 6: 2);
its riches	— His glory (Eph. 3: 16);
its praise	— His honour (I Cor. 1: 31);
its fellowship as a people	— His love (John 13: 34);
its sphere	— the whole earth (Rom. 10: 18);
its capital city	— the heavenly Jerusalem (Gal. 4: 26).

IV. Loving and Responsive Loving

Christ is the Lover and the church is His beloved (II Cor.
11: 2, 3). Christ is the Lord and she is to be His wife (Eph.
5: 31, 32). As affianced she has the pure and expectant love
(II Cor. 11: 2, 3); as the wife she will have the possessing and
enjoying love.

It is as if an oriental prince should see in the slave-market a
slave girl, and burning with sudden love, should buy her at a
high price, so as then to purify her, to robe her in splendid
garments, and finally to exalt her as his wife to the royal throne
—thus also Christ and the church. He has loved her, the former
slave of sin; has then given Himself up as the purchase price,
and now purifies her by means of "the laver of water in the
word," and will presently "present her to Himself" without
spot or wrinkle, that is, in holiness and the beauty of eternal
youth (Eph. 5: 25–27).

So in the picture of marriage we have the whole work of
Christ for His church:

her choice	— through His love (Eph. 5: 25);
her redemption	— through His devotion (Eph. 5: 25);
her purification	— through His lordship (Eph. 5: 26, 24, 33);
her glorification	— through His return (Eph. 5: 27).

As Augustine has already said: "Whom God has

foreordained	*before* the world was, He has also
called	*out of* the world,
justified	*in* the world, and will
glorify	*after* the world" (comp. Rom. 8: 29, 30).

Our life, therefore, belongs to Him alone. Our soul should
for ever glow with its first love (Rev. 2: 4), that is, the love as
it was at first when our union with Christ began. In the Lord's
letter to Ephesus it is associated with the tree of life of Paradise
(Rev. 2: 4, 7), for love is life, and "who loves not, lives not.
Who lives by that life, he cannot die" (Raymond Lull: died 1315).

Even in the Old Testament time there existed a relationship of

love between Jehovah and His people.   In a much more glorious
degree it exists today between Christ and His church.   Therefore
the Spirit of God takes the highest relationship of love which
general human experience knows and applies it to both Israel
(Hos. 2: 21, 22; Ezek. 16 and 23; Isa. 62: 5; Psa. 45; Song of
Songs) and also to the church (II Cor. 11: 2, 3; Eph. 5: 31, 32).
But the conjunction of both is the heavenly Jerusalem, the city
where in due time the redeemed from Israel will dwell (Rev. 21:
12), and which is the "mother of us all" for the church (Gal.
4: 26; Heb. 12: 22; Rev. 3: 12).   It is the "holy city," "the bride
and the wife of the Lamb" (Rev. 21: 9, 10; comp. 19: 7).

The objection that as the "body" of Christ the church cannot
be also "betrothed" and "wife" rests upon a mistake as to the
variableness of oriental and Biblical figures of speech.   In the
parable of the sower the field is the human heart (Matt. 13: 19),
in the parable of the tares it is the "world" (ver. 38).   Birds are
at times emblems of the good (Matt. 6: 26; 10: 16; 3: 16), in
other places they represent evil (Matt. 13: 4, 19).   The eagle, as
an unclean creature, is an abomination to the children of Israel
(Lev. 11: 13); nevertheless it is employed as a picture of the
powerful care of God (Exod. 19: 4; Rev. 4: 7).   Similarly the
Pauline picture language is everywhere fluid, living, and moving.
The slave status is now a picture of what our relationships to
God are *not* (as regards inward estrangement and fear—Gal. 4: 7;
John 15: 15); now of what they nevertheless *are* (as to possession,
obedience, protection) (Rom. 6: 15–23).   To say that because
the church is the "body" of Christ, she cannot be also the "bride"
would be as precipitate as to say that because she is a "body"
she cannot be "pillar" or "house" (I Tim. 3: 15).   In all these
instances it is a matter of *pictures*.   And the picture of the
"betrothed" and the "wife" lies unmistakably in II Cor. 11: 2, 3
and Eph. 5: 31, 32.   But behind all these pictures, and explained
by them, there are spiritual realities.

V. Quickening and Being Quickened
(Oneness of Life)

The basis of all is the organic fellowship in life of the members
with Christ.   This is already indicated in the picture of marriage:
"the two shall be *one* flesh . . . I speak as regards Christ and the
church" (Eph. 5: 31, 32).   Here also the New Testament has
a rich picture language:

Christ is the "vine" and we are the branches (John 15: 1–5).
Christ is the head and we are the members (Eph. 1: 22, 23).   The
believer is a tree rooted in Him (Col. 2: 7).   The individual is a
plant (Matt. 15: 13: I Cor. 3: 6–9) planted together with Him
(Rom. 6: 5, lit.).   They are all "*in* Christ."

A. THE RELATIONSHIP OF THE MEMBERS TO THE HEAD

The most important figure is that of the "body." It is used exclusively by Paul. It, as no other figure, sets forth the blessings of the Christian fellowship.

1. *Possession of Christ.* The church is *His* "body" (Eph. 1: 23).

2. *Dependent service.* In a body only *one* will rules, and the head governs the body (Col. 1: 18).

3. *Direct fellowship.* The individual member stands in direct relationship to the Head. No man or angel stands between (I Tim. 2: 5). Therefore it behoves us to "hold fast" the Head in all things (Col. 2: 18, 19).

4. *Love and Care.* "No man ever hated his own flesh; but nourisheth and cherisheth it, even as Christ also the church" (Eph. 5: 29). "He is the Saviour of the body" (Eph. 5: 23).

5. *Quickening and Upbuilding.* The Head is the source for the body of its building itself up. In the earthly the soul is the body-building element. Hence the connexion between bodily form and the powers of the soul. Thus also "out of" its Head the body of Christ grows with its God-appointed increase (Col. 2: 19). Only "out of" Him can it effect the "building up of itself in love" (Eph. 4: 16). Thus Christ is the builder (Matt. 16: 18) and we also are the builders (I Cor. 3: 10–15). In the New Testament the figure of building is employed only of the church, but not of the kingdom of God.

6. *The "fulness" of the Head.* Not as a Divine person, but only as the "last Adam" Christ would not be "complete" without His "body": the corn of wheat without its fruit would be "alone" (John 12: 24). A redeemer without redeemed were no redeemer. Thus the church is "the fulness of Him who fills all things in all"; that is, "the full formation of Him who brings to full formation all things in all" (Eph. 1: 23).

Through all this the church is

7. *The means of revelation of the life of Christ.* In the earthly life the body is the organ by which the spirit reveals itself. And in the spiritual life it is through the church that the very manifold wisdom of God is made known (Eph. 3: 10). The exalted Head continues through His body His life here below. The church is "God's sphere of life in history," the continuance on earth of the incarnation of Christ. Through the Spirit the church extends His life here below. It is not only in Christ, but also Christ is in it (Col. 1: 27). In the church He gains form (Gal. 4: 19), expresses in it His nature, and the Head reveals Himself through His members.

B. THE RELATIONSHIPS OF THE MEMBERS TO ONE ANOTHER

Also of the fellowship of Christians the "body" is the most

expressive of pictures. The chief passage is I Cor. 12. The redeemed are:

1. *An Unity,* much deeper than all national, and much wider than all international fellowship (Gal. 6: 10). Though they may not have seen each other, yet they know each other (II Cor. 6: 9), though they may be entire strangers, yet they *love* one another! (Col. 2: 1, 2; 1: 9). For "as the body is one, although it has many members, so also is the Christ" (I Cor. 12: 12). He is an organism and not an organization; not a corporation but a body, the body of Christ; a creation of God, and no work of man. Christ, the Head, is the unity of the body; His body is the "*one* new man" (Eph. 2: 15).

Seven particular features constitute the unity of the body. There is "*one* body (Rom. 12: 5; Eph. 2: 16) and *one* spirit (Eph. 2: 18; I Cor. 12: 11, 13), even as you are called in *one* hope of your calling; *one* Lord, *one* faith, *one* baptism, *one* God and Father of us all, who is over you all, and through you all, and in you all" (Eph. 4: 4–6).

The oneness of the church is threefold:

Oneness of the *spirit* (of the life) already exists. It is already a reality, which we have through *faith* (Eph. 4: 3);

Oneness of the *mind* ought to exist; it is our duty, which we fulfil through *love* (Phil. 1: 27; 2: 1–4; 4: 2);

Oneness of *knowledge* will come to exist. It is our goal, a portion of our *hope* (Eph. 4: 13).

Oneness of life is what we have, the foundation, which looks back to the *past*, to the work of Golgotha (John 11: 52);

Oneness of mind is that which we ought to have, the task which lies upon us in the *present*; that is oneness of purpose, not always absolute oneness of opinion (Rom. 14: 1–7);

Oneness of knowledge is that which we shall have, the "full measure" (Eph. 4: 13), which will be attained in the *future*.

But for the present the saying of Augustine holds good: "In things necessary unity, in things doubtful liberty, in all things charity."[1]

2. *Variety.* "For the body is not one member, but many. If the whole were an eye, where were the hearing? If the whole were hearing, where were the smelling?" (I Cor. 12: 14, 17; Rom. 12: 4–8). As on the breastplate of the high priest there shone twelve different jewels, representing the twelve tribes of Israel (Exod. 28: 15–21), so are the members of the new covenant borne on the breast of the Melchizedek High Priest. They are all different but they all shine, and the oneness of their light is the oneness of the Sun.

3. *Mutual dependence.* Each one of us is one-sided. Therefore

---

[1] "*In necessariis unitas, in dubiis libertas, in omnibus caritas.*"

each needs all. "The eye cannot say to the hand, I have no need of thee; or again the head to the feet, I have no need of you" (I Cor. 12: 21). Nay, they are all dependent upon one another, even the greatest upon the smallest, and the very least God has covered with greater honour, "that the members should have the same care for one another" (I Cor. 12: 22–25).

4. *Mutual sympathy.* "If one member suffers all the members suffer with it; or if one member is honoured, all the members rejoice with it" (I Cor. 12: 26).

5. *Common service.* Each member serves the other, and they all serve the whole body, and thus the whole body is "supplied through the joints and bands" (Col. 2: 19), and "held together by the help of all joints, which render their service according to the particular activity assigned to each member" (Eph. 4: 16). All members have duties. Not one individual is permitted to stand aside. Fellowship in the kingdom of God is fellowship in work. Only so will they have fellowship in victory.

6. *Common growth.* But all this is "till we all attain unto the unity of the faith, and of the knowledge of the Son of God, unto the ripeness of a fullgrown man, to the full measure of the stature of the fulness of Christ" (Eph. 4: 13).

VI. FOUNDING AND BUILDING UP

With the figure of the body there is closely connected in Scripture the figure of house building. The two figures are indeed interwoven: the house *grows* (Eph. 2: 21); the body is *built up* (Eph. 4: 12).

Christ is the corner stone and we are the superstructure (I Pet. 2: 6). The church is a house of God, a temple. This figure holds in a threefold manner—in reference to the whole church (Eph. 2: 21, 22; I Pet. 2: 4, 5), the local church (I Cor. 3: 16, 17; I Tim. 3: 15), the individual Christian (I Cor. 6: 19; Eph. 3: 17).

1. *The Foundation is the Lord Himself.* "Other foundation can no one lay than that which is laid" (I Cor. 3: 11). The testimony of the first generation speaks of Him. Therefore all that follows is "built upon the foundation of the apostles and prophets" (Eph. 2: 20). The truth which Peter confessed is the rock foundation of the church: the super-historical Sonship to God and the historical Messiahship of Jesus of Nazareth. "Thou art the Christ (Messiah), the Son of the living God"—"On this rock I will build My church" (Matt. 16: 16–18).

2. *The Stones.* They come out of two quarries, the Jews and the Gentiles (Eph. 2: 11, 12), and are joined together into *one* holy temple (Eph. 2: 21, 22). They are brought as dead stones to Him the living One, and through the Spirit of His life are made to live (I Pet. 2: 4). Their faith *in* Christ is at the same time

faith *on* Christ (I Pet. 2: 6; Rom. 9: 33), a repose on the corner stone in Zion (Isa. 28: 16), and a being built up on Him (Eph. 4: 29; Jude 20; I Cor. 14: 12–26).[1]

3. *The Purpose* of this house is that it shall be a *temple*. It is a *spiritual* house (I Pet. 2: 5), and the "stones" in the wall are at the same time priests at the altar (I Pet. 2: 5; Heb. 13: 10), and the leaders are "pillars" in the temple of their God (Gal. 2: 9; Rev. 3: 12).

By this it is already indicated that the church is a priesthood.

VII. Blessed and made a Blessing

Christ is the high priest and we are the priests (Heb. 8: 1; Rev. 1: 6). The church is a "holy" people (I Pet. 2: 9). As priests its members have a fourfold service:

1. *They offer.*

Their life is	— a sacrifice (Rom. 12: 1; 15: 16; Darby);
Their devotion	— a burnt offering (Mark 12: 33);
Their service	— a drink offering (II Tim. 4:6, R.V. mgn; Phil. 2: 17);
Their deeds	— spiritual sacrifices (I Pet. 2: 5; Heb. 13: 16);
Their prayers	— an incense offering (Psa. 141: 2; Rev. 8: 3, 4);
Their worship	— a praise offering (Heb. 13: 15).

2. *They pray.* They pray for others; they give thanks for others; in the quiet chamber they embrace the whole world (I Tim. 2: 1, 2); and in heaven the Spirit intercedes for them with inexpressible groans and imparts to their prayers Divine energy (Rom. 8: 26, 27).

3. *They witness.* "The priest's lips should keep knowledge, and they should seek the law from his mouth, for he is the messenger of Jehovah of hosts" (Mal. 2: 7).

4. *They bless.* "Speak unto Aaron and unto his sons saying, On this wise ye shall bless the children of Israel. . . . They shall put My name upon the children of Israel, and I will bless them" (Num. 6: 23–27). Thus "to bless" means "to put the name of God on some one." Therefore he only is a blessing who brings others into touch with God through word and walk.

But in the new covenant there is a universal priesthood. They all enjoy the priestly portion at the altar (Heb. 13: 10; I Cor. 9: 13). They are all, what Israel should have been, "a kingdom of priests" (Exod. 19: 6), and in even the least of them the promise can be fulfilled: "I will bless thee and thou shalt be a blessing" (Gen. 12: 2).

---

[1] Therefore the New Testament speaks not only of a faith *in* Christ (*pisteuein eis Christon*) but also of a faith *on* Him (*pisteuein ep' autō*), Rom. 9: 33; I Pet. 2: 6.

CHAPTER III

THE NEW COVENANT OF GOD

A LL blessings of the church, taken together, form the acme of the content of salvation under the "new covenant" (Matt. 26: 28). This is the heavenly calling of the covenant with Abraham (Heb. 11: 10; Eph. 1: 3), the unsearchable riches of Christ (Eph. 3: 8).

I. THE OLD AND THE NEW COVENANTS

But the New Covenant is "new" only in relation to the "old" covenant (Heb. 8: 13), and this was given only to Israel (Psa. 147: 19, 20). The nations were "strangers as regards the covenants of promise" (Eph. 2: 12). The name "new covenant," "new testament" thus itself expresses that the church cannot be separated from the ground of the Old Testament promise. "Salvation comes out of the Jews" (John 4: 22; Rom. 9: 5). "Thou bearest not the root but the root bears thee" (Rom. 11: 18). Nevertheless since the kingdom of God has been opened to the Gentiles also, there exists no more a "difference" as regards the enjoyment of its blessings (Acts 15: 9; 11: 17; 10: 17), and the believers from the peoples are exactly as the believers from Israel, partakers of the saving benefits of the new covenant.

As to its content the new covenant is infinitely greater than the old. The *Hebrews* letter shows this especially. In a sevenfold contrast it displays the excellence of the New Testament salvation, and this in special comparison to four Old Testament persons (or groups of persons) and three Old Testament institutions.

In this it is like II Cor. 3, which also throws into relief a sevenfold glory of the new covenant: (1) stone—flesh (vv. 3, 7); (2) letter—spirit (ver. 6); (3) death—life (vv. 6, 7); (4) lesser—greater (vv. 8–10); (5) condemnation—righteousness (ver. 9); (6) passing—remaining (ver. 11); (7) veiling—unveiling (vv. 12–18).

In *Hebrews* it is shown that

A. CHRIST IS GREATER

(1) than the angels—the heavenly mediators of the old covenant (chs. 1 and 2), and comp. Heb. 2: 2 with Acts 7: 53;

(2) than Moses—the earthly mediator of the old covenant, the prophetic leader (Deut. 34: 10);

(3) than Joshua—the rest-giver of the old covenant, the political leader (ch. 4).

(4) than Aaron—the high priest of the old covenant, the priestly leader (chs. 5 to 9);

Furthermore, in Hebrews, it is shown that:

B. CHRIST IS GREATER

(5) than the covenant itself—the saving content of the old covenant (ch. 8).

For according to Heb. 8: 8–13 and Jer. 31: 31–34, Christ makes:

(a) the sovereignty an inward rule,
(b) the prophetic office universal,
(c) the priesthood perfect.

He is greater

(6) than the tabernacle—the place of revelation under the old covenant (ch. 9);

(7) than the sacrifices—the means of salvation under the old covenant (ch. 10).

Thus He is greater than all that which the old covenant included, for in Him we are made to share in:

1. a better covenant   — 7: 22; 8: 6;
2. a better Mediator   — 1: 4; 3: 3;
3. a better sacrifice   — 9: 23; 12: 24;
4. a better priesthood   — 8: 6; 7: 7;
5. a better possession   — 6: 9; 10: 34;
6. a better promise   — 8: 6; 11: 40;
7. a better hope   — 7: 19;
8. a better resurrection — 11: 35;
9. a better fatherland   — 11: 16.

Therefore in His power we can tread the "new and living way" (10: 20), that is:

in the faith that looks above (ch. 11),
in the hope that sees things ahead (ch. 12),
in the love that contemplates all things around (ch. 13).

II. THE COVENANTS WITH ABRAHAM AND WITH DAVID

In its essence this new convenant is the fulfilment of two Old Testament covenants, that with Abraham and that with David. In the Abrahamic covenant lay the breadth, the blessing for all peoples (Gen. 12: 3); in the Davidic covenant was the height, the royal throne of Messiah (I Chron. 17: 11–14). In the one lay expansion, the pressing outward to the circumference; in the other was the holding together, concentration on the centre. And therefore both are often mentioned together, as in Gabriel's message and Mary's song (Luke 1: 32, 55); in the prophetic praise of the Spirit-filled Zacharias (Luke 1: 67, 73); and in the chief scriptural proof of justification in Paul's letter to the Romans (4: 1–3, 6).

But the New Testament fulfilment takes an opposite course to the Old Testament promise. First Christ appears in Israel and works principally among the circumcision and especially as Son of David (Matt. 10: 5, 6; 15: 24); and then comes the time of salvation for the peoples of the world (Acts 13: 46; Rom. 11: 25), the calling of the nations, and thus the blessing of the covenant with Abraham embracing all mankind (Gal. 3: 8, 9, 14).

III. COVENANT AND TESTAMENT

Taken strictly it is less "covenant" than "testament." For

1. A covenant is two-sided, a testament only a one-sided disposal by the will of the testator ("last will"). But in salvation all proceeds from one side, God's side, and the faith of man is no equivalent (no "consideration"), but simply the hand that lays hold of what is offered.

2. A covenant is dissolved by death, but a testament only becomes legally effective on death. But salvation is wholly a testament, a disposition as one's "last will." Only by the death of the Crucified did it first become operative and valid (Heb. 9: 15–18). Its presupposition is Christ's death, its property is the eternal inheritance, and itself a holy Divine appointment. "Divine appointment" is therefore the best translation of the Greek *diathēkē* (Heb. *berith*), when it is used in this sense in the history of salvation.

IV. COVENANT PEOPLE AND WORLD

Outwardly the covenant people is the witness to covenant grace experienced. It is first its product, then its organ; first the object of salvation, then the instrument of salvation. This relation to the world is expressed most connectedly in that very chapter which most leads into the inner realm, the holy place, apart from the world, the High Priestly prayer (John 17). Here the Lord Jesus mentions seven chief relationships. His own are:

1. as to their surroundings—living *in* the world (vv. 11, 15).
2. as to their position—taken *out* of the world (6).
3. as to their sentiments—separated *from* the world (16, 14, 9).
4. as to their service as witnesses—*sent into* the world (18, 21, 23).
5. as to their treatment—*hated by* the world (14).
6. as to their victorious strength—*kept from* the world (15, 11).

The basis of the whole is:

7. the loving plan of God before *the foundation of the world*.

Before all time the Father had given the church to the Son as a love-gift, and this love of the Father to the Son *before* the foundation of the world is the basis of the church being glorified at the *end* of the world.   "Father, I will that those whom thou hast given me may be with me where I am, that they may behold my glory . . . *for* thou hast loved me before the foundation of the world" (John 17: 24).   Thus the love of the Most High *before* time and *after* time arches itself as a rainbow *over* all time.   The end returns to the beginning because the beginning guarantees the end (Rom. 11: 36).

But in the present the saints are the messengers of God to the world;

    i. the "pillar and basis of the truth" (I Tim. 3: 15);
   ii. His witnesses (Acts 1: 8);
  iii. His "letters" (II Cor. 3: 1–3);
   iv. His ambassadors to the world (II Cor. 5: 20);
    v. His "exhibitions of the word of life" (Darby, *darstellend,* Phil. 2: 16);
   vi. His stars in the dark night (Phil. 2: 15);
 vii. His seven golden lampstands with Himself in the midst (Rev. 1: 12, 13).

CHAPTER IV

THE PRESENT, PERSONAL SALVATION

He who denies certainty of salvation rejects faith.—Luther.

Not that I have already laid hold.—Paul.

R EDEMPTION in Christ is at once being and coming to be. The individual has through faith a full, free, present salvation, which, nevertheless, he at the same time experiences only in most effective, combined counter-workings.

I. A FULL, FREE, PRESENT SALVATION

Paul especially pictures his Christian experience in ever new colours. In harmony with his preference for juridical thought he describes it in five chief sets of pictures all taken from the realm of law. For him it is justification, redemption, forgiveness, reconciliation, and adoption as a son. To the apostle his experience of salvation is as a clear shining sun, with its full brightness—Christ—in itself, but with five chief rays which go out from it in all directions, unlimited, immeasurable.

With Paul all the five chief pictures are no mere theological conceptions, but first and foremost are purely everyday expressions of Roman-Greek legal life, especially:

dikaiōsis, acquittal   — justification;
apolytrōsis, buying out   — redemption;
aphesis, remission of debt   — forgiveness;
huiothesia, adoption, acceptance as son — sonship.

All theoretical "dogmatic" lies far from Paul. "He is far more a man of prayer and witness, a confessor and prophet, than a learned exegete or philosophical theologian."

1. In justification the sinner stands before God as the accused and is declared free (Rom. 8: 33).

2. In redemption he stands before God as the slave and receives freedom by ransom (Rom. 6: 18–22).

3. In forgiveness he stands before God as a debtor and receives his discharge (Eph. 1: 7; 4: 32; comp. Matt. 18: 21–35).

4. In reconciliation he stands before God as an enemy and is led to peace (II Cor. 5: 18–20).

5. In adoption he stands before God as a stranger (or slave) and receives adoption, sonship (Eph. 1: 5).

But each of these five chief pictures displays another side of the same experience of salvation.

1. Forgiveness refers to the fruit, the individual deeds of our life, the sins (Eph. 1: 7; comp. Rom. 3 and 4).

2. Redemption refers to the root, our whole condition of life, that is, slavery under sin (Rom. 6: 18–22; chs. 5 to 8).

3. Justification is the sum of forgiveness and redemption. In the first place, that is, in the narrower fundamental sense, it is acquittal from the guilt of sins (Rom. 3: 23, 24), and this is equivalent to forgiveness; but then it is also the declaration of freedom from the power of sin (Rom. 6: 7, 10), that is, emancipation.

4. Reconciliation is the concluding of peace, the removal of the enmity; it is connected with the will and the renewal of the mind (Rom. 5: 10); and

5. Sonship is finally the greatest of all; it is associated with our standing and gives heavenly dignity (Rom. 8: 17).

Thus is everything accomplished! Sin and sins, root and tree, sin's power and sin's guilt, heart condition and heart position—all this Christ has brought under His cross: "No one is holier than a sinner who has received grace" (Zinzendorf).

And yet! though everything has *come to pass*, everything—except justification—is *coming to be*. Until the return of Christ the believer—viewed in himself—experiences certain most effective, powerful, combined

II.   COUNTER WORKINGS

Future and present, position and condition, God's work and our work, heaven and earth, eternity and time, spirit and body—these all continue in him in a living, vital, unresolved conflict.

1. *Future and Present.* We *have* redemption (Eph. 1: 7; Col. 1: 14) and we *await* redemption (Rom. 8: 23). Therefore is the "day of redemption" still future (Eph. 4: 30; 1: 14).

We *have* eternal life (John 3: 36) and we *lay hold of* eternal life (I Tim. 6: 12).

We *are* sons of God (Rom. 8: 14) and we *await* sonship (Rom. 8: 23).

We *are* already in the kingdom (Col. 1: 13; Heb. 12: 22) and we *enter hereafter* into the kingdom (Acts 14: 22), we *inherit* the kingdom (I Cor. 6: 9, 10; Eph. 5: 5; I Thess. 2: 12).

God *has* glorified us (Rom. 8: 30) and He *will* glorify us (Rom. 8: 17).

This is the contrast between present and future, being and coming to be, not having and yet having. "Faith brings the fulness of the future into the poverty of the present." Christ the firstfruits (I Cor. 15: 20) gives to His own even now the gift of firstfruits (Rom. 8: 23).

We enjoy the present, and at the same time it is not yet the fulfilment. In Christ the new age is livingly present and yet the old is not yet gone. Salvation is at once present and future, for it is eternal.

All that we have we await, all that we await we already
have. We are "saved in hope" (Rom. 8: 24). The centre
of gravity lies in the past—at Golgotha: the zenith lies in
the future—the appearing in glory. But it is the future that is
the background of all New Testament ideas. The gaze toward
the goal is the pulse-beat of all sanctification and salvation. For
Christ is at once the embodiment of both promise and fulfilment.

From this arises the New Testament conception of all things
becoming manifest (Col. 3: 4; Rom. 8: 19; I John 3: 2), for only
things already existing can become manifest (uncovered). The
faithful and super-temporal God vouches to us the future as
already present, yes, as having already taken place in the past.
"He *has* glorified us" (Rom. 8: 30).

Thus we already have everything, but our enjoyment is as
yet only partial. Until the redemption of the body, our coming
of age (Rom. 8: 23), our invested capital is reserved in heaven
(I Pet. 1: 4; II Tim. 1: 12; Col. 1: 5). And that which we
already have is a proof that the capital sum is ours, and thus
our present possession is a guarantee of the future, a firstfruits
of the full harvest (Rom. 8: 23), an earnest, a pledge of the coming
sum total (Eph. 1: 14; II Cor. 1: 22; 5: 5).

But it is precisely the certainty of the "now" which establishes the high contrast of the "not yet." The very greatness
of our today causes us to look longingly for the still greater
tomorrow. Our very longing is a blessed enjoyment, and by
being satisfied our hunger grows (Phil. 3: 12; Matt. 5: 6).

2. *Position and Condition.* We *are* dead (Col. 3: 3; Gal. 2:
19, 20; 5: 24; Rom. 6: 6) and we *put to death* our members (Col.
3: 5).

We *are* new men (Col. 3: 10; Eph. 4: 24; II Cor. 5: 17) and
we *become* renewed (Col. 3: 10; Eph. 4: 23).

We *are* light (I Thess. 5: 5) and *ought to* shine as the light
(Eph. 5: 9; Matt. 5: 16).

We *are* saints of God (Col. 3: 12; Eph. 1: 1) and we *become*
sanctified (I Thess. 5: 23; Heb. 12: 14; II Cor. 7: 1).

We *are* perfect (Col. 2: 10) and we *pursue after* perfection
(Phil. 3: 12).

Christ *dwells* in us (Col. 1: 27) and He *should* dwell in us
(Eph. 3: 17).

This is the contrast between position and condition, dignity
and duty, reality and realization, standing in grace and character.
The poverty-stricken beggar is taken from his miserable hut and
set among princes, but then he is exhorted to behave as a prince
(Eph. 4: 1). The nobleman must be noble. Position imposes
duty. Here enters the strife between flesh and spirit (Gal. 5: 17),
between the old man and the new man (Rom. 6: 6, 11), and the
constant work of faith, which is sanctification.

G

But just here we continue to experience the contrast which follows next and which is related to strength.

3. *God's Work and Our Work.* It is God who works all things, yet we also are the workers. It is all a gift, yet everything must be acquired by effort (II Pet. 1: 3; Col. 4: 12). Holiness is wholly *His* work (I Thess. 5: 23; I Cor. 6: 11), and also wholly *my* work (Heb. 12: 14; I John 3: 3), wholly a present and wholly a command, wholly gift and wholly task.

As to the choice of the called, it was *before* all ages (Eph. 1: 4, 5; II Pet. 1: 10);

as to the sanctifying of the chosen, it is in the *course* of the ages (John 17: 17; II Cor. 7: 1);

as to the glorifying of the sanctified, it will be at the *end* of the ages (John 17: 24; II Tim. 2: 5).

This harmonious contrast is valid, "*Work out* your own salvation with fear and trembling, *for* (!) it is God who works in you both to will and also to perform, according to His own good pleasure" (Phil. 2: 12, 13).

All human attempts at explanation are here inadequate. They only show, especially if pushed to the extreme, that the kernel of the question remains unexplained. Even in Rom. 8: 29 and I Pet. 1: 1, 2 the question is not finally answered. The freedom of the human will (Matt. 23: 37; Rev. 22: 17) and its lack of freedom (Rom. 9: 11, 15, 16, 18; 11: 5, 7; Acts 13: 48) is a mystery of the kingdom of God. They are two parallel lines which meet first in infinity. Faith accepts this contrast without being able to explain it. That it exists is enough. It is the contrast between God's choice of grace and man's responsibility, between the lack of freedom and the freedom of the will of the creature, between grace and reward (Rom. 4: 2–6; I Cor. 3: 14; 4: 5; Col. 3: 24; II Cor. 5: 10).

The next contrast is that between:

4. *Heaven and Earth.* Christ is the One exalted in heaven (Eph. 1: 20; 4: 10; Heb. 7: 26; 8: 1) and who at the same time dwells in us on earth (Eph. 3: 17; Gal. 2: 20).[1]

The Christian lives here below on earth (John 17: 11, 15; Phil. 2: 15) and yet at the same time he sits together in the heavenly places (Eph. 2: 6; 1: 3; Heb. 12: 22; Phil. 3: 20)[2]

[1] This is the mystic-transcendental polarity between the transcendence and immanence of Christ. Hence the 164 times when Paul uses "in Christ," as also the 19 times "in the Spirit," and the Pauline *genitivus mysticus*, as e.g. peace of Christ (Col. 3: 15), blessing of Christ (Rom. 15. 29), faith of Christ (Rom. 3: 22), love of Christ (II Cor. 5. 14), obedience of Christ (II Cor. 10: 5), circumcision of Christ (Col. 2: 11); etc.

[2] The expression "in the heavenly places" (*en tois epouraniois*) is found in *Ephesians* only (five times), and is always to be understood locally, as is proved especially by Eph. 1: 20 (comp. 2: 6); also 3: 10 and 6: 12. The Christian has experienced with Christ not only crucifixion (Gal. 2: 19) and resurrection (Col. 3: 1), but also through the Spirit His ascension to heaven (Eph. 2: 6). Therefore is Eph. 1: 3 to be translated "heavenly *places*," not "heavenly possessions."

The connexion of the two is the Spirit. The Spirit came down from above, from "Christ *above* us," from heaven to earth (Acts 2: 33); and the Spirit as "Christ *in* us" leads from below upwards, from earth to heaven (Col. 1: 27; II Cor. 3: 17, 18).

But the basis of all is the contrast between

5. *Eternity and Time.* Eternity is more than merely unending time. Not only as to continuance but also as to content it is different in *essence* from everything temporal. It is something other, something higher, therefore not only a "before" and an "after." Eternal is no bare notion of quantity, but above all of quality. One must guard against introducing the idea of time into that of eternity. "We do not arrive at the idea of eternity by any sort of adding together of time." Therefore "eternal life" is indeed endless life (comp. Matt. 25: 46), but at the same time more than deathlessness. It is *divine* life.

Yet faith even now experiences the eternal God always within the limits of time. For faith this both elevates and humbles at the same time. All fellowship with God, especially by prayer, is a partaking of the life of God. By it man, in the midst of time, stands in the timeless. In the midst of movement and change the stable and abiding break through. The super-historical is experienced in the historical.

This is what Holy Scripture means when it teaches that the believer already "has" the eternal life. It does not begin after death but already today, on earth, in this life. "He who believes on the Son, he *has* the eternal life" (John 3: 36, comp. 17: 3; I John 3: 14; 5: 12).

6. *Spirit and Body.* Nevertheless all this comes to pass within the limits of time. We are "in Christ" and yet still "in the world" (John 17: 11); we are "in the Spirit" (Rom. 8: 9) and yet still "in the body" (II Cor. 5: 6); we are at once superior to death yet liable to die (II Cor. 4: 11, 16). What a weak organ is our soul! What a fragile "tent" is our body! (II Cor. 5: 1, 4). Indeed, what a contrast between God's Spirit and man, between strength and weakness, between contents and vessel! We have our treasure "in earthen vessels" (II Cor. 4: 7).

So, therefore, at the same time we are both "ready and waiting, resting and hastening (Heb. 4: 3, 10; Phil. 3: 12), released yet constrained, singing of victory yet groaning" (Rom. 8: 31–39; II Cor. 5: 4; Rom. 8: 23). We are "dying, and behold we live;" we are "sorrowful, yet always rejoicing;" we are "poor, yet making many rich;" we "have nothing, yet possess all things" (II Cor. 6: 9, 10). Our gaze is a looking *above,* on the eternal as the *super*-historical, as it is a looking *forwards,* to the eternal as the *end* of history; it is a "now" and a "soon," a having and a waiting, a today and a tomorrow, a *faith* and a *hope,* a double experience at the one time (I Pet. 1: 21), but both born from the eternal *love*.

But finally the day will come when all this tension will be relaxed. The return of Christ is the release of all constraints. The basic contrast and strain of the present age is that between the manifestation of the kingdom of Satan and the concealment of the kingdom of God, in spite of the victory of Golgotha. But at the appearing of Christ all this will be resolved. His revelation then will be

1. The revelation of the spiritual body, and
2. The passage of the church from time into eternity.
3. Then the present will be transfigured in the future;
4. Our condition will correspond perfectly to our position;
5. His divine work will perfect our human work in Himself; and
6. We shall be rapt above, away from the earth into the heavenly world.

Section III—The Hope of the Church

CHAPTER I

THE RAPTURE AND FIRST RESURRECTION

Marâna thâ. Our Lord, come! (I Cor. 16: 22)

THE present age is Easter Time. It begins with the resurrection of the Redeemer and ends with the resurrection of the redeemed. Between lies the spiritual "resurrection" of those called into life (Rom. 6: 4–11; Col. 3: 1). So we live between two Easters, as those who have been raised between two resurrections, as burning and shining lights (Phil. 2: 15) between two outshinings (*epiphaneiai*) of the Eternal Light (II Tim. 1: 10; Titus 2: 13). And in the power of the first Easter we go to meet the last Easter. The resurrection of the Head guarantees the resurrection of the members. The tree of life of the resurrection bears fully ripe fruit.

The hope of the church includes four features:
The rapture and first resurrection (I Thess. 4: 13–18);
The judgment seat of Christ (II Cor. 5: 10);
The marriage of the Lamb (Rev. 19: 7, 8);
The coming World Rule (I Cor. 6: 2, 3).

I. THE MOMENT OF THE RAPTURE

1. *The Two Resurrections.* Holy Scripture does not teach a general simultaneous resurrection and a single all-embracing final judgment of righteous and unrighteous. It speaks rather of a "resurrection *out of* the dead" (Luke 20: 35), of a "first" resurrection (Rev. 20: 6), indeed, of an "*out*-resurrection *out of* the dead" (Phil. 3: 11; lit.). It speaks of "divisions" and "classes" *within* the resurrection (I Cor. 15: 15–24), and emphasizes that these are separated from one another by intervening periods. "As in Adam all die, even so in Christ will all be made alive. But each in his own class (the word denotes at the same time military 'divisions'): the firstfruit, Christ; *thereafter* those who belong to Christ when He shall come: *thereafter* the end (that is, the end of resurrection, namely, of the remainder of the dead)" (I Cor. 15: 22–24).

In the Old Testament both of these—the resurrection "unto eternal life" and the resurrection "unto eternal reproach and shame"—were indeed viewed together in one picture (Dan. 12: 2, 13), even as in the prophecies of the Lord Jesus when on earth (John 5: 28, 29; comp. Acts 24; 15). But in the progress of prophetic revelation (John 16: 12, 13) these two became separated as two chief events: the resurrection of the righteous before Messiah's kingdom begins, and the general resurrection after the kingdom, at the end of the world.   The key is Rev. 20; 4, 5: "These (the priests of God and Christ) lived, and reigned with Christ a thousand years. But the rest of the dead were not made to live until the thousand years should be ended."   "It belongs to the glorifying of the Christ as the Head that His members should share in a *special* resurrection, one like his own, a 'resurrection *out of* the dead'" (Mark 9: 9, 10; Luke 20: 35).   These and similar expressions occur 34 times in connexion with the resurrection of Christ (e.g. I Pet. 1: 3; Gal. 1: 1) and 4 times in connexion with the resurrection of His people (Mark 12: 25; Luke 20: 35; Acts 4: 2; Phil. 3: 11).

This resurrection is:

as to its time—the first resurrection (Rev. 20: 5, 6);

as to its extent—an out-resurrection (Phil. 3: 11; Luke 20: 35);

as to its character—a resurrection of the righteous (Luke 14: 14);

as to its saving benefit—a resurrection unto life (John 5: 29; Dan. 12: 2).

Therefore, "Blessed and holy are they that have part in the first resurrection" (Rev. 20: 6).

2. *The Days of God.*   With the first coming of Christ there begin in the calendar of God the "last days" (Acts 2: 17). According to early Christian conviction, with the incarnation of Christ began the "End time" (Heb. 1: 2; I John 2: 18).   For Christ is the goal toward which the long previous ages strove (Heb. 9: 26).   "His first appearing is the beginning of the End, and with His second appearing begins the end of the End." Therefore the closing points, the "ends" and the goal of the pre-Messianic (pre-Christian) ages have in Christ come upon us who live in the Messianic (Christian) age (I Cor. 10: 11).   "The church of Christ is the goal of history" (Ph. Bachmann).   The history of the End, in the New Testament sense, is therefore not simply the history of the final future, but the whole New Testament history of salvation is the history of the End developing progressively.   In Christ the beginning of the completion has appeared.   Therefore ever since then everything is already the history of the End time.

The present is:

i. *The "day of salvation"* (II Cor. 6: 2), the "day" in which grace is seeking (Heb. 4: 7), the "hour" of the full proclamation of salvation (John 16: 25; lit.), the "hour" of the worship of the Father in spirit and truth (John 4: 21-23).   The goal is

ii. *The "day of God"* (II Pet. 3: 2), the new creation of heaven and earth, the "day of eternity" (II Pet. 3: 18, lit., comp. R.V. note).   Between these two days lies

iii. The "last day." This also is a long period (II Pet. 3: 8). It begins with the resurrection of the righteous (John 6: 39, 40, 44, 54; 11: 24) and ends with the judgment of the lost (John 12: 48). Since the Messianic kingdom lies between those two events, it covers a stretch of time of more than one thousand years (Rev. 20: 5). It begins with the rapture, the "day of Jesus Christ" (Phil. 2: 16; 1: 6, 10; I Cor. 1: 8; II Cor. 1: 14),[1] and the "day of the Lord" (II Thess. 2: 2–4), the "day of Jehovah" of the Old Testament prophets (Joel 2: 1, 2; 3: 14). It continues through the glorious kingdom of Messiah, through "those days," the brilliant period of the old earth (Jer. 3: 16; Joel 3: 2; Zech. 8: 23), and it ends with the "day of judgment" (Matt. 10: 15; 11: 22, 24; 12: 36), the recompensing of men and angels (Jude 6), the final settlement before the great white throne (Rev. 20: 11–15; II Pet. 2: 9; 3: 7; Rom. 2: 5). Thus it can be compared to a day with the morning star at dawn (II Pet. 1: 19; Rev. 22: 16), with tempest before midday (Rev. 6–19), with sunshine at noon and in the afternoon (Mal. 4: 2, that is the Millennial kingdom), and with flaming lightning towards evening (Rev. 20: 9, Gog and Magog). But at last the new sun arises, "at evening it will be light," and out of world destruction comes forth world transfiguration.

3. The Completion of the Age, the coming and appearing of the Lord. The exact time of the rapture cannot be ascertained.[2] "It belongs not to you to know season or hour" (Acts. 1: 7; Matt. 24: 36; Mark 13: 32). The time of glory is near, for the Lord says, "Behold, I come soon" (Rev. 22: 20; II Pet. 3: 8, 9). The time of glory is distant, for He said that the bridegroom "tarried" (Matt. 25: 5). The nobleman who receives the kingdom went into a distant land (Luke 19: 11, 12), and only "after a long time" came back so as to reckon with his servants (Matt. 25: 19). Thus in the prophetic view long-sight combines with present near-sight. The lesson is that we should "watch" (Matt. 25: 13; Mark. 13: 32–37; Luke 12: 40). God desires in us instant expectancy and readiness for eternity. With us the last things should be always the first. "Let your loins be girded and your lights burning, and ye yourselves like unto men who wait for their lord" (Luke 12: 35, 36).

Upon the details of this subject much difference has always existed. Equally great saints and scholars support divergent

[1] Comp. Eph. 4: 30; II Tim. 1: 12; 4: 8; I Cor. 3: 13; II Pet. 1: 19; I John 4: 17; Heb. 10: 25.

[2] How fruitless is all computation here has been shown by the contradictions of tne greatest minds that have attempted it. Luther expected the end of the world in 1556, the writer of the hymn "Waken up, the voice is calling" in 1670, the celebrated expositor John Cocceius in 1667, Amos Comenius in 1672, the scientist Isaac Newton in 1715, J. A. Bengel in 1836, not to speak of the contradictions among the Seventh Day Adventists.

views. This should rebuke dogmatism, induce forbearance, and provoke inquiry.

In this spirit we look toward the last time.

In reference to the world reign of Christ it is
the "completion of the age;"[1]

in reference to the absence of Christ it is
His Kingly coming (*parousia,* advent);[2]

in reference to the concealment of Christ it is
His revelation and unveiling (*apocalypse*);[3]

in reference to the light of Christ's glory it is
His brilliant appearing (*epiphany*).[4]

II. THE NATURE OF THE RAPTURE

"Behold, I tell you a mystery; we shall indeed not all sleep, but we shall all be changed" (I Cor. 15: 51). "For the Lord himself will descend from heaven, with a war cry and the voice of the archangel and with the trump of God, and the dead in Christ will first arise. Thereafter we who live and remain over will at the same time as they be caught up in the clouds to meet the Lord in the air, and thus we will be at all times with the Lord" (I Thess. 4: 16, 17).

The rapture as to its nature is a fivefold event: catching away, catching up, transfiguration, triumph, blessedness.

1. *A Catching Away.* It is a catching "away," a taking out of all distress of soul and body (II Cor. 5: 2, 4; Phil. 3: 21), out of all persecution and oppression by the foe, out of the entire sphere of sin (comp. Rom. 6: 6) and of death (Rom. 7: 24). Thus it is rest with all saints (II Thess. 1: 7) in "the day of the (coming) redemption" (Eph. 4: 30: Rom. 8: 23).

As such it is:

an act of Divine *grace*, "the grace which will be brought to us by the revelation of Jesus Christ" (I Pet. 1: 13), and which will free us from all sin;

an act of Divine *mercy*, the mercy for which we wait unto eternal life (Jude 21) and which will free us from all misery.

---

[1] Five times in the New Testament: Matt. 13: 39, 40, 49; 24: 3; 28: 20, lit.

[2] Seventeen times in the New Testament of the advent of Christ: e.g. Matt. 24: 3, 27, 37; I Cor. 15: 23; I Thess. 2: 19; 3: 13; etc. The term does not signify "future" or "return" but "presence," or more strictly the entrance of the one present (I Cor. 16: 17; II Cor. 7: 6). In the whole eastern world of Paul's time *parousia* and *epiphany* were the technical terms for the visit of a king or emperor (e.g. the *parousia* of Nero, the *epiphany* of Hadrian). Thus the element of the kingly rule of Jesus is contained in the conception of the early Christian hope of the *parousia* and *epiphany*. It is the arrival of Jesus as the "King of glory." "Behold, thy King comes to thee" (Zech. 9: 9).

[3] Five times in the New Testament of the return of Christ: I Cor. 1: 7; II Thess. 1: 7; I Pet. 1: 7–13; 4: 13.

[4] The Greek word is connected with "shine" (*epi—phan—eia*: comp. *phaino,* I shine; e.g. John 1: 5).

"Grace takes away the sin, mercy the misery" (Bengel);

an act of Divine *omnipotence,* the omnipotence which transfigures us into conformity with the Redeemer and elevates us to the most glorious spiritual body.   At that time the same power which moves the whole universe will act upon our body!   "He will change our body of humiliation that it may be fashioned like unto his body of glory, according to the power by which he is able to subdue the whole world" (Phil. 3: 21).

Therefore Paul uses for "rapture" a particularly strong word (*harpazo,* I Thess. 4: 17), which really means, to seize hastily, to rob with violence, to draw to oneself by swift, sudden movement, which word Luke uses in the Acts to describe how Paul was torn away by the Roman soldiers from the mob of his oppressors (Acts 23: 10).   And in I Thess. 1: 10, where Paul calls the rapture a "salvation from the coming wrath" he uses a word (Gk. *rhuo*) which means strictly a "rescue with power," the same word by which in II Tim. 4: 17 he describes his preservation in Nero's judgment court, his "rescue out of the jaws of the lion."   Therefore he describes the taking home of the church by an accumulation of powerful military figures.   The Lord Himself will descend from heaven with an "alarm signal," with a "word of command," a "battle cry," with a "trumpet clang" of the "trump of God."   And then will He, the royal Conqueror, accompanied by the armies of heaven, unite with Himself for ever His earthly warriors.

And this is of all the most important, for the rapture is

2. *A Catching Up,* and as such it is

A uniting of the members to the *Head;* for the Lord Himself will descend and we shall be *with Him* for ever (I Thess. 4: 16, 17).   He will present the church to "Himself" glorified (Eph. 5: 27) for the purpose of perfecting His glory as the Redeemer (Eph. 1: 23).   "I come again and will receive you to *myself,* that where I am ye also may be" (John 14: 2, 3).   And the rapture is

A uniting of the members to *one another*; for the living will be caught up at the same time with the dead (I Thess. 4: 17), and for the first time the church of all times and all lands will be with one another.   Thus the completed church will exist for the first time, but not on the earth but in the air (I Thess. 4: 17).   Till then there exist only churches (in the plural, Rev. 22: 16), and the church of a *generation* living at any one time on earth.   "But then there will be an ascent, not of a solitary Elijah with fiery chariots and horses, but millions of saints will rise, drawn upwards by the holy power of God, and all together will fill the heavenly regions with their Hallelujah."   But yet more.   Those thus lifted above will receive their transfiguration.

3. *Transfiguration.* "In a moment, in the twinkling of an eye, at the sound of the last trump"—then will they be changed from the body of humiliation into the body of glory (Phil. 3: 21), and this corruptible will put on incorruption and this mortal immortality (I Cor. 15: 51, 53).

And this all in the air! (I Thess. 4: 17). What a triumph!

4. *Triumph!* For the air is the very base of operations of the Enemy. It is from the air that the world is at present ruled by demon powers. Therefore Satan is called "the prince of the power of the air" (Eph. 2: 2 comp. 6: 12). But now exactly in the region of his power, at the very headquarters of the conquered foe, there takes place the meeting of the Conqueror, and His victorious hosts. The triumph cannot be greater; a more glorious festival of victory cannot be. Christ has conquered completely. His church has overcome absolutely. Therefore the crowning of the persecuted takes place at the headquarters of their defeated Persecutor.

5. *Blessedness.* This is the "blessed hope" of the redeemed (Titus 2: 13). "Awake and rejoice, ye who lie in the dust; for thy dew is as the dew of the heavenly lights, and the earth will again bring forth the shades [Heb. *Rephaim*] to the light of day" (Isa. 26: 19; comp. 35: 10; 51: 11).

III. THE COMING SPIRITUAL BODY

1. *Its necessity.* But why exactly *bodily* resurrection? Why not simply pure spirit? Because the body is not a prison of the soul, but belongs to the *essence* of man, for without a body the man is "naked" (II Cor. 5: 3). Because even here below the earthly body was ennobled by being the temple of the Spirit and therefore cannot be left deserted (Rom. 8: 11; I Cor. 6: 19). Because through sin there has come the separating of the spirit and soul from the body, and in consequence without bodily resurrection something of the effects of sin would remain in the redeemed. But God created man as a whole, and therefore as a whole He will redeem him. Mere permanence of the spirit as immortal were only a partial continuance of life and so a partial redemption. God does not abandon the works of His hands: matter also is a thought and a work of His power as creator. Therefore no part of His own redeemed ones can be allowed to remain in death. Only so will "death be swallowed up in victory" (I Cor. 15: 55–57; II Cor. 5: 4; Isa. 25: 8; Hos. 13: 14). There cannot be permitted a redemption *from* the body, but there must be a redemption *of* the body (Rom. 8: 23). Therefore Christ looks on the raising of the dead as His special work as Saviour, indeed, He Himself is the living resurrection (John 11: 25). "No one can come to Me except the Father draw him; and I will raise him up at the last day" (John 6: 44). "He who

eats my flesh and drinks my blood, he has eternal life, and I will raise him up at the last day" (John 6: 54, comp. 39; 5: 28, 29).

2. *Its actuality.* "Embodiment is the end of the ways of God." This is proved most distinctly by the resurrection body of Jesus. It could be seen with the eyes (Luke 24: 40) and touched with the hands (Luke 24: 39; John 20: 27). It could eat honey and fish (Luke 24: 41–43; comp. Acts 10: 41); indeed, according to the Lord's own testimony, it even had flesh and bone: "See my hands and my feet, that it is I myself: handle me and see, for a spirit has not flesh and bone, as ye see that I have" (Luke 24: 39). The Greek has *ostea,* bone, the same word as in John 19: 36 and Heb. 11: 22. The teaching therefore is false that the Risen One had no actual body but only a power of embodying Himself; that as to His nature He had become pure "spirit" and had taken a resurrection body solely for the purpose of making Himself visible to men, but always to lay it aside after His appearances. This at once contradicts the above passage, Luke 24: 39, where the Lord says expressly that He was no "spirit." According to that erroneous opinion He would have been usually a spirit without flesh and bone, in which case He must have completely misled His disciples by what He said; for instead of saying, "a spirit has not flesh and bone, as ye see that I *have*," He must have said, "a spirit cannot *take* flesh and bone."

But the Risen One is the standard and prototype of all the perfected ones at the heavenly throne (I John 3: 2; Rom. 8: 29). To His body of glory ours will presently be conformed (Phil. 3: 21: I Cor. 15: 49). Therefore in *His* body we can perceive certain basic features of our own future body; and if *His* body has glorified matter as its outward foundation, so also ours.

I Cor. 15: 50 says nothing against this; for, as the context shows, Paul speaks there only of the unglorified flesh and blood that it cannot inherit the kingdom of God. Nor will appeal to I Cor. 15: 54 hold. The new body is indeed called there a "spiritual" body, but this does not signify that it is wholly immaterial and consists purely of spirit. This is as little the case as that the "soulish" (psychical) body we at present have consists only of "soul." Much rather by "soulish" and "spiritual" the *basic nature* of both kinds of body is indicated. In the earthly body the soul dominates, in the heavenly body the spirit. The change of the one into the other does not consist in a putting *off* of the material, but, exactly the reverse, in a putting *on* (I Cor. 15: 53, 54), not in an "unclothing," but in a "clothing upon" of this corruptible matter with immortality and incorruption (II Cor. 5: 2–4). But the nature of this change is wholly inexplicable; it is a marvel which, as also that of the heavenly material, will be perceived only in eternity.

Because, therefore, of the reality of the heavenly body the

Scripture speaks of the resurrection of *bodies* out of the *graves*. "The hour comes in which all that are in the graves shall hear the voice of the Son of man" (John 5: 28, 29). *This* body of humiliation will be glorified (Phil. 3: 21); *this* mortal body will be made alive (Rom. 8: 11); *this* body sown in corruption will be raised incorruptible and immortal (I Cor. 15: 42, 43, 53, 54; comp. Job 19: 25, 26).

But if there were no spiritual body and no direct relation between the present body and the future, why the opening of the graves? Why then a resurrection at all? In that case the new body would be quite another, not the same, not "this" body which had been sown in the grave. No, there must be a connexion between the old and the new body, a connexion not only of soul and personality, but also of the body.

In the earthly body the atoms are continually in flux. The change of matter completes every seven years a full transformation of the whole material constitution of the body, so that with the passing of this period not a single atom of the former material is any longer present; and yet it is "the same" body. By means of the power given by the Creator the soul continually builds of the material which surrounds it a "new" body. The body itself is composed of the material taken from Nature which the soul quickens and governs and, corresponding to its own character, moulds into a higher unity of nature.

Thus in even the earthly body it is not the material that is the deciding element, but the body-building power of the soul; nevertheless there must be already present in the old, corruptible body an indestructible element which at the resurrection and transfiguration will be "clothed upon with the house which is from heaven" (II Cor. 5: 2). Only so it is conceivable that the old body must "rise" and that it can be described as the "seed" of the future body. The process in view is at one and the same time both breaking down and building up, dissolution and connexion, new creation and preservation.

"Even as in the dying plant only an element survives, which then, drawing to itself new material, under the influence of the light and the earth, forms to itself a new plant body, which because of that element is the same with the dead plant and nevertheless another," so also after the dissolution of the human body there survives an element with the possibility of new formation. The soul is, as it were, the magnet of the body which effects the conjunction of the millions of its atoms. In death it loses its magnetic power and the atoms fall apart; but in resurrection it receives it again, and indeed in far higher and more perfect degree. Therefore now the soul puts on the powers of heavenly light and clothes itself (II Cor. 5: 2-4) with a new, perfect body of glory.

We can form no conception of the heavenly material. Only figurative language is possible. It is related to earthly material as the flashing diamond to the dark carbon out of which it is formed,[1] as the luminous body of the gas flame to the black coal out of which it is made; as the radiant jewel to the dull soil out of which it is taken. Thus do the graveyards of man become the seed-plots of resurrection and the cemeteries of the people of God become through the heavenly dew the resurrection fields of the [promised] perfecting (Isa. 26: 19).

NOTE on the Intermediate State.

Concerning the circumstances of the soul between death and resurrection Scripture says but little. It is certain that the perfecting of the individual is attached to his resurrection, and so does not take place at death. Holy Scripture mostly looks on to the goal, passing over the interval with only a few hints and laying upon it no special stress. We should wait for the return of Christ, not for death. For the believing dead it is first of all a blessed waiting time in Paradise (Luke 23: 43), with Christ (Phil. 1: 23; Acts 7: 59), in "Abraham's bosom" (Luke 16: 22), where it is "far better" than here (Phil. 1: 23). For the unsaved dead there begins at once the "fire" (Luke 16: 22–24). Therefore for the believer the first "gain" is not at the rapture but at death (Phil. 1: 21); for the unbeliever there is a fearful expectation of the righteous judgment of God. But in both cases the completion is the resurrection either of life or of judgment (John 5: 29).

IV. THE SEVENFOLD GLORY OF THE RESURRECTION BODY

The nature of the new body is indescribable. The Scripture gives only figurative intimations.

1. *Spirituality.* The body of humiliation is a "soulish" body, the body of glory will be "spiritual" (I Cor. 15: 44–46), which means that in the former the soul predominates, in the latter the spirit.

2. *Subjection.* The body of humiliation is often a limit and restraint: the body of glory will be entirely serviceable. The body of humiliation, as a "soulish" body, has a certain independence of the spirit, an independence which quite often amounts to conflict between body and spirit (Rom. 7: 5, 23; I Cor. 9: 27; Rom. 6: 6). But the body of glory will be completely ruled by the spirit. In unrestricted dependence it will be at the disposal of the spirit, a perfect instrument of the perfected life.

But in the natural world the reverse condition rules.

---

[1] Through heat (comp. II Pet. 3: 12) the coal, volatilized to gas, crystalizes becomes as it were "glorified") into diamond.

3. *Superiority.* The body of humiliation, which is in measure independent as regards the spirit, as regards natural conditions is dependent and bound; the body of glory, which is dependent upon the spirit, is independent and free as regards these natural conditions. Therefore with the former there is the necessity of nourishment and the danger of sickness and misfortune; with the latter, however, is royal freedom and it is superior to the restrictions of matter, space, and time.

So it *can* eat, but without its being *necessary* (Luke 24: 41–43)—
superiority over the material;

so it can appear in a room with closed doors (John 20: 19; comp. Luke 24: 31, 36)—
freedom from the restrictions through space;

so it is immortal in eternity (I Cor. 15: 54, 42)—
freedom from all limitation through time.

4. *Exaltation.* The body of humiliation, because it is such (Phil. 3: 21), is a body of "dishonour" (I Cor. 15: 43). But the body of glory will be a body of exaltation. The lowliness of the present body is shown by sickness and death, as also by conception, birth, and the manner of its being nourished (I Cor. 6: 13); it therefore belongs to the dignity of the future body that these conditions shall cease: "in the resurrection they will neither marry nor be given in marriage; but are as the angels of God in heaven" (Matt. 22: 30).

But this does not mean "they will be themselves angels," but only in this point "as angels." No man becomes an angel when he dies. We shall indeed be in fellowship with the angels (Heb. 12. 22; Luke 16: 22); but we shall be more than angels (I Cor. 6: 2, 3). We are "firstfruits of his creatures" (Jas. 1: 18), and "sons of God" (Rom. 8: 14).

5. *Happiness.* The body of humiliation goes through sorrow and pain (II Cor. 5: 2, 4); the body of glory will be full of bliss. "They shall neither hunger nor thirst" (Isa. 49: 10; Rev. 7: 16, 17). "Neither mourning nor crying nor pain shall be any more: the first things are passed away" (Rev. 21: 4). "It is sown corruptible, it is raised incorruptible. It is sown in dishonour, it is raised in glory. It is sown in weakness and is raised in strength" (I Cor. 15: 42, 43).

6. *Splendour.* The body of humiliation is a poor tent, the body of glory is a transparent, radiant palace. "The righteous ... shall shine forth in their Father's kingdom" (Matt. 13: 43):

as dazzling white snow (Mark 9: 3; Phil. 3: 21);
as transparent dew (Isa. 26: 19);
as the moon and the stars (Dan. 12: 3);
as the brightness of the firmament (Dan. 12: 3);
as the sun in its might (Matt. 13: 43; 17: 2; Rev. 1: 16);
as the Lord Jesus Himself in the light of His glory (Phil. 3: 21;

I John 3: 2; II Cor. 3: 18).   "The teachers will radiate brightness as the heaven, and those who turn many to righteousness as the stars for ever and ever" (Dan. 12: 3).

This is the grandeur for which we wait.   Compared with this the earthly body is as a seed to the fully unfolded flower (I Cor. 15: 35–39, 42–44).   As little as one can see that a brilliant plant is contained in a tiny poppy seed, or the mighty oak in the acorn, or the apple tree in the apple pip, so little can one discern in the present body the glory of the future body.

7. *Conformity to Christ.*   But the most glorious feature is that the redeemed will be conformed to *HIM.*   "We shall be like him, for we shall see him even as he is" (I John 3: 2).   We shall be "conformed to the body of his glory" (Phil. 3: 21).   We shall bear on us His "image" that "He may be the firstborn among many brethren" (Rom. 8: 29; Col. 1: 18; comp. II Cor. 3: 18). "For the first man is of earth, of dust; the second man is of heaven. But as he who is of dust, so are they who are of dust; and as the heavenly One so are also the heavenly ones.   And as we have borne the image of the one from dust, so shall we bear also the image of the One from heaven" (I Cor. 15: 47–49; Darby).

THE JUDGMENT SEAT OF CHRIST

THE return of Christ is the "blessed hope" of the church (Titus 2: 13). Nevertheless it is connected not only with heavenly privileges but also with holy responsibility. Even as the rapture is a refreshment for the heart, so is the judgment seat of Christ a spur to the conscience.

There are seven facts as to this which especially the Holy Scripture permits us to know:

1. The time — the "day of Christ" (I Cor. 1: 8).
2. The judge — Christ Himself (II Tim. 4: 8).
3. The persons — "We all" (II Cor. 5: 10).
4. The severity — its fire (I Cor. 3: 13).
5. The standard — our faithfulness (I Cor. 4: 1–5).
6. The result — reward or loss (I Cor. 3: 14, 15).
7. The goal — glory (I Pet. 5: 4).

1. *The time* is the "day of Christ, or of the Lord" (six times in the New Testament, I Cor. 1: 8; 5: 5; II Cor. 1: 14; Phil. 1: 6, 10; 2: 16), "that day" (II Tim. 4: 8; 1: 12), "at His coming" (*parousia* II Tim. 4: 8), which means, according to the testimony of the whole New Testament, the time *before* the setting up of the visible kingdom of glory, and therefore *before* the Millennial kingdom. In consequence the "judgment seat of Christ" (Gk. *bema*) is to be distinguished from the "great white throne" (Gk. *thronos*). This latter will be set up only *after* the visible kingdom of glory, indeed, *after* the destruction of the whole of the old universe (Rev. 20: 11).

But it is also to be distinguished from the judgment at the *beginning* of the Millennial kingdom (Matt. 25: 31–46; Rev. 20: 4). For after the return of Christ the then living nations will there be judged. The "last day" will thus include three judgments to be distinguished as to time:

(*a*) The judgment upon the church, i.e. the raptured; at the "judgment seat of Christ" *before* the Millennial kingdom.

(*b*) The judgment upon the nations, i.e. upon the then living: at the "throne of His glory," at the *beginning* of the Millennial kingdom.

(*c*) The general judgment, i.e. of the dead (Rev. 20: 12); at the "great white throne," *after* the Millennial kingdom.

2. *The judge* is Christ, "the Lord, the righteous Judge" (II Tim. 4: 8). For the Father has committed all judgment unto the Son (John 5: 22). Therefore also before the Millennial

kingdom it is both the judgment seat of *Christ* (II Cor. 5: 10) and also the judgment seat of *God* (Rom. 14: 10).

3. *The persons* are "we all" (II Cor. 5: 10; Rom. 14: 10), the "at home," and the "away from home," all redeemed, the then living and the already asleep when the Lord comes (II Cor. 5: 6–10 and context). True it is that he who believes on the Son is free from the final judgment of condemnation (John 5: 24; Heb. 10: 14, 17), for "there is no condemnation for those who are in Christ Jesus" (Rom. 8: 1): but the question of faithfulness (I Cor. 4: 2–5) and the determining of the reward (I Cor. 3: 14; Col. 3: 24), or of the loss (I Cor. 3: 15; II John 8), demand a special day of judgment (I John 4: 17) even for believers. Here it is not a question of salvation but definitely as to the measure of the reward of grace.

4. *The severity.* "The Lord will judge his people" (Heb. 10: 30). Even for His own the day will be "revealed in fire" (I Cor. 3: 13). Therefore, in strict connexion with the judgment seat of Christ, Paul speaks of a "terror of the Lord" (II Cor. 5: 10, 11). "Damage" and "loss" (I Cor. 3: 15; II John 8), a shrinking with shame from Him at His presence[1] (I John 2: 28), "burning up" of one's whole life work (I Cor. 3: 13–15), oneself saved, but only as a brand out of the fire, as one who escapes from a burning building with his bare life (I Cor. 3: 15; comp. Amos 4: 11 and Gen. 19: 16, 29, Lot)—these are possibilities which *we* must look in the face.

Indeed, in II Cor. 5: 10, the Scripture says that we shall receive not only according to our good works, but also according to our bad works. "We" (that is, all members of the church, whether "at home" or "away from home" when the Lord comes, vv. 6–9) "must all be made manifest before the judgment

---

[1] The exact translation is not as A.V. "ashamed before Him at His coming" but as the R.V. margin "ashamed *from* Him." The Greek *apo* in *ap' autou* is not equivalent to "before." This "from" does not speak of an unfaithful Christian being driven away by the Lord into the shame of eternal condemnation and destruction as being eternally lost; but it stands in contrast to the boldness and confidence which the Christian ought to have at the coming of Christ, which is mentioned in the immediately preceding words in the same verse: so that this "being ashamed from Him" shows that for an unfaithful Christian there will be at the coming of the Lord a "shrinking with shame from Him at His presence." So Alford rightly translates, and Westcott adds the telling explanatory words "as a guilty thing surprised." Darby renders "and not be put to shame from before Him at His coming."

Foremost German translators give the same sense, as
    Professor Menge:
"So that we are not obliged to turn aside with shame from Him."
    Dächsel's Bible Work:
"So that we are not obliged to step back with shame from Him."
    Elberfeld Bible:
"So that we may not be put away with shame from Him."
    Professor Lange:
"So that we may not be put away with shame from Him in His coming" (Day).

H

seat of Christ, that each one may receive the things done by means of (*dia*) the body, according to what he hath done, whether good or bad"; and in the Colossian epistle (Col. 3: 24, 25), in connexion with the receiving of the coming recompense, and in reference to the everyday life of the members of the church, it is declared that "he that doeth wrong shall receive again the wrong that he hath done; and there is no respect of persons." With this compare I Cor. 3: 15; Luke 19: 24; 12: 45–48. Let us, therefore, not blunt the point of the sword of the Spirit (Heb. 4: 12). To be made manifest before the judgment seat of Christ is a more serious matter than perhaps we often think. Mere reference to "gain" or "loss" seems scarcely to do full justice to such extremely serious statements of the New Testament.

With our present powers of understanding it does not seem possible to comprehend the matter more in detail, and, above all, to see how glory and solemnity can here combine, because it belongs to the eternal realm. In many respects our perceptions and sentiments there will be quite other than those here, which suit the present conditions of life.

But the Scripture gives us these so very serious words to impress upon us the necessity of practical holiness and faithful, self-sacrificing service. With all the certainty of salvation and all the efficiency of the Divine work in us, this word still applies: "Work out your own salvation with fear and trembling" (Phil. 2: 12).

5. *The standard* is our faithfulness (I Cor. 4: 1–5; Matt. 25: 21, 23), the sum total of our life, the product of our development: not only our deeds but also our possibilities, not only what we were but what we might have become, not only our actions but also our omissions (Jas. 4: 17); not the work but the worker, not the number but the weight of our deeds (I Sam. 2: 3); not only what we attained but also what we strove after. Of our works, sacrifice counts for most; of our disposition, only selfless love; of our possessions, only what we employed in service. As to our sins that word applies: what we have judged He will not judge again (I Cor. 11: 31); what we have uncovered He will cover (I John 1: 9; Heb. 8: 12); what we have covered He will uncover (Luke 12: 2). And in everything He will take note of the most inward elements, of the impulses and motives, of the counsels of the heart, of the secrets of the soul hidden in darkness (I Cor. 4: 5; I Sam. 16: 7; Heb. 4: 13; Psa. 139).

6. *The result* will be very varied. Even with His own people the Lord is "the righteous Judge" (II Tim. 4: 8). One has built of wood, hay, and stubble—his work will be burned up; the other has built of gold, silver, and costly stones—his work will stand the fire (I Cor. 3: 12–15).

These have served faithfully—they will be great in the

kingdom of heaven (Mat. 5: 19; 25: 21; Luke 19: 17); others have sown to the flesh—they will reap the corruption of their life-work (Gal. 6: 6–8).

These are pure, faultless, and irreproachable (Phil. 1: 10; I Cor. 1: 8)—they will win the prize (Phil. 3: 14); others are [spiritually] poor (Rev. 3: 17) and disapproved (I Cor. 9: 27)—they will suffer loss (I Cor. 3: 15; II Tim. 2: 5).

These have boldness in the day of judgment (I John 4: 17); shame will be the portion of others (I John 2: 28).

Thus each receives his due (Heb. 6: 10; I Cor. 4: 5; II Tim. 4: 8), without respect of persons (I Pet. 1: 17; II Cor. 5: 10; Col. 3: 24, 25). Salvation depends upon faith, reward upon faithfulness. As sons we receive His life, as servants His recompense. "Behold, I come quickly, and my wages with me" (Rev. 22: 12).

But finally all will be saved and all will shine, if in different degrees of glory and splendour (I Cor. 15: 40–42). There will be great and small vessels in the future, but all will be filled. There will be degrees and stages of glory (Matt. 25: 14–30), but no difference in happiness (Matt. 20: 1–16). For the servants and the service are many, but there is only one Lord.

But the faithful will be specially crowned:
> the victorious warrior—
>> with the crown of righteousness (II Tim. 4: 8);
> the steadfast racer—
>> with the unfading crown (I Cor. 9: 25–27);
> the one faithful unto death—
>> with the crown of life (Rev. 2: 10; Jas. 1: 12);
> the unselfish worker—
>> with the crown of honour (I Thess. 2: 19, comp. 3–6;
>> Phil. 4: 1);
> the example to the flock—
>> with the crown of glory (I Pet. 5: 3, 4).

7. *The glory.* Through all this will come the consummation for the church. "And I heard as it were the voice of a great multitude, and as the voice of many waters, and as the voice of mighty thunders, saying, Hallelujah: for the Lord our God, the Almighty, reigneth. Let us rejoice and be exceeding glad, and let us give the glory unto Him: for the marriage of the Lamb is come, and his wife hath made herself ready. . . . Blessed are they who are bidden to the marriage supper of the Lamb" (Rev. 19: 6–9).

But simultaneously has broken the great day on which the Lord will punish the host of the high ones that is in the height and the kings of the earth upon the earth (Isa. 24: 21), and on which it will seem good to Him to give the great kingdom of power and glory to His "little flock" (Luk. 12: 32). "I saw thrones and they sat thereon, and it was granted to them to exercise judgment" (Rev. 20: 4). "The saints of the Most High will receive the kingdom" (Dan. 7: 18, 22). Those who at the judgment seat of Christ had been adjudged worthy of the prize will be made judges of the world. They will be the ruling aristocracy in the eternal kingdom of heaven.

And because they are "one body" the individual will not be glorified before the community. It is all *one* "inheritance of the saints in the light" and the individual has only a portion therein (Col. 1: 12). It is together that they are a royal realm, a kingdom (Rev. 1: 6; 5: 10), and the individuals are priests and kings therein. The whole is superior to the individual. The individual is set in his place in the entire course of the whole. Therefore the individual cannot be perfected as an individual but only in personal living connexion with the perfected community.

Therefore the waiting of those who sleep for the perfecting of the future generations (Heb. 11: 40; Rev. 6: 10, 11).

Therefore the clothing of the "soul" with the coming body of glory (I Cor. 15: 23)[1] does *not* take place directly at death (Rev. 6: 9; Heb. 12: 23).

Therefore there takes place at the same time the resurrection of the dead in Christ and the "clothing upon" (II Cor. 5: 2–4) of the then living by the rapture (I Thess. 4: 15). For the goal of the whole is an *organism*; not only the salvation of the individual, but the gloryfying of the community; not only individual blessedness, but the "kingdom of God" (Matt. 6: 10).

And even as now God's cosmic universal State is under the government of regional angel princes (comp. Dan. 10: 13, 20), so then will the company of the glorified saints reign as kings, with Christ their Head, over suns and worlds (Rev. 22: 5; comp; Heb. 2: 5). "Know ye not that the saints shall judge the world? know ye not that we shall judge angels?" (I Cor. 6: 2, 3). Therefore "he that overcometh to him will I give to sit down with me in my throne, as I also overcame, and sat down with my Father in his throne" (Rev. 3: 21). "Blessed are those servants whom the Lord when he comes shall find watching: verily I say unto you, that he shall gird himself, and make them sit down to meat, and shall come and serve them" (Luke 12: 37). This is the greatest promise of the Bible (J. A. Bengel).

---

[1] This takes place only "at His coming." The appearing of Moses and Elijah at the transfiguration (Matt. 17: 3), and the resurrection of many Old Testament saints at the resurrection of Jesus (Matt. 27: 52, 53), are exceptions for the sake of the personal glory of Jesus, in the one case, and because of the triumph of His work on Golgotha, in the other case.

PART III

THE COMING KINGDOM OF GOD

Section I—The Antichristian World System

CHAPTER I

THE PERSON OF THE ANTICHRIST

I. THE COMING OF THE ANTICHRIST

THE final goal of Christianity is Jesus Christ; the end of nominal Christendom is the Antichrist. It is the unmistakable teaching of the Bible that the goal of history is not the product of history, that the kingdom of God does not reach sovereignty through growth and ascent but only after worldwide collapse and catastrophe. Lawlessness will take the upper hand, the love of many will grow cold (Matt. 24: 12), and when the Son of man comes He will find but *little* faith on earth (Luke 18: 8). Not Christianizing of the world with consequent Christianizing of civilization, but increasing enmity of the world unto the expulsion of Christianity by civilization—this is the path foretold by Biblical prophecy.

Therefore it is not because the world is not Christian enough that Christ has not yet come but He has not yet come because the world is not unbelieving enough (II Tim. 3: 1–4; 4: 3, 4; II Pet. 3: 3; I Tim. 4: 1–3). It is a basic principle of the Divine government of the world that all things, the good as the evil (Matt. 13: 29, 30; Rev. 14: 15, 18), must reach ripeness; only for the evil the patience of God leads to the severer judgment. "Let no one mislead you, for the day of the Lord will not come except the apostasy comes in advance, and the Man of Sin be manifested, the Son of perdition, the opposer, the Wicked One, whom the Lord Jesus, when he comes, will destroy by the breath of his mouth" (II Thess. 2: 3, 4, 8).

Thus not by reconciliation but by intensifying of the conflict to the end, not by the glorifying of human development but by its collapse, not by a compact between God and civilization, but by the shattering of the kingdom of the world by the kingdom of God (Dan. 2: 34, 35; Rev. 19: 11–21)—this is the manner by which the affairs of the Lord will triumph. The end of history is not its natural perfecting. The "ascending" line will be suddenly torn to pieces; the stormers of heaven will be thrust down by heaven (Gen. 11: 4, 6; Rev. 18).

At first, indeed, all things appear the reverse of this. For according to the testimony of Scripture a system of civilization will arise which appears to fulfil all the longing of mankind through thousands of years. At its head stands a mighty ruler who, by a genius for organization, is at once a world ruler and benefactor (Rev. 13: 7, 4; 11: 10), a counsellor of the nations who secures them against all danger of war (I Thess, 5: 3), an organizer of mankind who brings order into the hopeless chaos of the masses. As the acme of human greatness, he will inflame men with the utmost enthusiasm, as the supreme leader in all undertakings he will call forth a consciousness of rest and security, and as the ruling head he will receive divine honour (Rev. 13: 3, 4, 12). Thus will he exalt the world spirit to the highest height, and for world culture it will be a time of greatest upward progress and brilliance.

But all this will be *without God*, with the exclusion of grace, solely in self-confidence, to the glory of one's own strength, and with the deifying of the spirit of man (II Thess. 2: 4).

Therefore the Most High will not withhold His answer (Jer. 17: 5), He will not give His honour to another, nor His praise to dust-begotten rebels (Isa. 42: 8). His answer to the challenge of the Antichrist will be to send His Christ (Acts 3: 20); and him whose "arrival (*parousia*) was according to the energy of Satan" will He destroy "through the outshining of *His* arrival" (the epiphany of *His parousia*) "in flaming fire, when He shall requite them who know not God, and those who obey not the gospel of our Lord Jesus Christ" (II Thess. 1: 8). Thus the summit of civilization will become the closing drama of its history, and through the red sunset of the world there will, as it were, flame as a sign of the judgment:

"*Mene, mene, tekel, upharsin,*"
"Numbered, numbered, weighed, and found too light"
(Dan. 5: 25–27).

II. THE NAMES OF THE ANTICHRIST

The title "Antichrist" is found only in the writings of *John,* but there five times, with a threefold sense: of the personal Antichrist (I John 2: 18), of the spirit of the Antichrist (I John 4: 3), and of *the* antichrists (in the plural, I John 2: 18, 22; II John 7). It had been remarked of old (as *e.g.* by Augustine) that by this "Antichrist" John doubtless means the same person whom *Paul* calls the "man of sin," the "son of perdition," the "lawless one," the "opposer" (II Thess. 2: 3, 8); and who, according to the *Revelation,* is the Beast that comes out of the sea of the peoples (Rev. 13: 1–10), and, according to the prophecies of *Daniel,* is the "little horn" that rises out of the fourth world-empire (Dan.

7: 8, 23–25). Thus the Scripture gives in all seven chief designations of this same baneful figure, amounting to a sevenfold description of the opposition to God of this demonic rebel.

III. THE PERSONALITY OF THE ANTICHRIST

The Antichrist is at once a person and a system. As an individual he is the personal head of a system, the leader and embodiment of a general human revolt. As an inspiration and tendency he is indeed always present (I John 2: 22; II John 7), even as the "mystery of lawlessness" (II Thess. 2: 7) and "the spirit of the antichrist" (I John 4: 3)—hence through millenniums runs the line of his harbingers and forerunners, the antichrists (in the plural, I John 2: 18); but as the complete exhibition of the closing history he is an individual, a demonic genius, a *super*human figure, a Devil's Messiah. The universality of a movement does not exclude individual personal figures; on the contrary, all marked progress in the world has been brought about by individual men. "The history of a people is the biography of its great men" (Carlyle). Therefore it was a thoroughly historical and true conviction when the early Christians expected the perfecting of antichristianism through an individual man. "I am come in my Father's name, and ye receive me not; if *another* comes in his own name, him ye will receive" (John 5: 43). The opposed "I—another" place beyond doubt that this "another" (the Antichrist) must be an individual as certainly as Christ is such, who here speaks of Himself by this "I."[1]

This further arises from the teaching of Christ as to the future found in Mark 13: 14, when read strictly: "When ye see the abomination of desolation standing where he ought not (let him that readeth take notice of it), then let them that are in Judæa flee unto the mountains." The "abomination of desolation" is very plainly connected with the antichristian period. But the striking fact is that, although in the original text the noun "abomination" is of the neuter gender, its dependent participle "standing" is not neuter but masculine in form.[2]

---

[1] There are different answers to the question whether Antichrist will be a Jew or a heathen. That he will be a Jew, and apparently of the tribe of Dan, Irenæus based upon Jer. 8: 16 and the absence of that tribe in Rev. 7: 5–8. Hippolytus grounded it upon Deut. 33: 22; Gen. 49: 16, 17, and the consideration that as the opposite to Christ he must descend from Israel. Ambrose refers to John 5: 43; Prof. Schlatter to II Thess. 2: 4; that he sets himself in the temple of God, not of idols. According to others he comes from heathendom, for his chief prototype, Antiochus Epiphanes, a Greco-Syrian, was a heathen king (Dan. 8: 8–12; 11: 21 ff.), and that he himself, as the first beast of Rev. 13, arises out of the "sea," that is, the nations (Rev. 13: 1, comp. 17: 15; Isa. 17: 12, 13).

[2] Gk. *to* bdelygma (neuter) . . . heste*kota*, accusative masculine, not heste*kos*, accusative neuter. (The R.V. marks this by the above rendering "standing where *he* ought not.")

This unmistakably signifies that the "abomination of desolation" is not to be merely an image or some other such object or action, but that a *person*, a *man*, is to stand in the holy place. Thus the profaning of the sanctuary will proceed from an individual man who, as an idolatrous human abomination, as a false god will stand forth as the enemy of the true God, and will demand for himself divine worship (II Thess. 2: 3, 4).

Finally, that the Antichrist is an individual person is shown by this further fact, that he, as well as Christ, will have his *parousia* (coming). It is he "whose coming (*parousia*) is according to the working of Satan with all power and signs and lying wonders" (II Thess. 2: 9). And just as Christ, as an individual person, after this period of His being hidden, will in God's hour come forth at His revelation (*apocalypse*, II Thess. 1–7), so also will His counterfeit, the Antichrist, as an individual person, in his season (which will be at once Satan's hour and God's hour), receive his revelation (*apocalypse*)! "The Lawless One will be revealed" (II Thess. 2: 8).

IV. THE FORERUNNERS OF THE ANTICHRIST

1. In Bible history these, among others, were:

Cain—the originator of religious war—the anti-Abel. As the first "war" was, as it were, a religious war (Gen. 4: 4–8), so will be the last of this age, the Anti-christian (Rev. 19: 19).

Lamech—the boaster who deified "I"—the anti-Enoch. Deifying self is the Lamech character of Antichristendom (Gen. 4: 23, 24; Rev. 13: 1; II Thess. 2: 4).

Nimrod—the founder of world power. With Nimrod began, with the Antichrist will end, the history of Babylonian world power. Babel on the Euphrates is the forerunner of Imperial Rome, and Imperial Rome of the antichristian End-time (Gen. 10: 8–12; Rev. 17: 1–14).

Balaam—the seducer into fornication—the Anti-Moses, as the Rabbis have said (Num. 31: 16; II Pet. 2: 15; Rev. 17: 4, 15; 18: 3, 4; 19: 2).

Goliath—the blaspheming popular orator—the anti-David, the representative terrorist. So the Rabbis (I Sam. 17: 8, 10, 25; Dan. 7: 25; Rev. 13: 6).

Antiochus Epiphanes—the devastator of the sanctuary. He is the chief type of the Antichrist (Dan. 8: 11; 9: 27; Rev. 11: 7; 13: 7). As such he is the "little horn" of the third world empire (Dan. 8: 9–14), even as the Antichrist himself is the "little horn" of the fourth world empire (Dan. 7. 23–25). In Dan. 11: 21–45 the two merge into one.

2. In church history and world history the following are forerunners:

Nero—the persecutor of Christians (Rev. 13: 7; 17: 6). Regarded as Antichrist by the first Christians. "Neron Kesar" (Nero Cæsar) written in Hebrew letters, has the numerical value 666.

the Emperors of Rome—representative of world power (Rev. 17: 3, 9). Comp. Kesar Romim, "Cæsar of the Romans," in Hebrew letters=666.[1]

Mohammed—the false prophet; as was considered by many believers at the beginning of the Middle Ages.

the Papacy—the sham religion, was regarded as Antichrist by the early evangelical churches of the Middle Ages (Waldenses, Wicliffites, Hussites), also by Dante, Luther and the Reformers, Bengel, and others.[2]

Napoleon—the world conqueror. In so far as Napoleon represented absolute rule, which had grown out of radicalism, he is certainly a type of the Antichrist.[3]

These are all advance messengers of the Antichrist.

Two lines run through the history of mankind: the line of Christ and the line of Antichrist, the line of the Woman's seed and that of the serpent. The Christ line begins with Adam,[4] passes via Golgotha, and leads to the heavenly Jerusalem. The Antichrist line begins with Cain, passes via Babel, and leads to the lake of fire. Each of us today belongs to one or the other line and is at the same time the preparer of his own future. He is introducing and furthering his own final completion, of which he is both type and pre-representation. He is either of Christ or of the Antichrist.

[1] Also "Latcinos," "Roman," written in Greek characters. So Irenaus (about A.D. 200). Further the Greek *titan*, the gigantic= 666 (Irenæus). So also the "harlot" (Rev. 17: 1, 3, 9, 15), who is throned on the seven hills and the many waters, unmistakably the "gathering of the whole earth," the seven-hilled city (*urbs septicollis*).

[2] Comp. the Latin title of the Pope, *Vicarius filii Dei*, Vicar of the Son of God, in Latin letters = 666.

[3] Further, the Greek word for "beast," written in Hebrew characters, has the value 666. But too much worth is not to be given to the different attempts to explain the number 666.

[4] Adam at once believed on the good news of the coming seed of the woman (Gen. 3: 15). This is shown by the name Eve (Heb. *Chavva* life) which he gave to his wife (*Ischa* woman, Gen. 2: 23) immediately after that first promise and certainly directly before the expulsion from Paradise (Gen. 3, context). "Sunken in death he nevertheless has given his wife so proud a name" (Calvin), and thereby expressed his confidence in the conquest of death by life. Thus it was "an act of faith that Adam named his wife Eve" (Delitzsch), and from that time her name was for mankind the "memorial of the promised grace of God" (*mnemosymon gratiæ Dei promissæ*, Melanchthon). As Luther said of the first promise: "Adam believed this and so was saved from his fall."

ANTICHRIST'S SYSTEM

ACCORDING to Rev. 13 the Antichrist comes as the head of
a human system at enmity with God.

In quite open opposition to and imitation of the Divine
Triunity this system is an unity of three trinities:

Three persons: the Dragon, the Beast, and the Prophet;

Three cities: Jerusalem, Babylon and Rome;

Three principles: political, economic, and religious world
unity.

It is like a three-sided pyramid with the Satanic trinity at the
pinnacle. It is the "tower of Babel" in final historical completion. So again shattering and judgment are God's answer to
this challenge of mankind (Rev. 19: 11–21; comp. Gen. 11: 7).
Correspondingly the nature of Antichristianism (apart from the
three cities) displays itself as follows:

a. The personal trinity:
(i) the anti-God; (ii) the anti-Son; (iii) the anti-Spirit.

b. The cultural trinity:
(i) the political unity; (ii) the economic unity; (iii) the
religious unity.

A. The Personal Trinity

Three persons are the spiritual summit of the system (Rev.
16: 13; 20: 10): the "Dragon," as the demonic authority (Rev.
12: 3, 9, 17; 13: 2); the Beast as the political (Rev. 13: 1–10); and
the "false Prophet" as the religious (Rev. 16: 13; 13: 11–18).
The Dragon is the anti-*god*, the Beast the anti-*son* (Antichrist);
the false prophet the anti-*spirit*.[1]

I. THE ANTI-GOD

The Dragon is the counterpart of the Father. He is the
"first" person in the infernal trinity (Rev. 16: 13), the ringleader
and seducer of the whole system, the chief enemy, "the old
serpent, which is called Devil and Satan" (Rev. 12: 9; John 8: 44).
He stands to the Beast in a similar relationship to that of the
Father to the Son in the Godhead:

[1] Of the two "beasts" in Rev. 13 the *first* is Antichrist, the second his prophet.
This is shown by all that is said above concerning the "anti-son" and the "anti-
spirit." Further: of these two the *first* Beast stands always in the foreground
(Rev. 13. 12). The second has only the authority of the first Beast (Rev. 13: 12).
The number 666, exactly as does the "image" of the Beast (Rev. 13: 14; comp. 3: 4),
unmistakably relates to the first Beast, not to the second (Rev. 14: 11; 15: 2; 19: 20).
Almost all noted expositors so explain. According to Rev. 16: 13; 20: 10, the anti-
spirit, the second Beast, is the "false prophet."

as the Father sent the Son into the world (John 6: 57), so
Satan, after being cast out of heaven, sends the Antichrist (Rev.
12: 7–12; 13: 1, 2);

as the Father has given all authority to the Son (John 17: 2;
Matt. 28: 18–20), so the Dragon gives to the Beast "his power
and his throne" (Rev. 13: 2, 4);

as the Father through the Son, after the resurrection, receives
all honour (I Cor. 15: 28; John 12: 27, 28; Phil. 2: 11), so the
Dragon through the Beast, after his resuscitation, receives the
worship of mankind (Rev. 13: 4).

II. THE ANTI-SON (ANTICHRIST)

The Beast is the "second" person in the demonic trinity
(Rev. 16: 13), the opposer (II Thess. 2: 4), the great parody of
Christ.

1. *His origin.* Christ came down "out of heaven" (John 6:
38; Phil. 2: 6–8); Antichrist comes up out of the Abyss (Rev.
11: 7).

2. *His coming.* Christ came in the Father's name; Antichrist
comes in his own name (John 5: 43).

3. *His nature.* Christ is the "Holy One" (Mark 1: 24) and
embodies the Truth (John 14: 6); Antichrist is the Lawless One
(II Thess. 2: 8) and embodies the Lie (II Thess. 2: 9, 11).

Christ, the mystery of godliness (I Tim. 3: 16), is the
Redeemer; Antichrist, the mystery of lawlessness (II Thess. 2: 7),
is the destroyer (Dan. 7: 25).

Christ, the Son of God (Luke 1: 35), is the effulgence of
His Father (Col. 1: 15; Heb. 1: 3); Antichrist, the son of perdition,
is the exact likeness of the Dragon.[1]

4. *His activity.* Christ served three and a half years in Israel
(John 2: 13; 6: 4; 13: 1); Antichrist lords it over the world
for three and a half years (Rev. 13: 5).

5. *His resuscitation.* Christ is He who has been raised from
the dead; Antichrist is he whose deadly wound has been healed
(Rev. 13: 3).

6. *His sphere.* Christ has the church, Jerusalem, the bride
(Eph. 5: 31, 32; Gal. 4: 26; Rev. 21: 9); Antichrist has the world
empire, Great Babylon, the Harlot (Rev. 17: 1–16).

Christ builds, out of living materials, an organism (Eph.
1: 23; 4: 12–16); Antichrist builds, out of dead materials, an
organization (Rev. 13: 17; Eph. 2: 1).

The church of Christ has "the cup of blessing, which we
bless" (I Cor. 10: 16); the world city of Antichrist has "the cup
of fornications" (Rev. 17: 4; 18: 3, 6).

---

[1] Both the Dragon and the Beast are, symbolically, monsters with seven
"heads" and ten "horns" (Rev. 12: 3; comp. 13: 1).

7. *His destiny.*   Christ leads His own into eternal life (John 3: 36); Antichrist brings his followers into destruction and judgment (II Thess. 2: 12).

Christ was Himself exalted in heaven (Phil. 2: 9); Antichrist is cast into the lake of fire (Rev. 19: 20).

III.   THE ANTI-SPIRIT

The "third" person in the Satanic triunity is the "false prophet" (Rev. 16: 13).   He is both the imitation of and the contrast to the Holy Spirit, the second Beast of Rev. 13: 11–18.

He is a prophet (Rev. 13: 11; 16: 13), even as the Spirit of God is the living energy of all prophecy (II Pet. 1: 21).

He receives everything from the Anti-son (Rev. 13: 12, 15), even as the Spirit of God derives all from the Son.   "He will take of Mine" (John 16: 14).

He magnifies the Anti-son (Rev. 13: 12, 16), even as the Spirit of God glorifies Christ (John 16: 14).

He gives life to the image of the Beast (Rev. 13: 15), even as it is the Spirit of God who gives life to believers (John 6: 63; Rom. 8: 11; Gal. 5: 25).

He causes the sealing of men with the mark of the Beast (Rev. 13: 16), even as the Spirit of God is our seal and earnest (Eph. 1: 13; II Cor. 1: 22).

He causes and quickens all worship of the Beast (Rev. 13: 12), even as the Spirit of God causes all the worship of the Holy One (John 4: 23, 24).

Thus the whole is an infernal trinity, a monstrous organism from the pit, with spirit, soul, and body.   The Dragon is the spirit, the Beast is the body, the false Prophet is the soul of it all. And in relation to the Persons of the Godhead the Dragon is— the demon *god;* the Beast is—Satan's *Messiah;* the Prophet is— the diabolical unholy *spirit.*

But thereby in the Devil's career the end is linked with the beginning; for now it is manifest that the antichristian system is nothing less than the acme of all Satanic rebellion, the carrying through to its conscious goal of his craving to be like God, the full, most blasphemous exhibition of his own presumption: "Ye shall be as God" (Gen. 3: 5; Isa. 14: 13, 14; Ezek. 28: 2, 6, 17).

B.   *The Cultural Triunity*

I.   POLITICAL WORLD-UNITY

If according to Rev. 13 "*all*" who dwell on the *earth*" worship the Beast (ver. 8), and "*all*" receive his mark, the small and the great (ver. 16), if *no one* can any longer buy or sell who does not do this (ver. 17), and *all* are killed who oppose the worship of his image (ver. 15), this signifies that a human system is about to come which will embrace politically and civilly all peoples of the world, which, most rigidly organized, supervises each individual, and which, proceeding energetically and tolerating no opposition, exercises supreme jurisdiction.

This means that Bible prophecy foretells a collaboration of all parts of the earth, a gigantic system of civilization composed of all systems, a universal union of mankind with one head. "To him was granted authority over all tribes and peoples, languages and nations" (Rev. 13: 7). Here is a union of opposites; of enthusiasm (Rev. 13: 4) with fear (Rev. 13: 5), of general happiness (Rev. 11: 7-10, esp. 10) with unrelenting severity (Rev. 11: 7; 13: 10, 17; 17: 6), of idealistic culture with despotism (Rev. 17: 6). The centripetal force of the whole overcomes the centrifugal force of the part. Here is the audacious tower building of the Babylonians of the End time (Gen. 11: 1-4; comp. Rev. 13: 7), the summit of all self-redemption of mankind without God.

Therefore also the figurative language of the Apocalypse goes on to picture this world situation of the End time as the gathering together and culmination of all former world-empires of prophecy, as the final product of all God-estranged world effort of the millenniums of man's ancient race, as the general sum of all the "beast" empires of Daniel's prophecies:

The Babylonian was a lion,
The Persian was a bear,
The Grecian was a leopard,
The fourth Beast was a terrifying beast (Dan. 7: 2-8).

But the antichristian Beast is all of these at once; its form as a leopard, its feet as a bear, its mouth as a lion's mouth, and as a whole a monster which is inspired by the Dragon (Rev. 13: 2).

The same idea arises from the number of the heads and horns. The Babylonian lion had one head, likewise the Persian bear, the Grecian leopard had four, and the fourth, the terrible Beast, one, thus together *seven*. And as to their horns,˙ the first three had none, but the last had *ten*. Thus altogether there were seven heads and ten horns, exactly the number of the first Beast in the *Revelation* (13: 1). But inasmuch as this is at the same time an exact reproduction of the Dragon, which likewise has seven heads and ten horns (Rev. 12: 3), it becomes plain that the entire development was controlled by the "god of this world," that the Dragon stands behind the whole labyrinth of human affairs (I John 5: 19), that the history of the sinner is a self-revelation of the Devil, a shocking perversion of the ancient gospel of the serpent, "Ye shall be as—Satan, your god."

But with all this it is clear that the rule of Antichrist does not extend to the whole world at the beginning of his career, but that he must first of all fight for his political position. Arising in one of the regions which had formerly belonged to the old Roman empire, he will surpass the neighbouring States in political power, will extend his rule over more distant lands, and in particular will gain supreme power over a group of the States which, in the End time, will exist in the area of the fourth world empire of Daniel (Rev. 17: 12). These correspond to the ten toes of the image of Nebuchadnezzar (Dan. 2: 41) and to the ten horns of the fourth beast of Daniel's vision (Dan. 7: 7, 24).

Among these ten horns he appears at first as only a small horn, but which at last surpasses all the rest in size and power. With this ten-horned kingdom as his own proper realm his influence will extend to all other peoples, even if these may not at first be incorporated with his own proper kingdom.

But in ever-increasing measure he will bring under his control the political, industrial and commercial, as well as the religious and philosophical life of all the world. He will solve their civil and social problems, excite their enthusiasm, suppress their religions (II Thess. 2: 4) and draw to himself their worship (Rev. 13: 4). Finally, having attained the summit of his power, he will dominate their whole outward and inward life in an imposing but at the same time God-defying manner (Rev. 13: 7).

But at last, as it appears, this world-wide, fascinating, bewitching influence over the peoples in some measure declines. In various parts of the world the enthusiasm wanes. Some nations revolt. Wars break out. The combination of mankind as an unity is imperilled. He is victorious against powerful opponents, especially Egypt (Dan. 11: 40-43), but at length his own overthrow comes.

Such military events at the end of the Antichristian period are intimated in the prophecies of Daniel. In ch. 11 the prophet gives first an outline of the then near future, the wars between the "king of the south" and the "king of the north," that is, of the political and military conflicts between Egypt and Syria in the third and second centuries before Christ. He has especially in view Antiochus Epiphanes (175-164), the chief enemy of the worship of Jehovah by Israel, the special type of the Antichrist.

But then the prophecy, viewing type and final fulfilment together, passes more and more to the actual Antichrist of the End days, and tells what will happen at the "time of the end." This expression "time of the end" is twice used in the context (Dan. 11: 35, 40). Quite apart from the obvious, proper meaning of the word itself, it is unmistakably connected by the prophet with the actual End time, for in *immediate* connexion Daniel says that "*in that time* shall Michael stand up, the great prince who stands for the children of thy people: and there shall be a time of trouble, such as never was since there was a nation even to *that same time*: and *at that time* thy people shall be delivered. . . . And many of them that sleep in the dust of the earth shall awake; these to eternal life, those to shame and eternal abhorrence" (Dan. 12: 1, 2).

This connexion makes clear that, allowing for the reference in the vision to the typical Antichrist (Antiochus Epiphanes) the prophet more and more carries forward his prophecy to the actual Antichrist, and ever more distinctly brings the antichristian End time into the centre of his message. It is in this exact connexion that he says that "at the time of the end shall the king of the south (Egypt) contend with him (that is, the Antichrist) . . . and he (the Antichrist) shall stretch forth his hand upon the countries: and the land of Egypt shall not escape" (Dan. 11: 40, 42). The whole passage, with ver. 44, intimates that final waning of his influence which has been mentioned above. Otherwise such revolts would not be possible, even though he is able to defeat them.

But at last Antichrist himself will "come to his end" (Dan. 11: 45). He himself with his central kingdom and all his many servants and vassals, will be brought to nought by Christ at His appearing with the armies of heaven in glory and power (Rev. 19: 11–21; II Thess. 2: 8).

Yet the Bible does not by this teach that God is against *every* union of the human race. On the contrary, the closest, most spiritual, and all-embracing fellowship of mankind is precisely His intention (Mic. 4: 1–4). But this fellowship is in Christ, His Son, whom He has appointed King (Psa. 2: 6; Eph. 1: 10; John 10: 16); it has Himself as its centre (Zech. 14: 9); and it brings blessing for mankind on the most world-wide scale. Understanding among the peoples, mutual esteem, reciprocal appreciation, co-operation in peace—all this is so little antichristian as to be exactly the will of God. That which the Scripture terms antichristian is not the outward form, but the religious revolt of the soul, the united rejection of Christ, the *conscious* decision against God. Thus antichristianism, as to its essence, lies on the plane of belief, not on that of culture in itself, but on that of the *cult* (that which one venerates as divine), not in the sphere of historical outlook, but in the sphere of religion. It is the concentration of the hatred of Christ, the revolt against the Most High, the attempt to dethrone the supreme Lord of the worlds.

II. COMMERCIAL WORLD UNITY

According to Rev. 13: 17 "*no one* on the *whole* earth" who does not receive the mark of the Beast will be able any longer to buy or sell. This is only possible if all traders, with all social and industrial undertakings, stand under one common oversight, if a centre exists in the world where everything is organized and centralized, a general collaboration of all men, which exercises an absolute control and rule over world trade. Thereby the New Testament foretells a gigantic organization of mankind to embrace each individual of its members, including the individual workers and the small employers,[1] and exercising over all the peoples the sole right of trade; a common Trade Authority directing all commercial life, without whose trade mark no one can continue to do business.

Here also it is not the commercial form that is antichristian. Only the grossest misunderstanding could so assert. Oversight of commercial life—exercised freely by each civilized nation—is a necessity in the life of the individual nation, an indispensable measure for guarding against social unrighteousness. Rightly exercised it is a pre-requisite for the preservation of life, for advance and ascent. The antagonism to God of the End time consists much rather in this, that this all will be misused in the fight against the Eternal, to the destruction of Biblical Christianity, to the brutal oppression of any who confess faith in God (Rev. 13: 17, comp. ver. 7; 17: 6; 18: 24; 20: 4).

III. RELIGIOUS WORLD UNITY

1. *Self-Deification of Mankind.* According to the prophecies of the *Revelation* the Antichrist will be worshipped (Rev. 13: 8, 12; 14: 9; 16: 2). He becomes the admired of the whole earth (13: 3), the honoured of all its inhabitants (13: 8), inflaming the enthusiasms of the masses (13: 4; 11: 10). It will be said of him: "Who is like to the Beast? Who is able to war with him?" (13: 4). He becomes the acme of mankind, the embodiment of its highest ideals, the visible perfection of all human genius, indeed "*the* man" in the highest sense of the word. In the deifying of his own power he will exalt himself above everything divine, set himself in the temple of God and represent that *he* is God! (II Thess. 2: 4).

But thereby the worship of *him* becomes the worship of mankind in general, and whoever resists *him* resists the body corporate; in the most offensive sense of the word he is of all men *the* Offender; he is Insurgent and Rebel, and therefore under sentence of destruction.

Through all this the antichristian system becomes a political-religious association with a welding of State and religion, a self-deifying World Church marked by intolerance of all opposing convictions. Thus will come withdrawal of religious liberty,

---

[1] Believers who refuse to receive the mark, and so are boycotted and even executed (Rev. 13: 15, 17), will doubtless, as in all times, be mostly of humble rank (I Cor. 1: 26–28).

religious compulsion, planned enslavement of conscience, mass execution of respectable[1] citizens solely for conscience' sake.

This is the religion of the Antichrist: it is the detestable doctrine of the divinity of man, faith in oneself, the deifying of one's own spirit. It is the most imposing attempt to escape the consequences of sin without laying aside the sin itself, the final outcome of "progress," the sum total and completion of all God-estranged civilization.[2]

2. *State Religion.* Antichristendom is thus not irreligious but a religious contrast to Christianity. It is not an eliminating of religion, but the establishing of a State religion; it is not a belittling of it, but the setting upon it of so high a value that the authority of the State is exerted in its favour. It is not simply heathendom but a super-heathendom. It is heathenism with conquest and rejection of Biblical Christianity. It is the glorifying and worshipping of self by an adulterous generation (Matt. 12: 39; Phil. 2: 15); it is the making of self a god and therefore is complete godlessness, the climax of all abomination and idolatry of the world. "It is not flesh but spirit, not folly but wisdom, not weakness but strength; it is not human but demonic, not simple but full of mystery, not darkness but blinding brilliance."

Outwardly it appears as a religious World Union, as a combination of business, politics, and faith; as a political blend of trade, external affairs, and religion; as a Union of State, commerce, and Church, that is, as a concentration of three already concentrated lines of life. Its head is a surpassing personality, an inventive, unique organizer, "a genius in statecraft, science, art, and social finance, of a religious type, and endowed with the occult powers of the unseen world" (II Thess. 2: 9).

But within it is hollow and empty, being nothing other than the fig-leaf philosophy of the first man (Gen. 3: 7), the self-redemption philosophy of the first murderer, the serpent gospel of the first deceiver, "Ye shall be as God."

And as the sum of all it is the summit of human revolt, the zenith of the civilization of the serpent's seed. The earthly kingdom of heaven, the rule of "God" without God and therefore of all the religions of history the most antagonistic to the true gospel. (Rev. 13: 7; 17: 6).

3. *The Pinnacle of Religion.* The Antichrist himself will be the "against" Christ because he is the "lying" Christ, the

---

[1] The "saints" of God (Rev. 13: 7; 17: 6; 18: 24), the "witnesses" (Rev. 11: 3, 7) and "prophets" (Rev. 16: 6).

[2] In this sense the purely symbolic number 666 is the motto of the Antichrist. For 6 is the number of man—on the sixth day man was created, on the sixth day (Friday) he was redeemed at Golgotha. But 666 is the total of all the numbers from 1 to 36, the square of 6 ($6 \times 6 = 36$: $1 + 2 + 3 + 4 \cdots 35 + 36 = 666$).

pseudo-false Christ (Matt. 24: 5, 23, 24). He will not only suppress Christ but supplant Him. As regards human culture, he will not deny outright the general expectation which Christians associate with the person of Jesus of Nazareth; on the contrary he starts with it and relies upon it; but he describes himself as its fulfilment and thereby would make the true Christ superfluous. Thus he confirms *intellectually* the Christ *idea* and proceeds to step forth as the "substitute" Christ; yet he denies the *personal* Christ of *prophecy* and is therefore the "opposer" (II Thess. 2: 4) and "anti"-Christ.

This double character corresponds to the two designations "pseudo-Christ" (lying Christ, Mark 13: 22) and Antichrist (against Christ). As Antichrist he sets himself *against* Christ; as the lying-Christ he declares himself, so to speak, *to be* "Christ." He is both at the one time, since he is the intellectual "substitute"-Christ.

Thus he is, so to speak, the Messiah of the world, its cultural Saviour, its saving Head. He sets himself before it as the centre of gravity of its order, the centre of its hope, the goal of its development. And against the heavenly truth that in Christ *God* has become *man* he sets the demonic lie that in him *man* has become God (II Thess. 2: 4).

Thus it is a fixing of faith *on this side,* a making the heavenly to be earthly, a humanizing of the conception of God. Conversely, it is a deifying of the human intellect, a claim to be oneself equal with God; indeed a will to supersede the Divine, and therefore it is the final, perfected sin.

CHAPTER III

SIGNS OF THE TIME

ACCORDING to the Scripture there will come at the end of the age a rebellion against God embracing all peoples, a denial of Biblical Christianity by all civilizations and cultures.

Is such a world situation possible? At least, is it not unlikely? What does the history of civilization say as to this?

In itself civilization is not ungodly, and still less antichristian. On the contrary, cultural achievements form a part of the paradisiacal nobility of man. Invention and discovery, science and art, refinement and improvement, in short, the progress of the spirit of man, are entirely the will of God. They are the taking possession of the earth by the royal race of mankind, the carrying out of a creative task by God's ennobled servants, a God-appointed service of government for the blessing of the earth. "Be fruitful and multiply and fill the earth, and subdue it and have dominion" (Gen. 1: 28). Only complete misunderstanding of the very simplest laws of revelation can therefore find fault with the Holy Scripture as being a retrograde form of thought and an enemy of culture. No, what the Bible rejects and what is contrary to God is not culture in itself, but the estrangement from God of millions of its representatives, the isolation from heaven of the sinner, the false "religious" shams, the denial of the sovereignty of the Most High, the spirit of haughtiness and rebellion, the conscious exclusion of God, in short, insurrection against the Lord Himself. "We *will* not that this One rules over us" (Luke 19: 14).

Thus the outward framework of civilization's history is not in opposition to God, much less antichristian. What matters is rather the *spirit,* the moral substance of deeds, the moral application of cultural advance, the attitude of heart of each individual to God. Moreover politics and history are in God's plan thoroughly interlocked (Prov. 21: 1; I Kings 11: 14, 23; Isa. 45: 1–7), and are overruled by the Most High as the supreme Lord of the world.

1. *The Mystery of the Fourth World Empire of Daniel.* The fourth world empire of Daniel's prophecy never died. The iron in Nebuchadnezzar's image reached from the thighs to the feet (Dan. 2: 33). In the sense of the prophecy it lasts till the end of the present age. Upon the empire being broken to pieces there follows *immediately* the setting up of the kingdom of the Son of man (Dan. 7: 7–14; 2: 33–35, 44).

Nowhere in Scripture is this fourth empire of Daniel expressly and directly described by the name "Rome." But there is no doubt that the ancient Roman empire was its *first phase*. The fourth empire begins with Rome.

But the old Rome collapsed. Even in the first two centuries after Christ, and in spite of all the splendour of the period of the Cæsars, it had declined in inward strength and outward power. By the division of the empire by the emperor Theodosius (A.D. 395) it was parted into two sections, the western empire with its capital at Rome itself (Emperor Honorious), and the eastern empire with its capital at Constantinople (Emperor Arcadius). Numerous expositors think that this was signified by the two legs of Nebuchadnezzar's image. The western empire was shortly afterwards destroyed by the northern invaders (Odoacer, 476), and the eastern a thousand years later (1453) by the Turks under Sultan Mohammed II.

Nevertheless from the lands which originally had been included in the Roman empire there went out the most powerful, decisive impulses for the further development of the surviving civilized peoples of the sphere of this former Roman empire. Only this fact enables us to understand why, in spite of all individual variations, and after the political collapse of Rome, Biblical prophecy views the consequent developments as connected with that empire, and sets it forth as one historical unity, even as being thĕ *one* fourth world empire of Daniel continuing from the early Roman time to the end of the present age.

The Roman administration lived on in the Church of Rome. The ecclesiastical provinces coincided with the State provinces; and Rome, the chief city of the world empire, became the chief city of the world Church, the seat of the Papacy.

The Roman tongue lived on in the Latin of the Church, and is still in use in the international technical language of law, medicine, and natural science.

Roman law lived on in legislation. The *corpus juris Romanum* (body of Roman law) of the Eastern Roman Emperor Justinian (A.D. 527–565) became the foundation of jurisprudence among the Latin and Germanic peoples throughout the Middle Ages and far into modern times.

The Roman army lived on in military systems. It became the model for armaments and western defence. We still use Latin words such as captain, major, general, battalion, regiment, army, infantry, artillery, and cavalry.

The rulers of central Europe were called *Kaiser*. In the Middle Ages they were often crowned in Rome, as Charlemagne in A.D. 800 and Otto the Great in 962.[1] The rulers of eastern

[1] Not until 1806, during the assaults of Napoleon, was the imperial dignity of "Roman" Kaiser given up by Francis II of Austria.

and southern Europe (Russia and Bulgaria) were called Tsars. Both titles were from the personal name of the Roman Caius Julius *Caesar*, which became a title (first century B.C.).

Also the spirit of the Roman conception of the State has survived. It was marked by severest discipline, iron will, centralization, subordination of the individual to the community, devotion to the State, belief in its eternity, expressed in "eternal Rome" (*Roma aeterna*), idolization of the State, as in the Roman emperor cult, merging of the man in the citizen.

Finally, a certain mystery hovers around the history of the *city* of Rome itself:

about 1000 B.C.	— a poor village.[1]
about A.D. 100	— a city of 1,000,000.[2]
in the Middle Ages	— a medium-sized provincial town.[3]
since the sixteenth century	— gradually increasing.[4]
since 1870	— strong and rapid growth.[5]
today	— again a million inhabitants as in the days of the Roman emperors.

Many of these facts are only historical incidents. Many of them appear for only a brief time and disappear. The value of observing them lies in this, that they enable us to perceive that, even after the collapse of Rome, in the subsequent development of the peoples of its area, and in the background of the whole process, there is at work a continuous, homogeneous, dynamic historical force which, in ever new forms, displays its permanence, vitality, and strength. This shows that in a wider sense the whole is actually *one* kingdom. At the same time this continuity, embracing centuries, becomes a sublime testimony to the reliability of the prophets and to their grasp of reality and to the accuracy of their historical foresight.

But the centre and weight of all Bible prophecy as to the fourth empire lies in the future. Actually and strictly the prophecy is not concerned with the "legs" of the imperial image of Nebuchadnezzar, but much rather with the "toes" of its feet. It shows clearly that, in the final development of the fourth empire, the antichristian empire will include a group of States corresponding to the toes of the image (Dan. 2: 40) and to the ten horns of the fourth beast of Daniel's vision, out of which the Antichrist will finally arise as the "little horn" (Dan. 7: 7, 8, 20–25).

[1] Rome is at least 300 years older than the official year of its foundation 753 B.C.

[2] 700,000 inhabitants, plus 300,000 slaves.

[3] 25,000 to 40,000 inhabitants. In 546, after being sacked at different times during the migration period, only 500 inhabitants.

[4] 1870. The unification of Italy. 215,000 inhabitants.

[5] 1950. Over 1,100,000 inhabitants.

But that at the end of the age the last phase of this fourth world empire will see an exact restoration of its first phase, that is, that in the antichristian time there will be a literal, territorial renewal and reviving of the Roman empire, with the same frontiers and without question the same capital city—this Holy Scripture nowhere plainly states.[1]   Even in the past the frontiers of the old Roman empire were not invariable, and in any case a kingdom remains the same kingdom even if its frontiers are extended far beyond their earlier limit, and indeed even if its capital is removed to another place.   Thus China remained China though its capital was removed from Peking to Nanking, some 570 miles south.   Russia remained Russia though its capital was no longer St. Petersburg but, as now, Moscow.   Or, to take an example from the history of western Europe, England has remained England though originally its capital was not London but, in the days of the old Saxon kings, Winchester, some twelve miles north of Southampton, and London became the capital only in the thirteenth century.   Similarly the fourth empire of Daniel will remain the same empire even if, in the final development, not the literal Rome, that is, its first capital, but some other city should become the capital.

A number of notable expositors think that they have found in the prophetic word abundant ground to believe that in the End time the ancient Babylon on the Euphrates will be rebuilt, to be the centre of the antichristian world empire.   Babylon the "mother of all harlotry and idolatry" (Rev. 17: 5)!   Babylon the centre "of all abominations on earth"!   Babylon the beginning, Babylon the end of all religious and moral apostasy of present human history without God!

World kingdoms have only come fully into the prophetic vision when they have united themselves with Babylon in the Middle East and have regarded it as their centre.   Thus Nebuchadnezzar, the sovereign of the first world empire of prophecy, had Babylon as his capital.   The Medes and Persians had existed for centuries, but they only became a world empire in the prophetic sense by the conquest of Babylon by Cyrus and the removal thither of the Persian capital.   It was the same with the Greeks.   The development of their high civilization through many centuries was not included in the prophetic outlook.   This did not come to pass until Alexander the Great, after the overthrow of the Persians, conquered the Orient and chose Babylon as his capital.   Only from then is the Grecian kingdom the third world empire within the meaning of prophecy.

[1] [This matter is of crucial importance.   The opinion is here offered that, not only does Scripture nowhere plainly state the view mentioned, but is plainly against it.   See my *Histories and Prophecies of Daniel* and *The Revelation of Jesus Christ*. Trans.]

And may it not be that Daniel's fourth world empire also will only have reached its culmination and perfection if it likewise rebuilds Babylon in Mesopotamia as the centre of Antichristianism?

We do not answer this question with full assurance. The possibility of such a development remains. But the fulfilment will be the complete explanation of the prophecy.

Until then we wait. In the consciousness of our insufficiency we search the prophetic word. But this we already see clearly, that the path of world history moves steadily to the Orient as its centre and that the course of events leads ever more plainly into the foreground of the final development.

2. Many signs of the times show unmistakably that the End draws near.

Rapid Development of Means of Communication. The peoples draw together. World events expand. Europe has been lifted out of its proud isolation. Since the nineteenth century there has come for the first time a oneness into world history. What before was so called was only a history of part of mankind, even if of the leading civilizations, western Asiatic, Egyptian, European, and American. Now all is as *one* cogwheel, with inter-action of all parts of the earth.

World Commerce. Nineteenth century. Absorption of small industries by *similar* great industries—horizontal building up. Twentieth century. Absorption of *different* small and great industries into giant "concerns," trusts. Conjunction of coal mines, machine factories, wharves, shipping concerns, sugar factories, film undertakings, newspapers, etcetera, for the production and distribution of goods from the raw material to the finished product—vertical building up.

Control of retail trade. Compulsory central combines. Ration cards, coupons. Possible prevention of all "buying and selling" (Rev. 13: 17). Modern system of boycott.

Ameliorative measures by governments. Reactions and reforms. New economic programs. But these also are possible only by centralization and organization; otherwise impossible. Only in this way salvation from threatening collapse. *In itself* organization is not antichristian, but rather a necessary measure in the life of nations for the common welfare.

Increase of world intercourse. Expedited tempo of world happenings.

Development of War Technique. Improvement of the most horrible weapons of slaughter. Danger of self-extinction of the leading civilized nations. Therefore, considered from even the technical standpoint alone, increasing necessity for an understanding among the nations for the maintenance of peace (I Thess. 5: 2, 3).

Armies numbering millions. "Twice ten thousand times ten thousand," that is, 200 millions (Rev. 9: 16). Already in the 1914–18 war, 40 millions were engaged. The killed alone were 9 million, and there died, including deaths by pestilence, another 35 million.

A third of mankind killed (Rev. 9: 15, 18). Certainly entirely possible now. Aeroplane attacks! Flying bombs! Atom and hydrogen bombs! A European total war—the destruction of Europe, literally. Over-civilization the murderer of culture.

Religious world Propaganda. The False Prophet will bring *all,* the small and the great, to worship the Antichrist (Rev. 13: 12, 16).

Suppression of Religious Liberty. Mass executions on account of spiritual convictions (Matt. 24: 9; Rev. 13: 15; 17: 6; 18: 24) still possible today? Notwithstanding "progress" and "world improvement"? Yes, even in this modern time there have been and there are persecutions on account of Christian faith.

Wars and Rumours of War to the End (Matt 24: 6, 7). Yet in spite of all this

World Evangelization. "The gospel of the kingdom will be preached in the whole world for a testimony to all peoples, and then will the End come" (Matt. 24: 14).

Up to A.D. 1500.   Printed Bibles and portions distributed in 14 languages.

1800.   In 71 languages.

1804.   Founding of the British and Foreign Bible Society.

1930.   According to Dr. Kilgour, Director of Translating in the London Bible house, in over 900 languages (including the translations of all Bible Societies). By this means "every five or six weeks a new language can be added to the lists of our Society."

1948.   The number of languages and chief dialects had risen to over 1,100, of which the British Society published 770, and issues every year over 11 million copies of Scriptures. (*The Gospel in Many Tongues,* 1948, pp. 187, 188).

A truly powerful preparation for the evangelization of the peoples at the End time (Rev. 7: 9–11).

Israel. On the one hand, August, A.D. 70, saw the destruction of Jerusalem by Titus, 1,100,000 dead. And

in 135 followed the collapse of the Jewish national State after the defeat of the "son of the stars," Bar Kochba (comp. Num. 24: 17), 500,000 dead. Expulsion of all Jews from Judæa and Jerusalem (Deut. 28: 64; Lev. 26: 33).

On the other hand, we see the indestructibility of the Jewish people, even under the Divine judgment (Isa. 66: 22; Jer. 33: 20–26; Matt. 24: 34). Today, after centuries of catastrophic judgments[1] there are more than twice as many Jews as in the most splendid days of David and Solomon. As about a quarter of the inhabitants of a land are capable of military service, it follows from II Sam. 24: 9, that the total population in the days of David was about 5,000,000. But today there are about 12,000,000 of Jews on earth. On the other hand, apart from Rome, note the collapse or decline of every other ancient civilized people.

Further: September 28, 1791, the French National Assembly annulled all special laws against the Jews. Since then in the Nineteenth century a rapid development of Jewish influence into a great power in politics, the press, and high finance.

1897. Founding of Zionism. Systematic endeavours to return to the land of their fathers.

February 27, 1919. Conference in San Remo. Palestine declared the national home of the Jewish people under British mandate, in virtue of the Balfour Declaration of 1917. On February 26, 1923, the Chief Council (Sanhedrin) held its first session for many centuries. After fifteen hundreds of years the "dead" Hebrew language is again the living language of common intercourse in *Erez Israel*, the land of Israel—1918 saw the establishment of the Hebrew University on Mount Scopus. In 1900 there were about 50,000 Jews in the land; by 1936 the number was already about 375,000. The Jewish population is now over one million.

1948. Saw the setting up of a Jewish government in Palestine more than eighteen centuries after A.D. 135.

This all is the awakening of the Near East. The "fig tree" of Israel has budded (Matt. 24: 32, comp. Luke 13: 6-9; Matt. 21: 19). The "dead bones" begin to stir and to come together (Ezek. 37: 7). Israel, the "pointer on God's world clock," already points to midnight.

Thus we see everywhere evidence of the historical possibility and literal sense of the Bible prophecies of the End (Matt. 16: 2, 3).

1. In political life:
the awakening of the Orient (Rev. 16: 12; 9: 14-16);
the return of the Jews to Palestine (Isa. 11: 11);
the general political world fermentation (Matt. 24: 6, 7).

[1] In addition to the figures given above, in May to July, 1096, 10,000 Jews were killed in the Rhineland, Germany.

Nov. 1, 1290: Expulsion of all Jews (over 1600) from England under threat of hanging. Return legally sanctioned only after 370 years, by Cromwell.

April 20 till autumn 1298, 100,000 Jews killed in Franconia, Bavaria, and Austria.

Sept. 1306: 100,000 Jews expelled from France under threat of death.

August 2, 1492: Expulsion of 300,000 Jews from Spain under threat of death by the Inquisition.

1648-58: Death of about 400,000 Polish Jews in the war between Russia, Poland, and Sweden.

1939-45: Murder of at least many hundreds of thousands of Jews in the second world war.

2. In economic life:
  tension between rich and poor (Jas. 5: 1–8);
  organizing and centralizing (Rev. 13: 17).
3. In technical life:
  development of world intercourse—drawing together of
  the peoples—improvement of war technique—necessity
  of world understanding on account of the danger of self-
  annihilation of the leading civilized peoples.
4. In religious life:
  self-deifying (II Thess. 2: 3, 4);
  spiritism (I Tim. 4: 1);
  pretended piety (II Tim. 3: 5; comp. 1);
  fanaticism (Matt. 24: 4, 5, 11, 23–26);
  false doctrines (II Tim. 4: 3, 4; II Pet. 2: 1, 2).
5. In moral life:
  fleshly security (Matt. 24: 37–39; I Thess. 5: 3);
  immoral conduct (II Tim. 3: 1–4);
  haughty mockery (II Pet. 3: 3, 4).
6. In Nature:
  Earthquakes[1] and natural disasters (Matt. 24: 7; Joel 2:3, 10);
  comp. signs in sun, moon, and stars (Matt. 24: 29).
7. In the life of the church of God:
  Bible circulation and world evangelization (Matt. 24: 14);
  Lukewarmness of many (Rev. 3: 16; Matt. 25: 5; Luke
    18: 8), but watchfulness of the faithful (Luke 12: 37).
But at midnight there will sound a cry: "Behold, the Bridegroom! Go ye out to meet Him" (Matt. 25: 6).[2]

[1] "Between the years 1600 to 1700 four great earthquakes were recorded;
between 1700 to 1800 seven, from 1800 to 1900 nine. In the past quarter of a century (1901–1925) there were already four—that of Martinique (30,000 killed), San
Francisco, Messini (100,000 dead) and Tokyo (230,000 dead)" (F. P. Keller).
Also at Quetta, India, 1935 (40,000 killed).

[2] Nevertheless there are still powers that work decidedly in favour of *delay*.
Therefore every attempt to date the fulfilment in advance should be avoided. In
particular there is one person who and one thing which "restrains" (II Thess. 2:
6, 7), but who and what these are cannot be pronounced with certainty. The view
of most of the Church Fathers was that it was the Roman Empire (so Irenæus,
Tertullian, Hippolytus, Jerome, and Chrysostom). Theodoret thought it was
heathen idolatry, J. P. Lange the moral spirit of the life of the State, Calvin the
preaching of the gospel, Darby the church and the Spirit of God, Bullinger the
Devil who "holds fast" his position in heaven and must be cast out by the archangel
Michael (Rev. 12: 7 ff.) before he permits the Antichrist to go forth on earth
(Rev. 13). Augustine well remarks: "The Thessalonians understood it ('Ye
know,' II Thess. 2: 6); I do not know it at all: yet I will not conceal the suppositions
of others."

[A more recent suggestion is that, as the Antichrist is a king who has formerly
lived on earth and is now in the abyss, the world of the dead (Rev. 17: 8, 11), and
would gladly return to earth before "his own season" (II Thess. 2: 6), it is the angel
ruler of that world who "restrains" him, that is, who will not let him come before
the time permitted of God. This "angel of the abyss" is mentioned in Rev. 9: 11,
where his names in Hebrew and Greek are given, the Greek name being that of
the well-known god Apollo. This conception was quite well-known in the
ancient world, which would explain why Paul says that the Thessalonians already
knew who was the restrainer. Trans.]

THE JUDGMENT UPON ANTICHRIST

T HE brilliant summit of human history is at the same time
its turning point to collapse (Dan. 2: 34, 35). The Lord
Himself executes the judgment.

I. THE GREAT TRIBULATION

The terrors of the judgment convulse the whole earth (Rev.
3: 10), especially the land of Judæa (Matt. 24: 16; Luke 21: 21).
The "great tribulation" (Dan. 12: 1; Matt. 24: 21, 29; Rev.
7: 14)—the "trouble of Jacob" (Jer. 30: 7)—breaks in upon
mankind (Rev. 6–19). Mighty are the catastrophes:
the breaking of the seven Seals and the blowing of the seven
Trumpets (Rev. 6–11);
the rolling of the seven Thunders (Rev. 10: 4), and the outpouring of the seven Bowls of wrath (Rev. 16);
the apocalyptic Riders and the coming World War (Rev.
6; 9: 13–21);
the destruction of Jerusalem (Zech. 14: 2), and the destruction
of Great Babylon (Rev. 17: 16);
the military Expedition of the Orient and the "Tumult in
the valley of Decision" (Rev. 16: 12–16: Joel 3: 14).
Of course many details are not disclosed, such as the figurativeness or literality of many prophecies of the End times;
whether the seventy year-weeks of Daniel 9: 24–27, are
fulfilled or not yet fulfilled;
the relationship of the Lord's Olivet discourse (Matt. 24) to
the other New Testament prophecies of the End times;
the interweaving of prophecies relating to the near and the
distant futures into one uniform total picture with features
sharply interpenetrating;
the God-opposing Seven-hilled city of Babylon and its
destruction by the even more God-opposing Antichrist
(Rev. 17: 16);
the area of rule of the Beast and the secret of his number 666
(Rev. 13: 18);
the Jewish State in Palestine and the devastating invasion
of the nations (Rev. 11: 7; Zech. 14:);
the decisive battle of Har-Magedon (Rev. 16: 16), and the
judgment of the nations in the valley of Jehoshaphat (Joel
3: 12)—
these are all prophetic hieroglyphs which no man has so far
deciphered with unassailable certainty.

But at last comes the final blow: the appearing of the Lord in glory and the destruction of the antichristian hosts at Har-Magedon (Rev. 19: 11–21; 16: 16).

Through all this, in an unexpected manner, will be fulfilled the word of Napoleon, the great world-conqueror: "World history will not be decided in the Occident (the west) but in the Orient (the east)." "Har-Magedon" means "mountain (Heb. *har*) of Megiddo," the chief town of the plain of Jezreel, at the foot of Carmel, the most important battlefield in Jewish history.

II. THE APPEARING OF THE LORD

The heavens are opened. The sign of the Son of man appears (Matt. 24: 30). The Lord comes as a rider on a white horse, accompanied by the armies of heaven. Out of His mouth goes forth a sharp two-edged sword, and He Himself treads the winepress of the wrath of God the Almighty (Rev. 19: 11–16).

With a rod of iron (Rev. 19: 15; Psa. 2: 9);
with blood dipped garments (Rev. 19: 13);
as one who treads the winepress (Isa. 63: 1–6); Rev. 19: 15);
as one who threshes the harvest floor (Mic. 4: 12, 13; Matt. 3: 12);
as one who reaps with the sickle of Divine judgment (Joel 3: 13; Rev. 14: 17, 18)—
thus will the despised Jesus of Nazareth again appear!

Then will all the families of the earth wail (Matt. 24: 30). Then has come the Day of the Lord (Joel 1: 15; 4: 14; Amos 5: 20), "the day of His fierce anger" (Isa. 13: 13), the "great and terrible" day (Mal. 4: 5), "a day of darkness and of gloominess, a day of clouds and thick darkness" (Joel 2: 2; Zech. 14: 6).

Then will they creep into the clefts and ravines (Rev. 6: 15). Then will they hide in the caverns of the rocks and the holes of the earth (Isa. 2: 19). Then will they call to the mountains, Fall on us! and to the hills, Cover us! (Luke 23: 30; Rev. 6: 16; 9: 6). But there will be no escape.

For the Lord comes as a flash of lightning (Matt. 24: 27), His chariots as a tempest (Isa. 66: 15), His eyes as flames of fire (Rev. 19: 12), His voice as the voice of a lion (Joel 3: 16; Isa. 30: 30), and the slain of the Lord will be many (Isa. 66: 15, 16; Psa. 110: 6).

In flaming fire (II Thess. 1: 8; Isa. 66: 15, 16),
as a fiery oven (Mal. 4: 1; Matt. 13: 41, 42),
as an inescapable snare (Luke 21: 35),
so will the sudden destruction "seize all" (I Thess. 5: 3),
as the flood in the days of Noah (Matt. 24: 38, 39),
as the fiery judgment overtook Sodom and Gomorrah (Luke 17: 28–32).

On the mount of Olives, whence He formerly ascended (Acts 1: 9, 12), will the Lord again first appear (Zech. 14: 4). *Every* eye will see Him (Rev. 1: 7; Matt. 24: 30); *every* contradiction will be silenced (Matt. 22: 12; Job 9: 3); *every* tongue will confess that Jesus Christ is the Lord, to the honour of God the Father (Phil. 2: 11).

III. THE DESTRUCTION OF THE SATANIC TRINITY

Upon the shattering of the military power of Antichristianism there follows immediately the breaking up of its threefold demonic high command (comp. Rev. 16: 13).   The Lord will slay the Lawless One with the breath of His mouth and destroy him through the outshining of His arrival (II Thess. 2: 8; Isa. 11: 4; Psa. 110: 6).   He, the Beast, and the False Prophet will be seized and cast into the lake of fire (Rev. 19: 20); the Dragon, the old Serpent, will be bound and be flung into the Abyss for a thousand years (Rev. 20: 1–3).   Thereby the Satanic trinity is broken asunder.   The first Person is rendered harmless for a thousand years; the second and third Persons are judged finally and for ever.

Thus the Lamb triumphs over the Dragon, the Son of man over the Beast, the Bride over the Harlot, the Divine Trinity over the Satanic trinity of lies.

But now there arises over Har-Magedon's field of devastation the health-bringing Sun of righteousness (Mal. 4: 2).   After the smashing up of the antichristian *union* of the peoples there comes on the scene the *fellowship* of the peoples of the Millennium. After the collapse of all man's faulty efforts it shall be now shown what GOD can do.

And now the way is free for the kingdom of God.   The binding of the Devil is an event in the spirit realm pre-requisite for the earthly kingdom of glory.   It must now still be decided which of the survivors can be permitted to enter this kingdom. This is effected through

IV. THE JUDGMENT OF THE NATIONS IN THE VALLEY OF JEHOSHAPHAT

The Son of man will sit on the throne of His glory and judge all nations of the earth.   They will all be gathered before Him, and He will separate them one from another, as a shepherd separates the sheep from the goats (Matt. 25: 31, 32).   The latter will go into eternal destruction, the former into the kingdom prepared for them from the foundation of the world (Matt. 25: 34, 46).

This is the great judgment of peoples at the beginning of the

Millennium (Matt. 25: 31–46; Dan. 7: 9–14; Rev. 20: 4). It is important to distinguish it from the final judgment before the great white throne (Rev. 20: 11–15).

1. *The Place.* It does not take place after the destruction of the old earth (Rev. 20: 11), but upon the soil of the old earth, namely, in the valley of Jehoshaphat (Joel 3: 12; Matt. 25: 31).

2. *The Time.* It will not be held after the end of the earthly kingdom of glory but at its beginning (Rev. 20: 11, comp. 7–10; Matt. 25: 31).

3. *The Persons.* It is not the "dead" who are judged, that is, those raised in the second resurrection (Rev. 20: 12, 13), but those then living and surviving from the catastrophic judgments without death and resurrection (Matt. 25: 32).

4. *The Decision.* The question is not destruction *or* simply the eternal, heavenly kingdom (comp. II Tim. 4: 18); but destruction *or* first of all the earthly kingdom of glory (Matt. 25: 34, 46).

This judgment at the beginning of the Millennial kingdom is (as it would appear, and according to the law of prophetic perspective) certainly viewed with the final judgment as one picture; so that prior judgment and final judgment, partial judgment and complete judgment coalesce in one single, mighty, mutually interpenetrating complete picture.

In a similar manner the first and second comings of Christ were viewed by the Old Testament prophets as one picture (e.g. Isa. 61: 1–3, comp. Luke 4: 18, 19); and in the prophecies of Jesus Himself the two resurrections before and after the Millennial kingdom, which by Paul and John are separated as to time (I Cor. 15: 23, 24; Rev. 20: 5, 12), were combined in a single sublime prophecy which does not further stress these gradations of time (John 5: 28, 29; comp. Dan. 12: 2, 3).

V. THE ESTABLISHMENT OF THE KINGDOM OF GLORY

All this together is the "outshining of His presence," the *epiphany* of His *parousia* (II Thess. 2: 8). It is the triumph of the Crucified One (Matt. 26: 64), the revelation of His glory (I Peter 4: 13), and the appearing of His kingdom (Luke 19: 11). His angels will accompany Him (Matt. 25: 31; II Thess. 1: 7), His redeemed will be with Him (I Thess. 3: 13; Jude 14), and He Himself will be admired in all His saints (II Thess. 1: 10). All the world will serve Him (Isa. 60: 1–3); He will reign without opposition (Rev. 12: 10), for He is the "King of all kings and the Lord of all lords" (Rev. 19: 16; 1: 5).

But the kingdom which *He* brings is the kingdom of God. It is not an earthly but a heavenly creation (Luke 19: 12; Dan,

7: 13, 14); it does not come through "progress" but by smashing to pieces [Dan. 2: 34, 44, 45]; it is not the result of human striving but is a gift of God.

1. Viewed from *without* it is the insignificant stone which shatters Nebuchadnezzar's imposing colossus (comp. Matt. 21: 44), but afterwards it increases to a great mountain and fills the whole earth (Dan. 2: 35, 44, 45).

2. Viewed from *within* it is the kingdom of the Son of man which prepares an end for the bloodthirsty Beasts of Daniel's world empire and, for the first time, exalts to the throne of international history true humanity in the sense of Holy Scripture, that is, humanity in the image and likeness of God (Gen. 1: 27; Dan. 7: 13, comp. 2–7; Matt. 26: 64).

3. Viewed from *above* it is the kingdom of heaven, which comes down from heaven, and therefore brings into this earthly world heavenly nature and heavenly happiness (comp. Dan. 4: 23).

4. But in everything it is the kingdom of God, which was:
   i. planned from the very beginning (Matt. 25: 34);
   ii. striven for the ages through (Matt. 6: 10);
   iii. founded by Christ (John 18: 36, 37);
   iv. preached by His followers (Acts 20: 25; 28: 31);
   v. expected by mankind (Rom. 8: 19), and now
   vi. set up on the old earth (Rev. 11: 15; 19: 6), so as, after the final catastrophe of the hitherto existing world (Rev. 20: 7–15),
   vii. to run on into the new eternal creation (Rev. 21 and 22).

With all this it is to be observed that in numerous places Biblical prophecy views together in one picture the visible kingdom of God on the old earth (that is, the Millennium) and the ages of the eternal kingdom of glory on the new earth and in the new heaven (that is, the eternal condition). All one-sided stereotyping of the picture is therefore to be avoided, even as is any over-emphasis upon the Millennium. The visible kingdom of glory on the old earth is not the proper and chief goal of prophetic expectation. It is the last stage toward the perfecting, like the immediate vestibule in a royal palace. And as in a palace the vestibule is built into and belongs to the palace itself, but is not of equal status with the throne room of the king, even so the Millennium belongs to the kingdom of glory, indeed is itself that kingdom of glory in the true sense of the term, yet the chief brightness of that glory and the full unreserved triumph lie beyond the thousand years in the kingdom of Christ and God (Rev. 22: 1; Eph. 5: 5), after the final catastrophe of the old earth, after world renewing and world transfiguration (Rev. 21 and 22). See our explanations on pp. 25, 152f., 156f., and above all in *The Dawn of World Redemption*, Part III, ch. 8.

Section II—The Visible Kingdom of Christ

CHAPTER I

ITS HISTORICAL REALITY

THE kingly rule of God is the final goal of salvation's history. "That God may be all in all" (I Cor. 15: 28). The kingdom is therefore the real basic theme of the Bible.

Belief in a visible kingdom of God on the old earth was originally the common spiritual property of all Christians.[1] Only with the start of the growing Catholicism was it lost, as by Clement, Origen (about A.D. 250) and Augustine (about 400). However, it has been again set on the lampstand during recent centuries.[2]

In fact only a threefold basic failure in expounding Scripture permits of this Biblical truth being overlooked: a confusing of Israel and the church, a hasty exchange of the present with the future, and a one-sided "spiritualizing" of the Old Testament prophecies of the kingdom.

Over against this the original Christian hope of an earthly, visible kingdom of glory stands on a fivefold, unshakable rock foundation. It is:

1. The only adequate confirmation of the truthfulness and covenant faithfulness of God to His promises.

2. The only logical interpretation of Old Testament Messianic prophecy.

3. The only explanation of the history of the End which agrees with the words of the Lord Jesus and His apostles.

4. The only complete conclusion of Divine self-justification in the history of salvation.

5. The only and necessary means of carrying forward human history from its present stage on to its goal in the eternal kingdom of the Father.

I. THE ONLY ADEQUATE CONFIRMATION OF THE TRUTHFULNESS AND COVENANT FAITHFULNESS OF GOD TO HIS PROMISES

[1] The so-called Chiliasm (from the Greek *chilioi*, a thousand), that is, the doctrine of the Millennial kingdom, was held, e.g. by Papias, Justin, Tertullian, Irenæus, Hippolytus, and generally, in the first to the third centuries. "Millennial kingdom" is from the Latin *millennium*, namely, *mille*, 1000 and *annus* year.

[2] As e.g. by Comenius, Labadie, Bengel, Lavater, v. Hofmann, Frank, Th. Culmann, Kurtz, Ebrard, Beck, Auberlen, Stier, Baumgarten, Bettex, Spener, Franz Delitzsch, even though in details they differ. Also to be mentioned are Mat. Hahn, Crusius, [B. W. Newton, J. N. Darby, Wm. Kelly, George Müller, R. Govett, G. H. Pember, A. T. Pierson, and many others.]

"God's gifts of grace and calling are beyond change of mind"
(Rom. 11: 29). To the believing natural descendants of Abraham
God had given the promise of the land (Gen. 15: 4-7, 18). It
was a promise that did not begin with Moses but with Abraham
(Gen. 12: 1-3; 13: 15), and thus was not founded on law but on
promise (Rom. 4: 13-15). Therefore it cannot be annulled by
Israel's failure, but abides unchanged for the sake of God's
honour (Ezek. 36: 22, 23) and His truthfulness (Rom. 15: 8), and
for the sake of Abraham His friend (Gen. 26: 2-5; Lev. 26: 42).
Holy Scripture shows this to be as secure as:

the firmness of the mountains (Isa. 54: 10),
the order of Nature (Isa. 54: 9),
the course of day and night (Jer. 33: 20, 21, 25, 26),
the laws of sun, moon, and stars (Jer. 31: 35-37; Psa. 89:
36, 37),
the everlastingness of the new heavens and the new earth
(Isa. 66: 22).

"Thus saith Jehovah, who giveth the sun for a light by day
and the ordinances of the moon and of the stars for a light by
night . . . If these ordinances depart from before Me, saith
Jehovah, then the seed of Israel also shall cease from being a
nation before Me for ever" (Jer. 31: 35, 36). "For as the new
heaven and the new earth, which I will make, shall remain
before Me, saith Jehovah, so shall your seed and your name
remain" (Isa. 66: 22). These prophecies of the kingdom were
meant literally. A spiritualizing of them and a transference of
them to some other corporate system were nothing else than a
covert breach of covenant by God as regards His promises.
But this is impossible.

Furthermore, the original Christian hope of the kingdom is:

II. The Only Logical Interpretation of Old Testament
Messianic Prophecy

The promises of the first coming of Christ were fulfilled
literally. The promises of the second coming often stand *in
the same sentence* with those. Who therefore can justify these being
taken merely "spiritually"? (e.g. Luke 1: 31-33). Christ came
literally out of Bethlehem (Mic. 5: 2), rode literally on an ass into
Jerusalem (Zech. 9: 9), was literally betrayed for thirty pieces of
silver (Zech. 11: 12), and His hands and feet were literally
pierced on the cross (Psa. 22: 16). Literally His bones were not
broken (Psa. 34: 20), literally His side was pierced by a lance (Zech.
12: 10). He died and was buried literally (Isa. 53: 8, 9, 12), and
also literally rose again on the third day (Psa. 16: 10; Hos. 6: 2).[1]

[1] Compare further the following prophecies of the first coming of Christ
and their literal fulfilment. Psa. 41: 9 (John 13: 18); Zech. 13. 7 (Matt. 26. 31);
Psa. 35: 11 (Matt. 26: 60); Isa. 56: 6 (Matt. 26: 67); Zech. 11. 13 (Matt. 27: 7-10).

K

What absurdity and contrariness, therefore, it would now be to evaporate into mere metaphors the predictions of His coming in glory. "Has then Jesus only metaphorically died on the cross? Has He drunk only *spiritual* vinegar (Psa. 69: 21), and were lots thrown only for His *spiritual* garments? (Psa. 22: 18). Has God only *figuratively* scattered His people among all the nations? (Deut. 4: 27), and are they at this moment only *metaphorically* 'without king, without prince, without sacrifice, without altar, without ephod, and without sanctuary'? (Hos. 3: 4). No, all came to pass *literally* and *actually*" (Bettex). How therefore would it be right, when God in the prophets repeatedly asserts that He will gather afresh the people of Israel out of all the peoples of the world and bring them again into the land of their fathers,[1] to suppose that all this is merely figurative turns of speech? Who gave us the right to make out of the Jews the Christians, out of Jerusalem the church, out of Canaan heaven? Has the "throne of David" ever stood in heaven (Luke 1: 32), and has "this" land and Lebanon, and the land of Gilead, where the Lord will re-plant His people (Jer. 32: 41; Zech. 10: 10), ever been anywhere but upon earth, and in the Near East?

Certainly the prophets often use poetic metaphors; certainly the Millennial kingdom is a typical forecast of eternity, and certainly as regards this earthly kingdom God has at the same time given in the church a spiritual fulfilment; so that the spiritualizing may not be *wholly* rejected, indeed, with the eye on eternity, it is even of the very greatest significance.[2]

But *mere* spiritualizing is a dangerous circumventing of the simplest meaning of Scripture: in view of the prophecies of the first coming of Christ it is arbitrary and illogical, and it makes God a liar as regards His promise. The Jews are already returning to Palestine. This is part of the Bible programme for their future.

Further, the early Christian expectation of the kingdom is

III. The only Explanation of the History of the End which Agrees with the Words of the Lord Jesus and His Apostles

1. *The Testimony of Christ.* In His judgment upon the Pharisees and upon Israel as misled by them, Christ said: "O Jerusalem, Jerusalem, which killeth the prophets, and stoneth them that are

---

[1] e.g. Jer. 16: 14, 15; Zech. 10: 8, 9; Isa. 27: 12, 13; Ezek. 11: 17; 28: 25.

[2] As the example of the New Testament writers shows: Rom. 15: 12 (Isa. 11: 10); I Pet. 2: 10 and Rom. 9: 25, 26 (Hos. 1: 10); Acts 2: 16–21 (Joel 2: 28–32); I Pet. 2: 9 (Exod. 19: 6).

sent unto her. .... Behold, your house is left unto you desolate.
For I say unto you, Ye shall not see me henceforth, till ye shall
say, Blessed is he that cometh in the name of the Lord" (Matt.
23: 37–39). By this the Lord said that the house of Israel shall
not always remain a desert; not for ever shall it remain under
judgment with withered soul and languishing heart: but a time
shall come when Israel shall recognize its Messiah and receive
Him with joyful song and glad acclaim. Being thus converted
they will devote themselves to Him with their whole heart and
greet Him as their Messiah and divine King.

The kingdom of the Lord Jesus is not "of" this world (as
to its origin or character) (John 18: 36), but it is certainly *for*
this world. The Lord Himself testifies: "ye who have followed
me, in the regeneration (that is, in the time of the re-birth of
the earthly creation in the visible kingdom of God), when the
Son of man shall sit on the throne of His glory, ye also shall sit
upon twelve thrones, judging the twelve tribes of Israel" (Matt.
19: 28). And when, after His resurrection, His disciples asked:
"Lord, dost thou at this time restore the kingdom to Israel?"
(Acts 1: 6), He did not rebuke them on account of their "fleshly
conceptions" or give a general denial of the coming of the
kingdom in the visible sense which they meant, but said only:
"It is not for you to know *times* or *seasons,* which the Father has
retained in his own power" (Acts 1: 7). Now this very prophetic
expression "times or seasons" proves that the kingdom of God
will some day be actually set up (comp. Matt. 8: 11; 26: 29).

2. *The Testimony of the Apostle John.* Beyond contradiction
the Revelation of John further testifies to the coming of this
kingdom of glory. In so doing it is the only book of the Bible
which speaks expressly of the "thousand years" (Rev. 20: 2–7).
The placing of the section in question *after* the account of the
appearing of Christ and the overthrow of the Antichrist (Rev.
19: 11–21) proves that this "thousand years" is to be reckoned
from the *return of Christ* and will lie between the "first" resurrection and the "great white throne" (Rev. 20: 11–15).

3. *The Testimony of Paul.* In his second epistle to the Corinthians Paul compares the glory of the old covenant with that of
the new, and in this connexion speaks of the unbelief of Israel in
the time of its blindness. "But their minds were hardened: for
until this day whensoever Moses is read a veil lieth upon their
heart. But whensoever it (i.e. Israel) shall turn to the Lord the
veil shall be taken away" (II Cor. 3: 14–16; comp. Exod. 34: 34).
The apostle here looks on to a time when Israel will turn to
Christ. Then the veil will be taken away from their heart and
they will attain to glory and true freedom. Thus this passage is a
clear testimony that Paul expected a future salvation and reception of Israel. "Because Paul had the promise concerning Israel

that Christ will reveal Himself to them, therefore the hour will come for Israel in which it will no longer honour a law which it did not understand, but it will understand its meaning and purpose. Then will come the hour when it will turn to Jesus." "Moses removed the veil every time he turned to God (Exod. 34: 34). Thus also when the people of God of the Old Testament turns itself to the Lord, is converted to Jesus, the veil will be taken away. Then will Israel perceive that the glory of Moses is not to be compared with the glory of 'the only-begotten Son of the Father full of grace and truth' (John 1: 14–17). This was a living hope in the heart of the apostle."

The second chief passage is the resurrection chapter, I Cor. 15. There Paul speaks of the bodily resurrection of the dead and, in a special section (vv. 22–24), of the times of the stages and order of the same. Of these he distinguishes three:

(a) Christ the firstfruits,
(b) "Then, those that are of Christ, at His advent (parousia),"
(c) "Then the end, when He gives over the kingdom to God the Father."

According to the context this "end" can mean only the end of bodily resurrection. With this takes place at the same time the giving over of the kingdom by Christ to the Father. Thus Paul also testifies to a kingdom of Christ between the resurrection of the church and the general resurrection, the end; and because, according to the Revelation, this coincides with the great white throne and the destruction of the old earth (Rev. 20: 12, 13, 5), this apostle also becomes a witness to a kingly reign of Christ upon the old earth. Only after this earthly time of glory does history run on into eternity.

But above all, here comes into the question Paul's great proof of his gospel as justified by the history of salvation (Rom. 9–11). Paul proclaimed a gospel free from law, without distinction between Jew and Gentile (Rom. 3: 9, 22, 23; 10: 12; Gal. 3: 29). In every Israelite who believed the Scripture the question must have arisen: Does not the fact of the choice and unique position of Israel, which has stood unshaken for two thousand years, give the lie to this message? (Psa. 147: 19, 20; Amos 3: 2; Exod. 19: 5). Is it not clear that either God must have broken His promises to Israel or—since this can never be the case (II Cor. 1: 20)—that this Jesus of Nazareth, as Paul proclaimed him, is not the Messiah promised to Israel?

To this Paul answers:

(a) *God's action is free* (Rom. 9). On the theatre of world history He moves the figures as He will. He certainly does not compel the believer to believe nor the unbeliever to disbelief; but *out of* the number of the unbelieving He chooses certain individuals to be special examples of His power to judge (as Pharaoh of Egypt, vv. 14–18), and *out of* the number of the believing He chooses others to be special agents for mediating His salvation (as Abraham, Isaac, and Jacob, vv. 6–13). Thus Rom. 9 does not deal with the call unto salvation but to certain purposes connected with the *history* of salvation. It speaks less of God as the Redeemer of the *individual* than of Him as the One Who directs *general* history. Here the individuals are more official persons than private.

Thus therefore also the choice of Israel rests entirely on God's freedom, and man, including the Jews, has no manner of right to demand anything from God.[1] Even when he does not understand God's dealings it is for him to be silent and simply acknowledge God's freedom, as the freedom of the potter over the clay (vv. 19–25). Nevertheless

(*b*) *God's action is ever righteous* (Rom. 10). His freedom is not arbitrary. He has just ground for treating Israel as He has done. For Israel has willed to be justified by law (Rom. 9: 30–10: 3), but God has appointed justification by faith. He has commanded it, He has made it possible (Rom. 10: 4–13), He has proclaimed it (10: 14–18); but Israel, on the contrary, has refused it. Therefore Israel is disobedient and guilty and has deserved the punishment which has overtaken it (10: 19–21).

(*c*) *God's action ever brings blessing* (Rom. 11). Even in judgment He has not "cast away" His people but only set them aside for a time (Rom. 11: 1). Even during the dispersion Israel still retains its hope (Lev. 26: 44, 45; Ezek. 11: 17). God's dealing with Israel brings blessing for all:

for the remnant who believe on Christ—for they attain pardon (vv. 1–10);

for the world in general—for it receives the gospel (vv. 11–15);

for Israel when at last spiritually renewed—for it will be received again (vv. 16–32).

So the hardening which has come upon Israel has befallen them only "in part", and only "until" the full number of the nations shall have come in (Rom. 11: 25). Then the branches broken out of the olive tree of God's kingdom will be again engrafted (Rom. 11: 23, 24, 16, 17), "and so all Israel shall be saved" (11: 26).

This is the solution of the apparent conflict between the calling of the people of Israel and the calling of the church from the peoples of the world. Only by the future can the past be recon-

[1] For example, God would have been able to choose Melchizedek, the contemporary of Abraham, the "priest of God Most High," instead of Abraham (Gen. 14: 18).

ciled with the present.   Only by the end is the intermediate period justified.

The whole Pauline gospel stands or falls with the acknowledgment of these propositions.   Therefore whoever denies these prophecies concerning Israel denies the basis of the church.   He denies, if he thinks logically, either the covenant faithfulness of God or the freedom of the gospel from law, that is, either Jehovah or Paul.

The question of the Millennial kingdom is therefore not only a question of final history, but touches at the same time the very heart of the gospel (freedom from law, universality of the gospel, gift by grace).   To deny it makes either God a liar in relation to His prophets or Paul a false witness in relation to us.   Rom. 9 to 11 is no mere justifying of God, but a justification of Paul's doctrine of justification.

According to the testimony of the apostle this reviving of Israel will have powerful effects upon the Gentile world.   It amounts to a widespread re-birth in the kingdom of the Risen One (Matt. 19: 28).   Paul says: "I ask now: Did they stumble in order that they might fall?   By no means!   Much rather through their trespass salvation has passed to the Gentiles. . . . But if their trespass has become a blessing to mankind, and their being *reduced* to a *little remnant* a blessing to the Gentiles, how much richer in blessing must be their *full* admission?   For if their rejection leads to the reconciling of the world, what can their acceptance bring other than life from the dead?" (Rom. 11: 12, 15).

In words which simply cannot be misunderstood Paul here confesses his belief in a full conversion of Israel, and explains that from it the greatest and most blessed effects will flow out to mankind.   In comparison with these new gifts of God and the living energies of a higher fulness of the Spirit, which will then spread forth over the nations, all former national life will appear as something *dead*, all former national riches as but *poverty*, and all former national well-being as *misery*.

But by this Paul declares not only his belief in a future spiritual and national salvation of Israel, but at the same time shows the significance of this event as including national and super-national affairs, affecting world history and the history of salvation.   It is "salvation" for the peoples of the world, "riches" for the nations, indeed, a spiritual resurrection festival for mankind generally, even "life from the dead."

This at once touches the question as to the meaning of this coming kingdom of God.   For still the question arises, to what purpose is such a visible kingdom?   Why did God give such promises to Israel?   What is the *meaning* of this coming kingdom period in His plan of redemption and salvation?

To this we answer that the visible kingdom of glory is

IV. THE ONLY COMPLETE CONCLUSION OF DIVINE SELF-JUSTIFICATION IN THE HISTORY OF SALVATION

1. *In reference to Christ.* Is not the Most High under obligation to give to His anointed King the opportunity to prove Himself to be the best Lawgiver and Judge, Regent and World-ruler, and the One Who understands how to direct world affairs better than all the hitherto existing great and mighty ones of the earth, and this especially within the framework of the *old* creation, in which indeed they have lived and have rejected Him as King? And is it not right that after Satan for thousands of years has shown all the world how he can lie and deceive and corrupt the peoples, that God now on His side should show how He, in Christ, can bless and save and give peace, and this likewise on the soil of this *old* world? "Yes, indeed, this same earth which has seen the ignoring and shame of God's Son, must also yet view His glory. This same earth which has drunk the blood of the All-holy, must also yet partake of His redemption. God's righteousness demands this." Here where Satan has triumphed must Jesus be crowned.

2. *In reference to Mankind.* "If one considers this belief in a Millennial kingdom free from prejudice, one must admit that it were a great and fine thought of God if He were to grant to this poor earth, and the weary guest upon it, after six hard days of burden and labour, a great sabbath in which Christ shall take the reins out of the hand of sinful man and, for a time, personally, rule this world in justice and righteousness according to the law of God" (Bettex). Hitherto it has never been displayed *how* happy and glorious a people can be on *this* earth if it has the Lord personally dwelling and enthroned in its midst. This is in fact the great world-transfiguring idea of the revelation, that the kingdom of God is still possible on the *old* earth. And by this God will prove that it was not the fault of circumstances and elementary powers that the peoples could not live in peace with one another, but simply the sin of man and corruption through the Devil.

Yet further, the end of this kingdom shows how hopelessly lost man is by nature. For what does mankind do after a thousand years of perfect Divine government? It rebels against the Lord and in armed millions takes the field against the Most High (Gog and Magog, Rev. 20: 7–10). So the last testing by God shows the hopeless wickedness of man.

Even from the most ideal economic and political conditions, from the most abundant proofs of the grace of the Most High, indeed from the direct rule of the Lord Himself, the nations will have learned so little, that at the end, seduced by the Devil, they will rush together in the most fearful of human revolts (Rev. 20: 8). Thus will it become clear that, not only is man unable to create ideal conditions, but also that even when they exist they cannot improve him. So this most brilliant period of human history will become the most catastrophic proof of the lost condition of the sinner, and it will be proved irrefutably that God was right when, in the matter of human redemption, he absolutely excluded man's own strength. Now is reached the summit and conclusion of Divine self-justification and it is proved publicly before all the world that from the outset there could be only one way that could lead mankind to peace, even the grace of God alone and the cross of Golgotha.

But, finally, the visible kingdom of glory of the Son at the conclusion of history is:

V. The Only and Necessary Means of Carrying Forward Human History from its Present Stage on to its Goal in the Eternal Kingdom of the Father

It is a fact that in the whole course of world affairs copy and original are at first commingled, but that the further affairs develop the more do the essential features come clearly to the fore. This is quite evidently the case in the New Testament history of salvation.

Out of its present hidden character the kingdom of God will at last step forth into world-wide display. "He (the Son) must rule till he has put all enemies under his feet" (I Cor. 15: 25). This is the kingdom which will finally be manifested, the consummation of all things visible on earth, the most splendid period of its history.

But the Son is not the Father, but the effulgence of His glory (Heb. 1: 3), the image of the invisible God (Col. 1: 15). In His Person therefore the *image* of God is present on earth in the visible kingdom of God. Therefore there remains the need of a historical transition period, which transfers the history of the kingdom of God to the Father Himself. This is the chief, the proper, the deepest divine meaning of the Millennial kingdom. "The activity of Christ in the Millennial kingdom conducts the history of revelation from this last preparatory stage into the final Most Holy place, into direct fellowship with the Father."

Therefore had Irenæus (about A.D. 190), the pupil of Polycarp, the pupil of John the apostle, justly perceived three chief stages in the New Testament unfolding of salvation, which correspond to the three Persons of the Godhead, so that the whole development of the New Testament revelation carries at once a historical and trinitarian stamp.

That is to say:

The present is the age of *the Holy Spirit* Who glorifies here on earth in His absence the Redeemer Who has gone to heaven, and Who calls and builds the church (John 16: 7–15; I Cor. 12: 3–13).

Then follows the return of Christ, and the setting up of the visible kingdom of God for the thousand years, that is, the kingdom of the *Son* (I Cor. 15: 25).

But finally the Son gives over the kingdom to the Father, subjects Himself to Him, and the kingdom of the *Father,* the eternal consummation, becomes manifest. Then *God* will be "all things in all" (I Cor. 15: 28).

In this connexion the Millennial kingdom is the only means for the carrying forward of human history, under the direction of the Son, into the kingdom of the Father. Then "the righteous will shine as the sun in the kingdom of their Father" (Matt. 13: 43).

Bible prophecy thus shows us two chief victorious advances of the coming kingdom of God, two chief exhibitions of power, which stand in special relation to the two divine Persons of the Son and the Father:

the appearing of the kingdom of the *Son* at the beginning of the Millennial kingdom, with the old earth as its scene; and

the manifestation of the kingdom of the *Father* in the triumph of the Consummation in the new heaven and on the new earth.

To these two chief stages of the renewing of the world correspond the two resurrections of mankind, the one before and the other after the Millennial kingdom, as well as the two chief sessions of the judgment upon the wicked and the satanic trinity. Comp. p. 174. It is the taking of all this together which alone enables us to perceive, not only *that,* but also *why* the final Consummation does not arrive with the coming of Christ to the Millennial kingdom but lies *beyond* the Thousand Years (Rev. 20 and 21).

THE GLORY OF THE KINGDOM OF GOD ON EARTH

THE coming kingdom of God is the time of world-wide "regeneration" (Matt. 19: 28). The whole earthly creation has part in its visible glory: Israel, the nations, Nature, and—as the heavenly aristocratic government of the whole—the church.

The glory of the Lord had reluctantly forsaken the temple (Ezek. 10: 18, 19; 11: 22, 23); suddenly the Lord appears again so as to come to His temple (Mal. 3: 1; Ezek. 43: 1–5). The one event is the beginning, the other the end of the "times of the nations" (Luke 21: 24). The goal is "the Lord is there" (Ezek. 48: 35), "the tabernacle of God is with men" (Rev. 21: 3).

I. CHRIST, THE DIVINE KING

1. *His Personal Glory.* "Governor of men, a ruler in the fear of God, as the light when morning breaks, when the sun goes forth, as a cloudless morning, when in the sunshine after rain the young grass springeth forth out of the earth"— so is Christ the Redeemer, David's son and David's Lord. Thus had the ancestor of the Descendant himself testified, the typical David of the anti-typical David (II Sam. 23: 2–4). In Him all kingly ideals are fulfilled.

He is Immanuel (Isa. 7: 14; Matt. 1: 23), the great Triumphant One (Phil. 2: 11), the victorious Hero (Zeph. 3: 17), the one Head over all (Eph. 1: 10; Hos. 1: 11; Ezek. 37: 24; Zech. 14: 9).

From *without* He is:
    the Uniter of His people—
        as the true David (Ezek. 37: 22–24; 34: 23, 24; Hos. 3: 5):
    the Prince of Peace on the throne—
        as the Lord of His ancestor (Luke 1: 32; Matt. 22: 45;
        Isa. 9: 6, 7):
    the Banner of the nations—
        as the root of Jesse (Isa. 11: 10):
    the lofty Tree of the nations—
        as the topmost twig of God's cedar (Ezek. 17: 22–24, 4):
From *within* He is:
    the One permeated with the sevenfold Spirit—
        as the shoot out of the stem of Jesse (Isa. 11: 1, 2;
        Rev. 5: 6; 4: 5). In Isa. 11: 1, 2, the prophet mentions
        a sevenfold spiritual equipment of the Messiah:
    the Priest-King with the golden-silver crown—
        as the Zemach, the Branch of the Lord (Zech. 6: 11–13);[1]
    the " Jehovah our righteousness"—
        as the Divine King and Redeemer (Jer. 23: 5, 6; 33: 15, 16).

[1] (See opposite page)

Thus is He in truth the glorious Nazarene, the *nezer* (Heb. shoot) out of Nazareth (Isa. 11: 1). For "under Him it will bud forth" (Zech. 6: 12, comp. Isa. 27: 6; 35: 1, 2; Hos. 14: 6–8), and He will build again the temple of God and the "fallen tent of David" (Amos 9: 11).

But this all will be from ("out of") God (Hos. 14: 8). The basic fact of Messiah is His eternal Deity. Therefore is He at once root and shoot, origin and crown, beginning and goal of David's royal race (Rev. 22: 16; 5: 5), He is promise and fulfilment in one, He is the star in the night and the break of day, that is, the "brilliant morning star," the herald and bringer of an eternal sunrise (Rev. 22: 16).

2. *His Worship by Mankind.* "From the rising of the sun unto its setting shall My name be glorious among the Gentiles, and in every place shall incense and a pure meal offering be offered to My name; for My name shall become glorious among the Gentiles, saith the Lord of hosts" (Mal. 1: 11). As it appears, a temple will again arise in Jerusalem (Ezek. 37: 26, 28; 43: 7). All the chief kinds of offering will be presented there—burnt, meal, thanksgiving, and sin offerings (Ezek. 43: 18–27; 44: 11, 15, 27, 29; 45: 17; Zech. 14: 20, 21); certain feasts will be solemnized, for example, the Passover (Ezek. 45: 21) and that of Tabernacles (Zech. 14: 16); the sabbaths will be kept (Ezek. 44: 24; 45: 17; 46: 3); and the priesthood will be in the hands of the sons of Zadok, the "righteous" (Ezek. 40: 46; 43: 19; 44: 15). At all events Ezekiel in his prophecy of the Messianic salvation pictures a future service of offerings with so many detailed appointments (e.g. 45: 23, 24; 46: 4–15), and a future temple with so many detailed accounts and measures (40: 6–15; 41: 1–4; 43: 13–17), that it seems scarcely possible to understand these as only figurative and spiritual (Ezek. 40 to 44).[2]

[1] As Zemach (Branch) Messiah is:
    (a) King (Jer. 23: 5): comp. Matthew's Gospel.
    (b) Servant (Zech. 3: 8): comp. Mark's Gospel.
    (c) Son of man (Zech. 6: 12): comp. Luke's Gospel.
    (d) Son of God (Isa. 4: 2): comp. John's Gospel.

[2] Holy Scripture mentions in all eight temples of God:
    (a) The tabernacle of Moses (1500 to 1000 B.C.).
    (b) The temple of Solomon (1000 to 586).
    (c) The temple of Zerubbabel (rebuilt by Herod, John 2: 20; (516 B.C. to A.D. 70).
    (d) The temple of the body of Jesus (John 2: 21).
    (e) The spiritual temple, the church.
        (i) the whole church (Eph. 2: 21),
        (ii) the local church (I Cor. 3: 16, 17),
        (iii) the individual Christian (I Cor. 6: 19).
    (f) The temple of the End days (Rev. 11: 1, 2).
    (g) The temple of Ezekiel (chs. 40–44).
    (h) The new Jerusalem as temple (Rev. 21: 3, 22). "Behold, the tabernacle of God is with men."

The difficulty that after the completed work of Golgotha, and in spite of the teaching of the Hebrews epistle (10: 10, 14; 8: 13; 7: 18), there should again be a service of offerings, might possibly be solved by regarding these offerings as on much the same footing as baptism and the Lord's Supper in the present time, namely, that they would be memorial tokens, representing the *completed* work of redemption, symbols looking backward, even as the Old Testament offerings, done away by the cross, looked forward to the *still to be completed* work of redemption, seen from their standpoint as still future.

But in any case this temple will differ from that of Solomon: there will be no ark of the covenant (Jer. 3: 16, 17), as also no lampstand, no table of shewbread, no veil between the Holy place and the Most Holy (comp. Heb. 9: 8; Matt. 27: 51).

Since the destruction of Jerusalem by Nebuchadnezzar Israel has never had an ark of the covenant. This was a great loss for the temple of Zerubbabel (516 B.C. to A.D. 70). For without the ark the temple was but a shell without a kernel, like a house without an inhabitant; for the ark of the covenant was the "throne" of the Lord, the symbol of His presence, the most holy object in the most holy place (Exod. 25: 22).

For the future temple, however, precisely this lack will be a great gain. And the reason is no less than this, that now *the Lord personally* is present, that Jerusalem is His throne (Jer. 3: 17), that the presence of God is the *shechinah,* the cloud of glory (Isa. 4: 5; Exod. 40: 34-38); so that the symbol, being fulfilled, can now give place to the reality.

This absence of the ark of the covenant expresses exactly the nature of the Millennial kingdom; it is the transition period of salvation to eternity. In the heavenly Jerusalem there will be no longer any temple at all, because everything is fulfilled in Christ (Rev. 21: 22). But here there disappears first a part, and indeed the chief part; but the "shell" still remains. The Messianic kingdom has certainly the germ of perfection, the visible presence of Christ; but the "shell"—the old world—is not yet done away. Thus it is at the same time both the fulfilment of the prophecy and the introduction to the consummation, both conclusion of this temporal condition and also the dawn of eternity.

As such it is the most perfect type of the glory. The earthly kingdom of God is really not the chief matter, but the eternal kingdom when all will be perfected; not the brilliant period of history on "this side," but the full unfolding of the final goal on " that side," not the closing age on the old earth, but eternity on the new earth. The essence of the kingdom of Messiah is the new world.

Yet they are related to each other as an introduction to the main portion, as a preliminary presentation to the final fulfilment, as an entrance hall to the royal palace. They are separated by the new creation, that is, by world destruction, world judgment, and world transfiguration (Rev. 20: 7–21: 1). These are the dividing wall between the "this side" and the "that side" of the earth.

But the Old Testament prophets viewed time and eternity as one. For them first step and conclusion, end time and the other side, earthly and heavenly Jerusalem, flowed together into one single magnificent picture.[1] Thus Isaiah speaks of a new heaven and a new earth (65: 17; 66: 22), on which nevertheless there are sin and death even if as exceptions (65: 20). This can only refer to the *earthly* kingdom of glory (comp. Rev. 21: 4). On the other hand, of the Jerusalem of the End time he says that it needs neither sun nor moon, because the Lord is its light (60: 19), which, however, in connexion with the New Testament, unmistakably alludes to the *heavenly* Jerusalem (Rev. 21: 23).

So the prophets view the close of "this side" and the eternal "other side" as one single continuous line with the nature of "this side," and they depict the new creation of the Consummation with the colours of the kingdom of glory of the old creation (e.g. Isa. 54: 11, 12; Rev. 21: 18–21). Here of course "spiritualizing," in the highest and noblest sense, is in place. It is only the New Testament which draws a clear diagonal line which divides eternity from time.

II. THE PEOPLE OF ISRAEL

1. *Israel's Return and Gathering to Canaan.* "I will gather, yea, I will gather thee, Jacob, all together: I will bring together, yea, I will bring together the remnant of Israel" (Mic. 2: 12; Isa. 27: 12, 13; 60: 4; Hos. 11: 10, 11). Even "if thy dispersed were at the end of heaven, so will the Lord gather thee thence, and thence fetch thee" (Deut. 30. 4).

By the agency of nations and kings (Isa. 49: 22, 23; 60: 9, 10; 61: 5; 66: 20);

With visible signs and wonders (Mic. 7: 15; Isa. 11: 15, 16; 35: 5–10; Zech. 10: 11); indeed,

Under the personal direction of the Lord (Isa. 52: 12; Mic. 2: 13; Hos. 1: 11; Jer. 31: 9)—so will the people of Israel return to their land.

Of this future return the return from Babylon is a type of the real fulfilment as an introduction is to the main matter (comp. Jer. 23: 7, 8). But in fact, with this "second" and decisive event (Isa. 11: 11, 12) everything is mightier.

---

[1] Thus also they viewed together in one picture the first and second comings of Christ (Isa. 61: 1–3; comp. Luke 4: 18, 19), and the first and second resurrections (Dan. 12: 2; comp. Rev. 20: 5; I Pet. 1: 11) (comp. The Law of Prophetic Perspective, p. 142).

The *extent* is greater. The return from Babylon was from among one people; the return from the present dispersion will be out of *all* peoples (Deut. 30: 3; Isa. 11: 11, 12; 43: 5, 6; 60: 9; Jer. 23: 8; 29: 14; 31: 8–10; 32: 37; Ezek. 34: 12). The return from Babylon was the experience of chiefly *two* tribes, the kingdom of Judah united with Benjamin (Ezra 2); but the return from the present dispersion will be shared by *all* twelve tribes, including the kingdom of Israel (Jer. 3: 18; 30: 3; 31: 1, 6; 33: 7; 50: 4; Zech. 10: 6; Isa. 11: 13; Ezek. 37: 15–24; Hos. 1: 11).

The *duration* is more secure. The return from Babylon ended with the destruction of Jerusalem and the driving of the Jews out of Palestine by the Romans (A.D. 70 and 135). The future return will be final and for ever. Jerusalem and her remnant renewed spiritually, will "dwell in safety" (Zech. 14: 11; Jer. 24: 6; 30: 10; 32: 37; 33: 16; Hos. 2: 20), and will "never again be torn out of the land" (Amos 9: 15). The city which in the course of history has been destroyed over twenty times, will thenceforward be no more destroyed so long as the earth remains (Jer. 31: 38–40; Isa. 54: 15; 32: 18; 52: 1; Joel 3: 17).

The *inward condition* is more spiritual. The return from Babylon was connected with an awakening; from that time Israel never again fell into idolatry. But the future return will be connected with the full Messianic salvation (Isa. 49: 8–13); thenceforward idolatry will disappear not only in Israel (Hos. 2: 17), but from the earth everywhere. And whereas the first awakening degenerated into orthodoxy and dead mental belief, this last will consist in a true heart faith and vigorous spiritual life.

This all proves that it is impossible for us to refer all these prophecies to the return from Babylon, 536 B.C., for

(*a*) Isaiah prophesies expressly of a "second" gathering of Israel from among the nations of the world (Isa. 11: 11);

(*b*) Zechariah, about 520 B.C., and so *after* the return from Babylon in 536 B.C., spoke of a return, then still future, of the whole of Israel from a dispersion (Zech. 9: 11–13; 10: 8–10); and

(*c*) the extent, duration, and content of the prophecy do not in many particulars agree with the event of 536 B.C. (see above), and therefore await fulfilment.

From this it follows, that many prophecies contemplate both events as one, but many others, either principally or wholly, the last only.

2. *Israel's Conversion to the Lord*. Even before the time of Antichrist the people of Israel will have returned to their land. This is proved by the facts

that it is in *Judæa* itself that Antichrist will oppress them (Matt. 24: 16–22; Rev. 11: 1–14);

that he will set up the abomination of desolation "in a *holy place*" (Matt. 24: 15; Dan. 9: 26, 27; 11: 31; 12: 11) (see p. 119);

that in the war against the Jews he invades and devastates *Palestine* (Zech. 14: 1, 2; 12: 2; Joel 3: 12); and

that Messiah, at the descent from heaven, will liberate His people by the victory at *Har-Magedon*[1] (Rev. 16: 16); and

by the judgment of the nations in the valley of *Jehoshaphat* (Joel 3: 12–18; Zech. 14: 3–5; 12: 3–9).

But this all (except the last) will take place while Israel is still in unbelief. Not as the "people of God" but as the "Jewish nation" will they return to Palestine, not so much from religious but from political motives. The dead bones which Ezekiel saw, and which signify the nation of Israel (Ezek. 37: 11, 12), come together before ever the breath of life, the Spirit of God, the Lord, is in them (Ezek. 37: 7, 8, 12–14).

Then events in Palestine follow one another very swiftly.

1. *The appearing of Messiah.* "Behold, he cometh with the clouds and every eye, including those who pierced him, shall see him" (Rev. 1: 7; comp. Zech. 14: 4; Matt. 26: 64).

2. *The mourning.* Then "all the tribes of the land will mourn because of him" (Rev. 1: 7; Zech. 12: 10), "as one mourneth for his only son, as one weeps for his firstborn" (Zech. 12: 10–14).

3. *Repentance.* They will weep over their sins, especially the murder of the Messiah (Zech. 12: 10). The Jew will himself recognize his Jewish naughtiness as abominable and abhorrent (Ezek. 36: 21, lit.), and they who in their sins had become loathsome to Jehovah will now loathe themselves in their own sight (Lev. 26: 30; Ezek. 20: 43; 36: 31). Yet, "continually weeping, will they come and seek the Lord their God" (Jer. 50: 4; Hos. 3: 5; Jer. 31: 9).

4. *Confession.* Then will they say of Christ, their Messiah: "We counted Him as nothing. We held Him to be one Who was tormented and smitten and tortured of God. But the Lord cast all *our* sins upon Him. On account of *our* transgressions He was wounded, and on account of *our* iniquities smitten. That we might have peace the punishment lay upon Him, and through His wounds we are healed" (Isa. 53: 3–6). This is the direct sense of Isaiah 53, this great central chapter of Old Testament prophecy. It is the repenting confession which Israel, at the time of the End, ashamed of its blindness, will make on the day when the Lord appears.

And then will occur the great miracle:

5. *The New Birth.* "On that day will a fountain be opened to the house of David and the inhabitants of Jerusalem for sin and for uncleanness" (Zech. 13: 1). God will forgive their

---

[1] Har-magedon means "mount of Megiddo," which last is in northern Palestine in the plain of Jezreel, on the slope of Carmel.

transgressions (Jer. 33: 8; 50: 20), cover their iniquities (Isa. 44: 22), wash away their filth (Isa. 4: 4) and heal their apostasy (Hos. 14: 4). Their stony heart He will take away (Ezek. 11: 19; 36: 26), quench their mercenary spirit (Zech. 14: 21), cleanse their blood-guiltiness (Isa. 4: 4), quicken their "dead bones" (Ezek. 37: 9; Hos. 6: 2). He will sprinkle them with clean water (Ezek. 36: 25–28; Lev. 14: 1–7), pour out upon them the spirit of grace and supplication (Zech. 12: 10), yes, put His own Holy Spirit within them (Ezek. 37: 14; 39: 29; Isa. 44: 3; Joel 2: 28, 29).

This is Israel's spiritual re-birth. From being *Lo-ruhama* she will become *Ruhama,* in place of being Not Beloved she will become the Beloved (Hos. 1: 6; 2: 1), instead of *Lo-ammi* she will be *Ammi,* from Not my People she will become My People (Hos. 1: 9; 2: 1, 23). Spiritually renewed, Israel will enter into the new covenant (Jer. 31: 31–34; 32: 40), into the blessings of its happy "betrothal" and "marriage" to Jehovah (Hos. 2: 18–20; Isa. 62: 5; 61: 10).

This all will take place in Israel's own land, in Palestine in the Near East, and all on *one* day. "Great is the day of Jezreel" (Hos. 1: 11). The Lord will carry out with speed His work of new creation (Isa. 60: 22), and thus "on one day a whole land shall be brought into the world," and "at one time" a nation be born (Isa. 66: 7–9), and "with the eyes shall it be seen when the Lord converts Zion" (Isa. 52: 8).

6. *Holiness.* Thenceforward Israel is a holy people. "It shall come to pass that he that is left in Zion, and he that remaineth in Jerusalem, shall be called holy, each who is written unto life[1] in Jerusalem" (Isa. 4: 3). "They will no more do evil nor act unrighteously on all My holy mountain, for the earth shall be full of the knowledge of the Lord, as the waters cover the bottom of the sea" (Isa. 11: 9). Indeed, upon the bells of the horses will stand the high priestly word "Holy to the Lord" (Zech. 14: 20; comp. Exod. 28: 36), and every cooking pot in Jerusalem and Judah will be holy unto the Lord of hosts (Zech. 14: 21).

Thus will Israel's righteousness be perfect, clear and lustrous, its salvation will be as a burning lamp (Isa. 62: 1), its purity as gold and silver (Zech. 13: 9; Mal. 3: 3), its beauty as a royal diadem in the hand of its God (Isa. 62: 3; 28: 5, 6).

Its capital is a holy city (Joel 3: 17; Isa. 52: 1), its people are a righteous nation (Isa. 26: 2), Palestine is the ornament of the whole world (Jer. 3: 19), and the individual Israelites are jewels that sparkle on the soil of their land (Zech. 9: 16).

Jerusalem is called the City of Truth (Zech. 8: 3; comp. Zeph. 3: 13), its walls are called Salvation (Isa. 26 :1; 60: 18), its

---

[1] [That is, who is registered in God's book as one who is to live and not perish.]

doors are named Praise (Isa. 60: 18), and the King in its midst is the Lord, the Rock of ages (Isa. 26: 4).

No wonder that every heart is full of joy (Isa. 65: 19; 12: 1–6).

7. *Blessedness.* "The ransomed of the Lord shall return, and come jubilantly unto Zion; and everlasting joy shall be upon their heads, and sorrow and sighing shall flee away" (Isa. 35: 10; 51: 11).

"They shall turn with trembling unto Jehovah and to His goodness at the end of the days" (Hos. 3: 5), "yea, they shall tremble and be moved because of all the goodness and all the peace" which the Lord their God will grant to them (Jer. 33: 9; Isa. 60: 5; Hos. 14: 5–7). "Behold," says the Lord, "thou unhappy one, storm-tossed, uncomforted, I will set thy stones in antimony, and lay thy foundations with sapphire, and will make thy pinnacles of rubies and thy gates of carbuncles and all thy battlements of precious stones" (Isa. 54: 11, 12). Here, it is true, the prophet describes, in splendid pictorial speech, the *heavenly* city, Jerusalem above, the golden city (Rev. 21); and true indeed it is that behind the Zion of the Millennial kingdom there lies a far greater and more glorious Zion, the Jerusalem of the Consummation, of which the former will be only a symbol; but here, in the first place, the prophet speaks of the *earthly* city, for the heavenly has never been miserable and without comfort, and very definitely the earthly city is "the city of the great King" (Matt. 5: 35; Psa. 48: 2), the "Zion of the Holy One of Israel" (Isa. 60: 14). Therefore He will build again the earthly city (Luke 21: 24; Isa. 58: 12), and "His magnificent house" He will again make magnificent (Isa. 60: 7, 13).

Then Jerusalem will dwell in safety (Jer. 24: 6; 32: 37; Zech. 14: 10, 11; Ezek. 28: 26; Jer. 23: 6). No foreigner will pass through it (Joel 3: 17; Isa. 52: 1), no sickness will threaten it (Deut. 7: 15; Isa. 33: 5, 6; 65: 20–23), no destruction will destroy its homes and dwellings (Isa. 60: 18). All danger will be banished, no distress can draw near. Indeed, the city will be in truth, what its ancient name expressed, a *Salem*, a city of peace.

Its inhabitants will be heroes, as a noble war-horse (Zech. 10: 3–5), the weakest among them as David, and the house of David as God, as the Angel of the Lord at their head (Zech. 12: 8; Isa. 33: 24). Indeed, Jerusalem will be inhabited as an *open* city, for "I myself," saith the Lord, "will be to it a wall of fire round about and will be its glory in the midst" (Zech. 2: 5; Zeph. 3: 17).

As the place of Messiah's throne (Jer. 3: 17; Isa. 24: 23) the temple mount will be higher than all other mountains and rise above all hills (Isa. 2: 2; Mic. 4: 1; Psa. 48: 1, 2). There will stand the throne of David, the throne of Messiah (Luke 1: 32, 33), surrounded by the thrones of His twelve apostles (Matt. 19:

L

28), who, at the head of a wider circle of judges and subordinate princes, will in His name rule in righteousness the twelve tribed people (Isa. 1: 26; 32: 1; 60: 17; Jer. 23: 4; Obad. 21).

Thus Israel reaches salvation, "to be a praise and a name in the lands of their reproach" (Zeph. 3: 19, 20; Isa. 61: 9), and as formerly the Jew had been a malediction (Jer. 24: 9; 25: 18; 26: 6; comp. 29: 22), so will he now be a benediction (Zech. 8: 13; comp. Gen. 48: 20), and when one wishes the good of another he will say: "The Lord bless thee as He has blessed Zion!" And these are the names by which the city will be called:

individually: Priests, servants of God, redeemed of the Lord (Isa. 61: 6; 62: 12; comp. 58: 12);

corporately: the holy people, My delight is in her (Isa. 62: 12, 4);

the land: the married to the Lord, the bride of Jehovah, the delight of the earth (Isa. 62: 4; Psa. 48: 3);

the capital: city of truth, mountain of righteousness, faithful city, holy mountain, Zion of the Holy One of Israel, "Jehovah is there"; indeed the very same as the name of the King Himself—Jehovah our righteousness (Zech. 8: 3; Isa. 1: 26; 60: 14; Jer. 33: 16; 23: 6; Ezek. 48: 35).

But all this is the work of God, not of human national strength. As regards its origin Israel was the smallest of all peoples (Deut. 7: 7), in its rebellion as a thorn bush (Mic. 7: 4; Exod. 3: 2), in its sins an abomination to Jehovah (Lev. 26: 30). Therefore can now its spiritual transformation at the beginning of the new era of salvation be only a miracle of God, to the glorifying of His name, to the display of His new creating power. "They shall be to Me a name of joy, for a praise and for an ornament before all the nations of the earth," saith the Lord (Jer. 33: 9; comp. 13: 11). The chief point is not Israel, but God and His honour (Isa. 11: 9); not man and his salvation but God and His glory. "Not on your account, O house of Israel, do I so act, but for the sake of my holy name, which *you* have dishonoured among the Gentiles. For my great name, which *you* have defiled among the Gentiles, will I bring again to honour, so that the peoples shall recognize that I am the Lord" (Ezek. 36: 22, 23; 20: 44; 39: 25). And therefore once again: "Not on your account do I so act, says the Lord Jehovah, be it known to you. Much rather be ashamed and blush because of your conduct, ye of the house of Israel" (Ezek. 36: 32; comp. 20).

Israel's transformation is therefore wholly for the Lord's sake. *For the Lord* will Zion be built (Jer. 31: 38), *His* blessing will be seen in everything (Isa. 61: 9), *His* glorious deeds be proclaimed in Jerusalem (Isa. 60: 6). Not on account of the Jews but "on account of the name of the Lord," the peoples will come together to worship (Jer. 3: 17); for *His* name will be hallowed through the healing of Israel (Isa. 29: 23; Ezek. 28: 25), and *His* glory be displayed before the eyes of all nations (Ezek. 39: 21). In everything He glorifies Himself (Isa. 44: 23).

But through this, Israel's re-acceptance becomes a world-wide glorifying of God. The meaning of its praise is *God's* praise (Isa. 60: 21; 43: 6, 7); it is entirely a symbol of and testimony to the mercy of God (Isa. 49: 10; 54: 10), and Israel itself is only the humbled and honoured bearer of the honour of its God: "Not unto us, O Lord, not unto us, no, to *Thy* name be honour, on account of Thy grace and Thy faithfulness" (Psa. 115: 1).

3. *Israel's Evangelistic Service.* Renewed Israel will be God's evangelist to the nations. "Out of Zion shall go forth the law and the word of the Lord from Jerusalem" (Mic. 4: 2; Isa. 2: 3). "This people which I have formed shall set forth my praise" (Isa. 43: 21; Psa. 79: 13), "that they may declare the name of Jehovah in Zion and his praise in Jerusalem, when the peoples are gathered together, and the kingdoms, to serve Jehovah" (Psa. 102: 21, 22).

Therefore also their special capacity for propaganda, their gift of learning languages, and their ability to accommodate themselves to all nations, in spite of the most tenacious holding fast of their own nationality. All this Israel will only comprehend when it comes to understand it as a national talent for its mission to the nations in the kingdom of Messiah. In its condition of unbelief, Israel, as the Old Testament has said, is only a malediction[1] among the peoples (Jer. 24: 9; 25: 18), but then, as messenger of God, it will use its gifts to their blessing (Zech. 8: 13), as bearer and embodiment of the good news of the kingdom (Matt. 4: 23; 9: 35; 24: 14). Therefore "Arise, shine; for thy light is come, and the glory of Jehovah is risen upon thee" (Isa. 60: 1).

But also from the saved of the nations God will send out messengers to the most distant peoples of the world. "The time cometh that I will gather all nations and tongues, and they shall come, and shall see my glory. And I will set a sign among them, and I will send such as escape of them[2] unto the nations . . . that have not heard my fame, neither have seen my glory; and they shall declare my glory among the nations" (Isa. 66: 18, 19).

Through this its mission service to the world Israel will become the "Paul" of the Millennial kingdom:

at first a persecutor and hater of believers (Acts 9: 1, 2; I Thess. 2: 15, 16);

[1] [*Fluchwort*, lit. "swear-word."]

[2] [That is, such as escape when the armies of Antichrist are destroyed, and therefore non-Jews (vv. 15–17; comp. Rev. 19: 19–21.]

then suddenly conquered by the appearing of the Lord (Acts 9: 4–8; Matt. 24: 30);

finally a chief apostle and messenger of Christ to the Gentiles. Israel's "Damascus hour" on Olivet (Zech. 14: 4; Rev. 1: 7) where it—in contrast to ourselves—passes from sight to faith (John 20: 29; II Cor. 5: 7), is the beginning of a world-wide mission to the nations (Isa. 12: 4). From that time Israel is God's witness to mankind (Isa. 55: 4), a blessing on earth (Isa. 19: 24), a dew among the peoples (Mic. 5: 7), and Jerusalem, its capital, is the birthplace of many nations (Psa. 87: 2–6).

III. The Nations

But God's goal is not Israel alone; God's goal is mankind (I Tim. 2: 4; Isa. 40: 5). "It is too little that thou shouldest be my servant only to raise up the tribes of Jacob and to bring back the preserved of Israel. I have set thee to be a light to the nations also, so as to be my salvation unto the end of the earth" (Isa. 49: 6; 42: 6, 7; Luke 2: 30–32).

1. *The Conversion of the Nations of the World.* The nations evangelized through the message of God's kingdom (Mic. 4: 2; Isa. 43: 21; Psa. 102: 21, 22; Isa. 66: 18, 19), will submit themselves to Christ as their Governor and King (Isa. 59: 19). All idol gods will be put down, all human religions will vanish (Zech. 13: 2; Jer. 16: 19–21; Isa. 2: 18–20), and "the Lord will be king over the whole earth" (Psa. 96: 10; 98: 9; 99: 1, 2). "In that day will the Lord alone be God and his name alone be acknowledged" (Zech. 14: 9; Isa. 54: 5). Then will He destroy in Zion the veil wherewith all peoples are veiled and the covering which is over all the nations (Isa. 25: 7), and as *peoples* and *tribes* they will come and turn to Christ, and perceive in Him, the despised Nazarene, the King of glory (Psa. 24: 7–10; Phil. 2: 11; Eph. 1: 10). Assyria entire, Egypt entire, Israel entire will come (Isa. 19: 21–25; Rom. 11: 26), and the Lord will receive them, bless them, and say, "Blessed be Egypt my people, and Assyria the work of my hands, and Israel my inheritance" (Isa. 19: 25).

Here Biblical prophecy does in fact offer its utmost as regards the extent of human redemption, for the hope here is not the incorporation of the converted Gentiles into the spiritually renewed people of God, but a spiritual salvation of Israel, the converted people of God, and of the converted nations on the one basis of the eternal divine redemption. Thus Israel in its land (Zech. 10: 10) and the peoples in their lands will experience a spiritual, divine, new birth (Psa. 87: 4–6), and as the Divine King the Lord will rule over the whole earth, and righteousness and peace will reign over all mankind. Yes, "many and mighty nations will come" (Zech. 8: 22) and "will join themselves to the Lord, and they will become *my people*" (Zech. 2: 11), saith the Lord.

The end will be the universal subjection of the world to Christ (Psa. 22: 28, 29; 47: 7–9; 50: 1, 2; 72: 8–11; 86: 9; 99: 1, 2; 113: 3, 4). Thus it is a mission to mankind under the sceptre of the Almighty, world evangelization with Christianizing of civilization, the proclamation of the kingdom with the winning of all peoples. It is thus to be the most important and most real missionary period of history, and for the first time on earth there will be Christian nations and associations of peoples within the meaning of Holy Scripture (Isa. 45: 22–24).

The fact that the peoples, as peoples, at this exact time turn to the Lord, and not as individuals only, as formerly, has its especial reason in this, that the nations will have seen with their eyes the mighty acts of God; the glorification of the church, Christ's coming in glory, the decisive battle at Har-Magedon, the judgment of the peoples in the valley of Jehoshaphat, God's salvation and wonders with Israel. " If the Lord will deliver the prisoners of Zion, we shall be as those who dream. . . . Then will one say among the heathen, The Lord has done great things for them" (Psa. 126: 1, 2). "Thou shalt arise and have mercy on Zion, for it is time to show her favour. . . . Then will the Gentiles fear the name of the Lord and all the kings of the earth thy glory" (Psa. 102: 13, 15). To this is to be added the facts that the hardened will have been killed at Har-Magedon and above all that the Devil is bound and therefore can no more mislead the peoples (Rev. 20: 2).

2. *The Sanctification of the Nations.* From conversion follows sanctification. "Then will I turn unto the peoples a pure lip, that they may call upon the name of the Lord, and serve him with one consent" (Zeph. 3: 9; Jer. 3: 17; Mic. 4: 2). There will be no more war (Isa. 2: 4), no striving after power, no will to oppress and plunder another; but in peaceable exchange and harmonious intercourse they will mutually and freely honour and enrich one another and serve the common Lord of all and Divine King (Isa. 19: 23; 66: 23; Zech. 14: 9). Health of the body (Isa. 35: 5, 6; 65: 20), profitable labour (Isa. 65: 21–23), social righteousness (Isa. 11: 3, 4), mutual assistance within the community (Isa. 58: 7), avoidance of giant cities (Zech. 3: 10), righteously fixed frontiers (Acts 17: 26), God-determined equality of rights (Isa. 19: 25; Matt. 8: 11; Zech. 2: 11), general disarmament (Mic. 4: 3)—these are everyday national blessings enjoyed by all. Thus the peoples continue their national life, yet at the same time form together an harmonious organism; as the members of a body they will promote mutual well-being, like a family of peoples, full of variety and yet an unity.

But sanctification is devotion, a striving after God, a heart devotion to Him Who has first loved us. Thus will the Shoot out of the root of David stand as "banner of the nations" and "after *HIM* will the peoples inquire" (Isa. 11: 10). On account of His name "they will gather as one" (Jer. 3: 17), and "the earth will be full of the knowledge of His glory as the waters cover the bottom of the sea" (Hab. 2: 14).

3. *The Worship of the Nations.* Knowledge of the Lord leads to worship. "From sunrise to sunset my name shall be glorious among the Gentiles, and in every place shall incense and a pure meal offering be offered to my name . . . saith the Lord of hosts" (Mal. 1: 11). And yet more: "It shall come to pass that from new moon to new moon and from sabbath to sabbath all flesh shall come so as to worship before me" (Isa. 66: 23). And they will then supplicate the Lord (Zech. 8: 21, 22), offer to Him their gifts (Isa. 56: 7; 60: 7), celebrate the feast of tabernacles (Zech. 14: 16), and serve Him alone (Psa. 102: 21, 22; 72: 11).

4. *The King of the Nations.* Immanuel, the Divine King, will be the centre of all. "Unto us a child has been born, a son has been given to us, and the government shall be on his shoulder. And he is called Wonderful, Counsellor, Strength, Hero, Father of eternity, Prince of Peace" (Isa. 9: 6). He will judge the peoples in righteousness (Psa. 67: 4; 96: 10; 72: 1, 2). He executes justice for the lowly (Psa. 72: 4, 12–14; Isa. 11: 3, 4; 29: 19–21), gives favour to the humble (I Sam. 2: 8), grants rest to the nations (Isa. 2: 4), and creates well-being for all the world (Psa. 96: 1–3; 100: 1, 2). He is the arbitrator of the peoples (Isa. 2: 4), protector of peace (Zech. 9: 10; Mic. 4: 3), Prince of the kings of the earth (Rev. 1: 5; 19: 16; 11: 15), the general Head of all (Eph. 1: 10). So will "justice settle in the wilderness and righteousness dwell in the fruitful field" (Isa. 32: 16, 17), and "as the earth bringeth forth her bud, and as the garden causeth the things that are sown in it to spring forth; so the Lord God will cause righteousness and praise to spring forth before all the nations" (Isa. 61: 11).

5. *The Blessings of the Nations.* Thus the peoples of the world reach the promised blessings, and there will be effected:
their final admission [i.e. to the blessings promised]—
through the judgment in the valley of Jehoshaphat (Joel 3: 12; Matt. 25: 31–46);
their spiritual renewal—
through national conversion (Isa. 2: 3; 19: 21, 24, 25);
their political ordering—
through the Divine Redeemer (Rev. 1: 5; Isa. 2: 2; 45: 22, 23);

their international concord—
    through the award of the King of the world (Isa. 2: 4;
    Zech. 9: 10);
their civil harmony—
    through just social measures (Isa. 11: 3, 4; 29: 19–21);
their outward happiness—
    through everyday blessings;[1]
their inward sanctification—
    through fellowship with the Eternal (Zeph. 3: 9; Hab.
    2: 14; Isa. 11: 10);
their common worship—
    through pilgrimages and Divine service (Mic. 4: 2; Zech.
    8: 21; 14: 16; Isa. 56: 7; 60: 3; 66: 23).

IV. THE CHURCH

But where is the church during the Millennial kingdom? As
it would appear, with Christ in heaven, not regularly on the earth.
Since the rapture the church is "always with the Lord" (I Thess.
4: 17). The Head is united with the members, and the members
share in the sovereignty and glory of the Head (II Thess. 2: 14;
Col. 3: 4; I Cor. 1: 9). They will reign with Christ (II Tim. 2: 12;
Rev. 20: 4–6; I Cor. 6: 2, 3). "He that overcomes to him will
I give to sit with me on my throne" (Rev. 3: 21; Matt. 19: 28).

Since being glorified they have no longer an earthly body, but
a heavenly body of light (Phil. 3: 21; I Cor. 15: 40–49), and are
therefore, as spiritually embodied, distinct from Israel and the
nations. The manner of their appearances on earth, therefore,
is apparently similar to the appearances of the Lord after His
resurrection; as glorified they belong to the heavenly world,
but even as He, so can they take part in earthly life, possibly
even so far as to eat and drink (Matt. 26: 29; Luke 24: 29–43;
John 20: 27). But in detail these questions are far beyond our
thought and comprehension. We rejoice at the coming glory.
All details we leave with God.

Thus the church stands far above Israel. The Jews are
subjects of Christ, the members of the church are His co-regents
(II Tim. 2: 12; Matt. 19: 28); the Jews belong to the kingdom,
the church is His wife; the Jews are God's earthly people (Isa.
60: 21), the church His heavenly people (Eph. 1: 3), and as
the heaven is higher than the earth so are the spiritual blessings
of the church higher than the earthly blessings of the at last
converted people of Israel.

The whole Millennial kingdom is thereby a mighty, triune

---

[1] Such as bodily health (Isa. 35: 5, 6), patriarchal longevity (Isa. 65: 20),
successful labour (Isa. 65: 21–23), avoidance of giant cities (Zech. 3: 10), fruitfulness
of Nature (Isa. 30: 23, 24; 41: 18, 19; 43: 20; 55: 13).

organism: the nations are the body, Israel the soul, the church, with Christ, the spirit.   The nations are the court, Israel the holy place, the glorified church, with the indwelling Christ, the most holy place.

But from the most holy place the blessing of God will flow out to the holy place and the court.   From the heavenly Jerusalem, the glorified church (Gal. 4: 26; Heb. 12: 22), the Lord will cause His grace and peace to stream out over the earthly Jerusalem, and from the earthly Jerusalem to the peoples of the earth (Isa. 2: 3).

V. NATURE

Along with mankind their dwelling place will be blessed. The whole earth shares in the glory of its Lord.   With the revelation of the sons of God the whole creation will be set free from the "bondage of corruption" (Rom. 8: 19–22).

1. *The Vegetable World.*   The field, cursed on man's account, will be freed from its curse (Gen. 3: 17; Rom. 8: 20, 21).   The dumb "prayer" which moves o'er plain and field will henceforth be answered (Hos. 2: 21, 22).   The "yearning hope" of the groaning creation will be fulfilled in glory (Rom. 8: 19).   "The wilderness and the parched land and the steppe shall rejoice and blossom as the narcissus. . . .   The glory of Lebanon is given to it, the splendour of Carmel and Sharon: they shall see the glory of the Lord, the magnificence of our God" (Isa. 35: 1, 2).   And, "I will cause rivers to break forth on the bare heights and springs in the midst of the valleys; I will make the wilderness a pool of water, and the parched land springs of water" (Isa. 41: 18), "and it shall be to the Lord for a praise, an eternal memorial that shall not be cut off" (Isa. 55: 12, 13; comp. 32: 15; 35: 6, 7; 43: 19–21; Joel 2: 21–23).

Canaan especially will be the land that "flows with milk and honey" (Joel 3: 18; Jer. 11: 5).   [The use of this phrase in ancient Egypt shows that it was a proverbial description of a fruitful region.]   It will be as the garden of Paradise (Isa. 51: 3), as Eden of old (Ezek. 36: 35).

With flowering gardens (Amos 9: 14),
With fruitful fields (Ezek. 36: 29, 30; 34: 27; Psa. 72: 16),
With mountains which run with corn, new wine, and oil (Joel 2: 19),
With rain of blessing (Ezek. 34: 26; Lev. 26: 4; Isa. 30: 23),
With overflowing harvests (Lev. 26: 5; Joel 2: 24; Amos 9: 13, 14),
With joy and delight in plain, field, and forest (Isa. 55: 12)—
this land especially will now be a delightsome land, and all other lands will share in measure in its prosperity.

Therefore: "Exult, O heaven; rejoice, O earth; praise, ye

mountains with shouting! for the Lord has comforted his people, and had compassion on his miserable ones" (Isa. 49: 13).

2. *The Animal World. Peace between beast and beast.* "Then shall the wolf dwell as guest of the lamb and the panther shall lie down near the kid; the calf, the young lion, and the fattened ox shall dwell together, and a little child shall lead them. Cow and bear will go together to the pasture, their young ones lie down together, and the lion will eat straw like the ox" (Isa. 11: 6, 7; 65: 25; comp. 30: 23, 24; Joel 2: 22).

Peace between man and beast. "In that day I will also make a covenant to their advantage with the beasts of the field and with the birds of the heavens, and with the creeping things of the ground" (Hos. 2: 18), and I "will cause hurtful beasts to disappear from the land, so that they shall be able to dwell safely even in the wilderness and to sleep in the woods" (Ezek. 34: 25; Lev. 26: 6). Indeed, even the serpent, though itself still unredeemed (Isa. 65: 25; Gen. 3: 14), will nevertheless be no more poisonous; for "the suckling shall play on the den of the adder, and the weaned child shall stretch out his hand on the hole of the basilisk" (Isa. 11: 8).

3. *The Starry World* also will be in some way drawn into the redemption: "For the light of the moon will be as bright as the sunlight, and the light of the sun as bright as the light of seven days, in the time that the Lord bindeth the hurt of the people and heals the stroke of his wounds" (Isa. 30: 26; comp. 24: 23).

Thus is it a redemption of world-wide extent; the new birth of creation (Matt. 19: 28), "the season of refreshing from the face of the Lord" (Acts 3: 19), "the restoration of all things of which God has spoken from of old through the mouth of his holy prophets" (Acts 3: 21).

"Let the heavens be glad, and let the earth rejoice;
Let the sea roar, and the fulness thereof;
Let the field exult, and all that is therein;
Then shall all the trees of the wood sing for joy;
Before the Lord, for he cometh;
For he cometh to judge the earth:
He shall judge the world with righteousness,
And the peoples with his truth." (Psa. 96: 11–13).

CHAPTER III

WORLD RUIN AND WORLD JUDGMENT

I. World Imperfection

IN spite of all its glory the Millennial kingdom comes at first to a terrible end. Not even the visible kingdom of peace on earth is the full consummation. Sin and death are still there, with the possibility of the guilty being accursed (Isa. 65: 20); indeed, the possibility of national disobedience by whole groups of peoples (Zech. 14: 17, 18). Righteousness indeed *rules* on the earth; it does not yet *dwell* absolutely in all. Much rather this will first be the case on the new earth (II Pet. 3: 13; Rev. 21: 3).

Nevertheless Satan is bound, which eliminates his power to mislead (Rev. 20: 2, 3). On the one hand this will be an easing of man's lot, because it will no longer be so hard not to sin; on the other hand it will involve an increase of their responsibility, if nevertheless they should sin. Hence also the severer judgment in the coming kingdom of God. Sin no longer stands, as before, under Divine forbearance (Matt. 5: 45; 13: 30; Gen. 8: 21; Rom. 3: 25; 9: 22; II Pet. 3: 9, 15), but is judged unsparingly. The nations that will not follow will be shepherded with an iron sceptre, those who resist will be shattered to pieces as a potter's vessel (Psa. 2: 8, 9; Rev. 19: 15; 12: 5; 2: 26, 27), and the lawless will be slain by the Lord with the breath of His mouth (Isa. 11: 4). Obedience or destruction—this is the alternative for all alike at the very beginning of the kingdom. Every false prophet will be killed (Zech. 13: 3), each people that does not worship will be visited with lack of rain (Zech. 14: 17–19), each nation that rebels will be stricken to the ground (Mic. 5: 7, 8; Obad. 18; Zech. 12: 6).

II. World Rebellion

But at last Satan *must* be let loose so as once again to attempt to seduce (Rev. 20: 3, 7, 8). "God's righteousness does not permit that unrighteousness shall be exterminated before it has become fully ripe" (comp. Rev. 14: 15; [Gen. 15: 16]). This is a Divine rule which will be followed in the case of even Satan himself. Even the Millennial kingdom *must* be tested for results. Even the nations of the kingdom of glory *must* be given opportunity to decide of their own free will. None shall be hindered from freely joining the host behind Satan. No one shall serve the Lord in eternity unwillingly. Even this brilliant period of human history *must* be shown to be incapable of breaking the inborn obstinacy of the sinner.

What in fact is the outcome of all that glory and blessing of a thousand long years? *Rebellion of the peoples over the widest area.* From all the ends of the earth they gather against Jerusalem, the massing of the peoples like the sand of the sea, under the supreme command of Gog and Magog (Rev. 20: 8, 9; Ezek. 38: 39; Gen. 10: 1, 2).

This is the last rebellion of history, the last religious war of the peoples, the last convulsive effort of human revolt against the Most High. Therewith sin has attained its full measure. Mankind has rejected even the visible lordship of the Godhead. They have despised the very greatest of His blessings with most disdainful ingratitude, and His personal glory they have trodden under foot.

And what was their choice? In place of the leadership of God they chose to be seduced by Satan. In place of unity and peace they chose conspiracy and insurrection. In place of the heavenly Christ they chose His deadly foe, the Devil.

To this there can be only one answer: destruction and ruin. But before it can come to a battle, fire falls from heaven and consumes them, and the Devil who deceived them is cast into the lake of fire and brimstone, where the Beast and the false Prophet are (Rev. 20: 9, 10). That of the three persons of the infernal trinity Satan will be the last to be judged has its own internal reason.

It is a fact that, in the whole course of world affairs, copy and original are at first commingled, but the further world development advances the essential elements come ever more clearly to light. This is the case in both kingdoms, both that of light and that of darkness.

Thus in the history of the revelation of the Divine Being we perceive three chief stages corresponding to the three Divine Persons: the age of the working of the *Spirit* (in the church age), the age of the visible kingly rule of the *Son* (the Millennium), the eternal kingdom of God the *Father* (in the ultimate perfect condition).

But the self-revelation of the Demonic also completes itself in three corresponding stages.

In the present age of the world Satan works under a veil, camouflaged as an angel of light (II Cor. 11: 14), as a "mystery" of lawlessness (II Thess. 2: 7), as the *spirit* of Antichristianism (I John 4: 3), for the more part even denying his own personal existence. But then, after he has throughout thousands of years plunged mankind into destruction by means of evil lusts, misleading religions, liars and deceivers in both personal and world history, at the end of the age he will speak to them through the appearing of his *Antichrist*, through the special revelation of himself in the Man of sin (II Thess. 2: 3), through his satanic counterpart to the heavenly Christ. But finally, when this Lawless One collapses and is cast into the lake of fire, he will himself, after the thousand years, step forth on to the battle-field and appear as the direct immediate Deceiver, but will *himself* also be conquered and thrown into the lake of fire (Rev. 20: 7–10). Thus

in the period of the church there corresponds
> to the *Spirit* of God
>> the demonic as an invisible *spirit* activity (I John 4: 3);
in the period just before the opening of Messiah's kingdom there corresponds
> to the manifestation of the *Christ* of God
>> the demonic as the coming forth of the *Antichrist;*
in the period immediately before the arrival of the perfect condition,
> to the final victory of God the *Father,* the *Head* of all the Divine realm, there corresponds
>> the demonic as the direct rebellion of the *head* of the demonic realm, as the final rebellion of Satan, himself the origin of all that is infernal.

Therefore must the "first" person of the Satanic trinity be the *last* to be judged, because as the origin of all that is demonic it is only at the last that he fully reveals himself. At the appearing of the Son the Anti-son (Antichrist) will be judged; at the manifestation of the Father, and so of God, the Anti-god, the Dragon himself, will be judged. The second Person of the Divine trinity triumphs over the "second" person of the demonic infernal trinity, the first Person of the Divine Being over the "first" person of the demonic. "For the attitude of the Father to the Son is the attitude of Satan to the Antichrist. As with the coming of the Father the deepest element of the kingdom of light is revealed, so in the kingdom of darkness the deepest element must be forced to the light and Satan himself be judged."

Thus it becomes manifest that in the whole universe there lies a mighty parallelism, an inner law of consequence, a spiritual law, clearly to be recognized, of historical and super-historical development and consummation.

III. World Destruction

Now the last judgment breaks loose. The universal structure goes up in flames. Earth destruction! Star destruction! World destruction! Heaven and earth are shattered (Hag. 2: 6; Heb. 12: 26–28), disappear as smoke, perish as a garment (Isa. 51: 6); all the godless are burnt up as in a fiery oven (Mal. 4: 1). The earth shivers to pieces (Isa. 24: 19); the stars melt (Isa. 34: 4); the heaven is rolled together as a scroll (Heb. 1: 12; Psa. 102: 26). The splitting of the atom! the dissolving of the elements (II Pet. 3: 12, 7)! the shattering of the universe with mighty roaring (II Pet. 3: 10)!

Such is the answer of the Almighty to this most despicable rebellion of His creatures. Such is the counterstroke of the Lord of the worlds against the most hellish revolt of His universe. Such is the final revelation of the righteous wrath of God over the whole scene of sin, earthly and heavenly.

But then out of this fiery judgment there emerges a new and glorious world. Not mere annihilation (Rev. 20: 11), but transformation was God's final goal in the destruction (Psa. 102: 26; Heb. 1: 12; 12: 27), not mere dissolution but new creation, not desolation but transfiguration. Out of the passing away of heaven and earth (Matt. 5: 18; 24: 35) there will come, under Divine government, a transition of both into a new heaven and a new earth (Rev. 21: 1; II Pet. 3: 13).

IV. WORLD JUDGMENT

"And I saw a great white throne, and him that sat upon it, from whose face the earth and the heaven fled away; and there was found no place for them. And I saw the dead, the great and the small, standing before the throne; and the books were opened; and another book was opened, which is the book of life; and the dead were judged out of the things which were written in the books, according to their works" (Rev. 20: 11, 12).

1. *The Throne.* The throne is great on account of its majesty, white because of its holiness. The earth must flee on account of the sins of men and its defilement with the blood of God's Son. The heaven must flee because of the sins of spirits and the wickedness of the World Rulers in the heavenly places, whose seat they had been (Eph. 6: 12; 2: 2). So heaven and earth must flee from before the great white throne, and every scene of sin is dissolved.

2. *The Judge* is Christ. For the Father has committed all judgment unto the Son (John 5: 22, 27), He is the Man whom the Highest has appointed to judge the earth in righteousness (Acts 17: 31), "the Judge ordained by God of the living and the dead" (Acts 10: 42; II Tim. 4: 8; I Pet. 4: 5), who exercises His judgment in accord with the Father (John 5: 30; 8: 16).

3. *The Standard* is the Word of God. "He who despises me, and receives not my word, has already his judge: the word which I have spoken to you, the same will judge him at the last day" (John 12: 48).

4. *Those judged* are all the dead, the great and the small, that

is, all men of all lands and all times, with the exception of those raised at the beginning of the Millennial kingdom. The Old Testament saints, as well as the members of the glorified church and the saved of the Tribulation time, had been already raised at the first resurrection before Messiah's kingdom (Rev. 20: 4, 5); had thus already been before the judgment seat of Christ (II Cor. 5: 10), and consequently had been already a thousand years in glorified spirit-bodies (Phil. 3: 20, 21).

At the coming of the Son those of the dead will be raised who belong to Christ and whose relationship to the Father is therefore that of *sonship* (I Cor. 15: 23). At the last judgment the deeper-lying regions will awake which had not been touched by the coming of the Son (Rev. 20: 5; I Cor. 15: 24). The final resurrection follows which includes all who stand in more general relationships to God than that of sonship (Rev. 20: 12). Thus the two chief stages of the resurrection of all men correspond to the two stages of the victorious march of the Divine plan for final perfecting: i.e. to the coming of the Son before the opening of the visible kingdom of God on earth, and to the appearing of the eternal kingdom of God the Father in the transfigured universe. Here also, in this parallelism of the events, is seen again that the Divine government of the history of salvation follows its own inner law.

5. *The Severity.* The others must now all appear before the judgment seat of God. All their works are recorded in "books," their deeds and thoughts, their acts and omissions (Rev. 20: 12). They must give account of every unprofitable word (Matt. 12: 36, 37), and everything will be manifest, even the most secret things of the soul (Heb. 4: 13). There the Lord will look into the eye of each, and each into His eye. There will the Judge, with glance of flame, instantly see through the most inward parts of each individual (comp. Rev. 1: 14; Dan. 7: 9, 10). There will the King, with holy unsparingness, drag completely into light every second of their life.

There will they be dumb, the vain babblers (Job 9: 3; Matt. 22: 12). There will they be broken to pieces, the haughty boasters (Jude 15). There will they be manifested in their pitiable wretchedness, all the "great minds" and "heroes" of human history (Psa. 2: 1–5).

There all supports snap. There all religions collapse. There all self-righteousness is seen as a filthy garment (Isa. 64: 6). Deceit is no more possible. No hiding-place is to be found (Psa. 139: 1–12). All self-deception becomes disappointment, unmasked by the truth. Each must bow (Rom. 14: 11; Phil. 2: 10). Each must yield assent (comp. Rom. 9: 20). Each must acknowledge that God is just.

6. *The Result.* Not all receive alike; each receives *his* portion,

that is, the portion that belongs to him (Matt. 24: 51), be it greater or lesser. It will go easier with Sodom and Gomorrah than with the cities that rejected the message of the kingdom of heaven (Matt. 10: 15); easier for Tyre and Sidon than Chorazin and Bethsaida (Matt. 11: 21, 22); easier with the land of Sodom than with Capernaum, the city of Jesus (Matt. 11: 23, 24; comp. 4: 13). The Queen of Sheba will condemn the contemporaries of Jesus (Matt. 12: 42), and so also will the men of Nineveh (Matt. 12: 41). To any teachers falsely called "Christian" God will add plagues (Rev. 22: 18); and, in general, to all pious shams and the stiff-necked He will cry: "Depart from me, ye cursed, into the eternal fire, prepared for the Devil and his angels" (Matt. 25: 41; 7: 23).

Nevertheless not all will be condemned. The doctrine that none who stand before the great white throne will be saved goes beyond Scripture. For the *Revelation* does not say, "Because *no one* was found written in the book of life they were *all* cast into the lake of fire," but "*If any one* was *not* found written in the book of life *he* was cast into the lake of fire" (Rev. 20: 15). The converted nations of the Millennial kingdom have not before been judged and must therefore appear before the great white throne. And when it is further said in the account in the *Revelation* that the dead were judged "according to their works," it is to be remembered that faith itself is a "work," the work and attitude which is the will of God, as Christ Himself declared in the words, "This is the *work* of him that sent me, that ye *believe* on him," etc. This was His answer to the question "What must we do that we may work the works of God" (John 6: 28, 29). And as regards particular deeds, there are two kinds of these: the works of the *flesh* and the *law* done by the unregenerate, through which, of course, no man can be justified before God (Rom. 3: 28), so that he who has these only will be cast into the lake of fire; and then the "good" works, the works of *faith* of the regenerate, which, according to Scripture, and in spite of all redemption and grace, are nevertheless required from the justified (Titus 2: 7, 14; 3: 1, 8, 14; Jas. 2: 26).

The Scripture does not deal fully with the question of how God will treat the Gentiles of the times before the Millennium who had not heard the gospel. Rom. 2: 1–16 should be considered. It is enough for us to expect by faith that God will act righteously. "Shall not the Judge of all the earth do right?" When Jesus was once asked, "Lord, do you mean that few will be saved?" He answered quite simply, "Strive that you enter in through the narrow gate" (Luke 13: 23, 24). At the close of the judgment each will recognize that he has received only his due. This is enough. The rest we leave to God (Rom. 11: 34).

7. *The Second Resurrection.* A resurrection is connected with

the great white throne, the so-called "second" resurrection in distinction from the "first" resurrection before the Millennial kingdom (Rev. 20: 12; comp. 5).

The Scripture plainly teaches a bodily resurrection of the lost. It calls it the "resurrection of the unrighteous" (Acts 24: 15), the "resurrection unto judgment" (John 5: 29), the "resurrection unto eternal disgrace and shame" (Dan. 12: 2). This also will be wrought by Christ, the Awaker of the dead (I Cor. 15: 21, 22; John 5: 26–29), and in it God is the one who is able to destroy even the body in hell (Matt. 10: 28).

Terrible is the difference between it and the resurrection unto life. In both cases the new body has in itself the nature and the essence of the old body, but each in a contrary direction and a fully matured form. In the case of the redeemed the earthly body had been a "temple of the Holy Spirit" (I Cor. 6: 19), its members, in principle, "instruments of righteousness" (Rom. 6: 13), and its resurrection element a seed *of God;* therefore it will be raised unto salvation. But in the case of the lost it had been only a body of sin and death (comp. Rom. 6: 6; 7: 24), its members "instruments of unrighteousness" (Rom. 6: 13), and its resurrection element a seed *of the Devil*; therefore will it now become a body of darkness and damnation.

Thus does all "seed" attain to ripeness (I Cor. 15: 42–44). Every body is at the same time an expression of inner spirit reality; and as the body of the saved bears the imprint of holiness, so the body of condemnation of the lost bears the imprint of godlessness, and it brings them to "shame and eternal abhorrence" (Dan. 12: 2).

Yet even their resurrection will show to the lost that they had no need to have remained in death, for *their* resurrection also is an outcome of the bodily resurrection of the Crucified One (John 5: 26–29; I Cor. 15: 20–22); and Christ, the Prince of Life, whose resurrection power they now experience in their own bodies for a purely judicial reason, would have been able to have freed them, exactly as the others, from the bands of every form of death.

But now this kind of resurrection grants them nothing. It is only, as the Scripture says, the "other death" (Rev. 20: 14; 2: 11); the passing from the forecourt of hell into hell itself, the transfer from the intermediate place, the place of "torment" (Luke 16: 23, 28), into the "eternal fire."

The Scripture gives a fearful picture of the lot of these the lost. It speaks of "tribulation and anguish" (Rom. 2: 9), of "howling and gnashing of teeth" (Matt. 22: 13; 25: 30), of "eternal destruction" (II Thess. 1: 9). It speaks of a "furnace" and of a "place of horror" [Topheth] (Matt. 13: 42, 50; Psa. 21: 9; Isa. 30: 33), of a "prison" and an "abyss" (Matt. 5: 25;

II Pet. 2: 4, [Tartarus], of a "hell" and "eternal torment" (Matt. 25: 46).   It speaks of a "worm that dieth not" (Mark 9: 48), a "fire that goes not out" (Mark 9: 43, 48; Matt. 25: 41), a "sea which burns with fire and brimstone" (Rev. 20: 15, 10; 19: 20). It says: "it is fearful to fall into the hands of the living God" (Heb. 10: 31).   "It were better for that man (Judas, for example) never to have been born" (Matt. 26: 24), and "the smoke of their torment goeth up for ever and ever" (Rev. 14: 11; 20: 10).

PART IV

WORLD CONSUMMATION AND THE HEAVENLY JERUSALEM

CHAPTER I

THE NEW HEAVEN AND THE NEW EARTH

The eternal ideas are God's, the changeable thoughts concerning them are man's. Bettex.

"AND I saw a new heaven and a new earth: for the first heaven and the first earth are passed away; and the sea is no more. And I saw the holy city, new Jerusalem, coming down out of heaven from God, made ready as a bride adorned for her husband. And I heard a great voice out of the throne saying, Behold, the tabernacle of God is with men, and he shall dwell with them, and they shall be his people, and God himself shall be their God" (Rev. 21: 1–3; Isa. 65: 17).

A new world will emerge from the flames of the old: in place of the fragile world of dust, a new creation formed of heavenly luminous matter; in place of the theatre of sin, a super-world of holy perfection; in place of formation and disappearance, eternal abiding and progress. "But we wait for a new heaven and a new earth in which righteousness dwells" (II Pet. 3: 13). This is the heavenly, final expectation of Christian faith.

We consider it here in a fivefold double connexion: old and new world, heaven and earth, eternity and time, spiritual body and (in)visibility, eternal world and symbolism.

I. OLD AND NEW WORLD

The new world will not be without connexion with the old world. The coming earth is not "another" but a "new" one. Otherwise it could not be called a "new *earth*." No, if John sees a new "heaven" and a new "earth," this proves that even in eternity the distinction between our planet and the heavenly places will in some fashion continue. With all transformation and transfiguration, even in that perfecting the new plan of the universe will in some way correspond to the old.

Doubtless the *material* also will be built in, even if in a manner still completely incomprehensible to us at present.[1] God does not forsake the work of His hands. Furthermore, He will never give over His glorious material to Satan, his arch-enemy, to possess and destroy. With the new creation of heaven and earth it is very similar to the new creation of the individual soul. In Christ the individual is "a new creature; the old is gone; behold, all is become new" (II Cor. 5: 17). And yet it is the same man with the same ego and the same soul. "He" has become new (comp. Rev. 21: 4, 5). Thus will God burn with fire His universal material, resolve it into its basic elements, split its atoms, free it from all restrictions, transform all things, and thus He will build the stones of the old structure into the new one according to a new plan. It is as if a piece of dirty coal were shut in a retort, by great heat made fluid as gas, and then afterwards crystallized again into a glorious diamond. Thus God will not annihilate but "change" (Psa. 102: 26), not reject but redeem, not destroy but set in order, not abolish but create anew, not ruin but transfigure.

II. HEAVEN AND EARTH

Not the earth only but also heaven will have part in the redemption. The offering on Golgotha extends its influence into universal history. The salvation of mankind is only *one part* of the world-embracing counsels of God. It stands indeed at the centre but does not occupy the whole circle. The "heavenly things" also will be cleansed through Christ's sacrifice of Himself (Heb. 9: 23). A "cleansing" of the heavenly places is required if on no other ground than that they have been the dwelling of fallen spirits (Eph. 6: 12; 2: 2), and because Satan, their chief, has for ages had access to the highest regions of the heavenly world (Job 1: 6; 2: 1; I Kings 22: 19–23; Rev. 12: 7–9; comp. Job 15: 15; Isa. 24: 23).

It has indeed pleased the Most High to crystallize the eternal thoughts of His redeeming love in us men—so that, without the history of the salvation of mankind there would have been no history of salvation at all (Rom. 8: 19), for Christ, the world's Redeemer has accomplished His redeeming work as *Son of man*. But things in heaven and in the universe are bound up with the redemption of man, things that surpass our whole present powers of thought and that in the Word of God are mentioned only in hints. Here we bow before the infinite and confess our ignorance.

Yet this one thing we see even now; the history of salvation has relation to humanity and to the universe at the same time. Its central sun is God, revealed in Christ His Son; its radiance

[1] For our chief evidence comp. "The Coming Spiritual Body: its necessity, its actuality," pp. 106–109.

passes throughout mankind; but single rays reach out into the wide spaces of the, for us, infinite universe.

But as consequently the Divine humanity of the Redeemer is the fundamental principle of all salvation in heaven and on earth, the earth, this dwelling place of mankind, will become the "dwelling place" of the Godhead, the capital of the universe of the Lord of all, and thereby the centre of the entire universe. The throne of God, which as yet is in the heaven (Psa. 103: 19), will then be on the earth, and the earth, the "footstool" of His throne will become itself the throne (Matt. 5: 34, 35). The heavenly Jerusalem descends to the earth (Rev. 21: 10); the other side becomes this side; eternity transfigures time; and this earth, the chief scene of the redemption, becomes the Residence of the universal kingdom of God. "The throne of God and of the Lamb shall be in it" (Rev. 22: 3). Not only to heaven will the perfected come (John 14: 2, 3), but the heaven will come to the earth; indeed, the new earth will itself be heaven; for where the throne of God is, there is heaven.

III. Eternity and Time

Eternity is more than mere endless time. Not only as to its continuance but also in content it is *essentially* different from everything temporal. It stands to time not in a purely temporal relationship so that it exists solely "before," "during," and "after" time, but in a creative, quickening, and transfiguring relationship. All time is at once "from" eternity, "in" eternity, and "to" eternity.

1. Eternity is the *origin* of time, for time originates from God: "*from* him are all things" (Rom. 11: 36).

2. Eternity is the *background* of time; for the "visible is temporal, but the invisible is eternal" (II Cor. 4: 18).

3. Eternity is the *abyss* of time; for everything eternal is without exception inexplicable. What "endlessness" is can no time-born creature conceive.

4. Eternity is the *substance* of time; for everything temporal has its stability only in the eternal (Col. 1: 17). In Him we live and move and exist (Acts 17: 28).

5. Eternity gives *meaning* to all time; for everything visible is interpenetrated by the invisible and is therefore a drapery and likeness of the eternal.

6. Eternity is the *goal* of all time; because for the Creator are all His works created. They are not only "from" Him, but "for" Him, and "unto" Him (Col. 1: 16; Rom. 11: 36). "Out of the invisible arises what shall come to pass in the visible; but when it has come to pass it flows again into the invisible" (Bengel)

7. Eternity is the *transfiguration* of time. Scripture knows

nothing of the cessation of time.[1]   On the contrary it speaks of æons upon æons, of ages upon ages, and so divides endless eternity into an inconceivable sequence of ever-rolling stretches and epochs of time.   Thus the contrast is not "eternity and time" but "eternal and temporal."   Eternity is not the negation of time but, on the contrary, the substantial form of time; the sequence of one thing after another remains in force in eternity also.   It is only the limitations of time which are absent, its restricting narrowness, its unreliable changeableness, its vanishing evanescence.   Why should God destroy His arrangement, the law of time, which He called into existence *before* all sin, even as it came to pass, "In the beginning God created"?   Why should He not further transfigure His law of time in eternity, and cause it to unfold more largely and gloriously in heavenly sabbaths and mighty Jubilees?   Why should a time-*less* eternity be more glorious than a time-*full* eternity?   No, it is God who is the Eternal in the sense of time-less.   He is *above* time, the absolutely free.   He is the Ruler, the beginning and the end, the Alpha and the Omega, the first and the last.   Time-*less* eternity is therefore God's alone, the time-*full* He has granted to His creatures.

IV. SPIRITUAL BODY AND (IN)-VISIBILITY

1. *Corporeality.* In eternity there will be "material." "Embodiment is the end of all the ways of God."   Holy Scripture knows nothing of a spaceless, timeless, non-material heaven; no pallid, anæmic Beyond for the soul, no mental structure of mere thoughts and ideas, but a blissful resurrection life in renewed bodies of light, a holy transfiguration in a materially transfigured universe.   Truly we can now speak of this inconceivable eternal "material" only in pictures and parables; but it is itself *more* than mere allegory, it is an actual, existing, spiritually embodied Reality.   Therefore the employment in the Bible of precious stones as symbols of the heavenly Jerusalem (Rev. 21: 18–21); therefore it speaks of the tree of life, the river of crystal, of the harps of the psalm-singers and the palms of victory of the overcomers.   Hence alone the justification of its symbolic portrayal of the glory of heaven.   For "in that which is said of God's

[1] Not even in Rev. 10: 6.   For when it is said there that "there shall be no more time," the word "time" is used in the sense of respite, delay, deferment: "from now there shall be no further respite; but when the seventh angel shall sound, then shall the mystery of God be completed"; much as we say, "I have no more time now."   There is no question at all of the abolition of time *in itself.*   Still later in the *Revelation* it mentions "days" (12: 6), "months" (13: 5), and "years" (20: 2, 3, 4, 5).   So Bengel, Zahn, Lange, Menge, Darby.   [So also R.V.   Time is a necessary accompaniment of finitude, for no finite being can conceive infinity; hence time can never cease for the creature, though never needed by the Creator. Trans.]

splendour and light, of paradise and the heavenly garden, of a blessed feast and of heavenly music there lies more than only a 'spiritual' sense. The earthly nature is a promise pointing towards an accomplishment."

Quite unbiblical, therefore, is the doctrine drawn from Grecian philosophy, and especially Plato, of an ideal state containing no bodily element. "Biblical eschatology knows nothing of this fleshless spiritualizing. From belief in creation and Easter it carries in itself the grand certainty of a transfigured new creation of this visible world. . . . God is a God who formed the bodily, the earthly, the visible. . . . He did not create simply a kingdom of ideas, of souls of flame and immortal spirits, but He constructed a world with colour and form. The bodily and earthly does not come from the abyss but is originally glorious and good. . . . Therefore Nature itself may go joyfully forward to meet an eternal Easter. . . . The very act of Christ becoming flesh shows how deeply God is concerned with the earth, but this is proved above all by the bodily resurrection of the Redeemer."

It has been justly said that "as Judaism applied the Messianic prophecies almost exclusively to this world, so did Alexandrian Hellenism apply them (also almost exclusively) to the life beyond. But with Paul we find full emphasis on this life and full emphasis on that life harmoniously conjoined." According to the Scripture the body is not a "prison" for the soul, not a house of correction for fallen spirits, but it forms part of the essential nature of man (II Cor. 5: 3, 4). Therefore Scripture does not teach a redemption *from* the body but *of* the body (Rom. 8: 23). Therefore also the bodily resurrection of the Lord Jesus (I Cor. 15). What inconsistence therefore on the part of so many, on the one hand, to believe in a Christ who rose with flesh and bones (Luke 24: 39–43) and who ate and drank (Acts 10: 41), yet, on the other hand, to conceive of the whole heavenly nature as only symbolic and allegorical. No, Jesus, risen *bodily* from the dead, is the King of this new world (Matt. 28: 18–20). Therefore it must correspond to Him, who ascended *bodily* to heaven (Acts 1: 9–11), and to His own people, who are to be transfigured in *body* to the likeness of His *body* (Phil. 3: 21).

2. (*In*)-*Visibility*. But "materiality" is not by itself equal to visibility. Visibility is not of the *essence* of materiality, but depends entirely on our eyes. So little is visibility an essential condition of earthly material that the latter can at any time lose it and at any time resume it without so much as one of its basic characteristics being lost. Thus at −202 degrees of cold "invisible" air will change into a cerulean fluid and beyond this into a block of crystal. So by heat the "visible" can be made invisible and by cold the "invisible" can be made visible. Therefore the material itself is neither "visible" nor "invisible."

"Visibleness" is of course a very narrow conception. Of all the millions of colours (compare the ultra-violet ray) we "see" in a ray of light extremely few, just as we "hear" only a few of all the millions of sounds. "The Lord God can magically paint around us the most glorious pictures; we do not see them unless they move between 400 and 800 billions of vibrations of the æther. He can encompass this earth with the finest music; we hear it not if the vibrations of air produced exceed 75,000 per second. How unintelligent therefore to object: 'No man has ever seen heaven or the angels,' as if their non-existence or non-materiality were in any wise thereby proved, and not much rather merely the fact that, as regards an angel we men are simply 'blind' and 'deaf.' No, all 'visibility' and 'invisibility' depends entirely upon our vision, but this upon the will of God" (Bettex).

But yet more: all visibility is simply a *lower* condition of the material. Cold and benumbing is its "death;" the crippling of all the powers of earthly material. At -328 degrees of cold not even the strongest acids are able to corrode metals. Only the heat, that makes the material invisible, also makes it strong and free and intensifies its life energy. Therefore also the warming of the material on being treated chemically, until it becomes heated, until indeed it is fluid and gaseous. Thus then it is a plain scientific fact in nature that precisely the higher conditions of earthly material are invisible.

The Bible says the same of heavenly *material,* and it is being shown how here also modern natural science comes ever nearer to the Biblical presentation of the world, and not, as the uninformed assert, departs more and more from it. And were we simply to assume that the angels and things of the invisible had a body of "æther," then the most modern physics, such as Röntgen rays or radio, must admit "not only that such a creation remains completely invisible to us, but also that it and its angels could roam, flow, and fly through our earth and our bodies without our observing it."

And yet, heavenly material is still more than merely æther or invisible earthly material. It is *essentially* higher, more perfect and more heavenly. It is *glorified* material, ruled throughout by spirit; it is *super*-worldly, *super*-earthly, exalted above all conception (see II Cor. 12: 4). Its invisibility does not depend on the degrees of heat and the blindness of our imperfect *eyes,* but on its essential nature, and above all on the incapacity for sight of our fallen *souls.* Only in eternity will our eyes be opened. Then first shall we know even as we have been known (I Cor. 13: 9–13). But then we shall know perfectly, and this seeing will be the true "seeing," this hearing the true "hearing." To a glorified body the spiritual body will be "visible."

V. The Eternal World and Symbolism

But even with the spiritual body it is not the bodily element but the spiritual that is the principal thing. It is a spiritual body because it is controlled entirely by the spirit. Even in eternal nature the spirit is the essence.

In germ it was already so in earthly nature. Every external object includes two characteristics, the one from time, the other from eternity; the one is revealed, the other concealed, and yet it is the concealed that constitutes the essence of the revealed.

Only thus does symbolism arise. All the figurative language of the Bible, all the parables of the Lord Jesus, and in general all picturing and comparing in the human spirit, have their roots in this alone, that the visible is a silhouette of the invisible, a clothing of ideas, a representation of the otherwise imperceptible. Symbolism therefore is the perception of ideas in material forms, a sort of "Jacob's ladder" between heaven and earth.

But this is to say at the same time that everything visible is *more* than a symbol. It is a house of the eternal. "The eternal resides therein." "The earth is full of heaven" (Plato). The eternal is not only the meaning but also the essence of the temporal, its spring, its root, its condition, its "soul." The heavenly ideas are "the melodies of things" (Carlyle), and the things themselves are "veiled" figures of their own future.

But then only the eternal nature can be the *true* nature. There above is the essential, here below the reflection; there above the supreme, here below the shadow; there above the original, here below the likeness; not the reverse. The inward meaning of all the world is what is behind and above all perceptibility. "The originals of things are in the heavens." There is the true eating, the true drinking, the true seeing, the true hearing. There is the true temple, the true altar, the true paradise, the true throne. What we call such here below, though actual in itself, in comparison is only a poor coarse fragment. Here below there is nothing that has not its origin there above.

Nevertheless those "trees" of life will be quite other than all the rough, material trees of this earth. Nevertheless that "river" will be quite other than all the waters and rivers of this side. Nevertheless that "transparent gold" (Rev. 21: 18) will be quite other than all the gold here in the palaces of kings.

Yet some sort of a relationship exists; and even if we do not perceive what this is,[1] but only know that the heavenly is the original of the earthly and the earthly the prophecy of the heavenly, nevertheless this one thing stands unchangeably firm, that there above we shall live in a reality which is far more real

[1] More exact knowledge lies beyond our power of perception. The eternal world is *totaliter aliter*, entirely different. Comp. II Cor. 12: 4.

than the most real things of earth, in a higher physical world of nature of which our present world is but a poor shadowy picture, in a kingdom of truth and of the heavens, which all things earthly yet resemble as does a shadow the substantial body.

But precisely the perfection of the heavenly implies the perfection of the symbol. In the earthly the symbol is only piecemeal. The spirit does not permeate. The material is not plastic. It is not interpenetrated, not completely controlled, not spirit-permeated enough. The eternal ideas are only partially perceptible. The earthly both unveils and veils them.

Not so the eternal. There the spirit rules unrestrained. There it forms the material, there it interpenetrates its essence; there it determines its measure, its form, its nature. There it brings itself to unlimited and perfect expression, and thereby makes the bodily a heavenly resemblance of the spiritual.

Therefore is symbolism eternal. Indeed, therefore, it is only in eternity that it really exists. Everything earlier was only a nascent, a destroyed, or an expectant symbol. But now for the first time the spiritual is *perfectly* seen in the bodily. Now the essential in Nature is perceived right through everything. Now the *whole* redeemed universe of God is a materially transfigured clothing of His Spirit's eternal power.

Therefore also in eternity, with all the materiality of the heavenly things, the symbolic in them is the chief feature. While holding fast the reality of the spirit-body of the things heavenly, yet the chief emphasis is to be laid upon the figurativeness of the speech. Even the heavenly Jerusalem, though an "actual" city —indeed, the first city that can properly be called a "city"— is nevertheless at the same time a spirit-embodied symbol of the glorified, perfected life.

CHAPTER 11

THE NEW JERUSALEM

THE goal is reached. The Consummation has come. The heavenly Jerusalem descends to the earth. The capital of heaven becomes the capital of earth, and the "heavenly" Jerusalem—the original of the earthly—becomes "new" Jerusalem, the glorifying of the earthly, a heaven in this world.

The designation "heavenly" Jerusalem is to be distinguished from the designation "new" Jerusalem. Both describe the same "city" with (finally) the same inhabitants. But "heavenly" Jerusalem refers to the city of God as the capital city in heaven, as the "mother" of the church, as the original of the earthly Jerusalem, until the glorifying of the universe (Heb. 12: 22; Gal. 4: 26). "New" Jerusalem describes it in contrast to the "old" Jerusalem, in Palestine, as the latter's goal, perfecting, and glorifying on the new earth (Rev. 3: 12; 21: 2). It is as "new" Jerusalem that the "heavenly" Jerusalem descends to the earth.

From the "wilderness" John saw Great Babylon, the harlot (Rev. 17: 1–3), from "a mountain great and high" New Jerusalem, the bride (Rev. 21: 9, 10). "Come hither, I will shew thee the bride, the wife of the Lamb." The Bible gives a threefold description:

as the new Jerusalem that descends from heaven (Rev. 21: 9–27);

as the perfected Temple of God, the actual eternal Holiest of all (Rev. 21: 15, 16, 22);

as the glorified Paradise, the super-historical perfecting of the earliest beginnings of history (Rev. 22: 1–5).

The Bible describes the first of these in a magnificent picture. It shows (1) its glory, (2) its foundations, (3) its jasper wall, (4) its pearly gates, (5) its inhabitants, (6) its municipal life, (7) its size.

I. THE GLORY OF THE CITY

"Glory is holiness displayed." Holiness is the soul of true beauty. Beauty is only beautiful if it is the radiance of truth.

Therefore Jerusalem is glorious (Psa. 87: 3). Therefore it shines in heavenly gold. Therefore it is, as it were, a translucent sunlit palace of crystal (Rev. 21: 18, 21, 23, 24). For Jerusalem is the city of perfection, the spiritualized Paradise, the illuminated, God-pervaded "Holy City" (Rev. 21: 2, 10, 27).

Therefore the Bible paints it in the most glorious colours. Therefore it takes the most precious things of earth—gold, pearls, precious stones—and uses them as a prophecy of the still more precious things of heaven, the original of all splendour, the coming city of God.

Hence its talk of the golden streets, the foundations of precious stones, the gates of pearl, the wall of jasper, and the crystal river of life. For the goal of all redemption is holy transfiguration: a holy transfigured humanity on a holy transfigured earth under the radiance of the glory of God which transfigures it by holiness (Rev. 21: 23–27).

II. THE FOUNDATIONS OF THE CITY

"And the wall of the city had twelve foundation stones, and on them the names of the twelve apostles of the Lamb." And the foundation stones were adorned with all kinds of precious stones, as with jasper, sapphire, emerald, with sardius, chrysolite, amethyst (Rev. 21: 14, 19, 20).

Why this foundation? Why precisely the names of the twelve apostles of the Lamb as inscription?

Because the Lamb is the foundation of the heavenly city, because the One crucified by the old Jerusalem is the crowned One in the new Jerusalem, because the apostolic message of the Lamb is the bejewelled foundation of all heavenly glory (comp. Eph. 2: 20).

In his picture of the new Jerusalem John seven times names the "Lamb" (Rev. 21 and 22). The word is literally "little lamb," thus everywhere in the *Revelation*—29 times. It sets the apparent weakness of the Crucified over against His triumph. To John the Lamb is:

1. *The foundation*—for the names of the twelve apostles of the *Lamb* are on the foundation (21: 14).

2. *The guard*—for only those whose names are in the *Lamb's* book of life are permitted to enter the city (21: 27).

3. *The spring of life*—for the river of life comes out of the throne of God and the *Lamb* (22: 1).

4. *The Light*—for the *Lamb* is its light, like jasper, as clear as crystal (21: 23, 11; Isa. 60: 19).

5. *The Beloved*—for the city is the wife of the *Lamb,* prepared as a bride adorned for her bridegroom (21: 9, 2; comp. II Cor. 11: 2, 3; Eph. 5: 31, 32).

6. *The Temple*—for the Almighty and the *Lamb* are its temple; therefore there is no other temple in it (21: 22).

7. *The King*—for the throne of God and of the *Lamb* is in the city: His servants will do Him service (22: 3).

III. THE JASPER WALL

"And it had a wall great and high . . . and he measured its wall a hundred and forty-four ells (250 feet) according to the measure of man, which is also the angelic measure" (21: 12, 17).

1. *Its height.* The wall is great and high, nearly 250 feet, almost four times as high as an ordinary modern house in a large city. Naturally the figures are to be taken as symbolic, and from the standpoint of the conditions of the civilized world of John's time the symbolism meant that the wall was not to be scaled by any human effort. Into the heavenly Jerusalem no one can enter by human progress, or ascent of culture, or climbing upward of man's spirit, or self-redemption by his own powers. The wall is too high. One must enter through the gates of pearl. But these are guarded by angels. Only the redeemed of God have access.

2. *Its lowliness.* And yet compared with the city itself the wall is low. About 250 feet to about 1,500 miles, as if a house in a big town 65 feet high had around it a railing about one-fortieth of an inch high. By this is indicated: So safe is Jerusalem! No enemy can disturb it, no adversary can disquiet it, so completely are all enemies of the Crucified conquered. Jerusalem shall be inhabited as an "open" city (Zech. 2: 4), with doors open all day long (Rev. 21: 25). Between the wall "salvation" and the fortress "rock of eternity" the redeemed shall dwell in safety (Isa. 26: 1–4; Psa. 122: 7). The Lord Himself is the wall (Zech. 2: 5; Psa. 125: 2), and no one can storm Him. "The Father is greater than all" (John 10: 29; Psa. 46: 6; 48: 14).

3. *Its Building material.* "The wall was of jasper," which allows the light of glory to pass through. The new Jerusalem radiates light over the whole earth. It does not retain its light; others shall share it. The glory of God is appointed for all. Therefore the peoples walk in the light of the city and the kings of the earth bring their glory into it (21: 24). The city which has the Lamb as its sun (21: 23) becomes itself a sun (Matt. 5: 14).

4. *Its preciousness.* On every side the wall is 12,000 furlongs, that is, 1,500 miles long, all of jasper, thus 6,000 miles of jasper, everywhere 250 feet high. What are all the jewels of earth in comparison? The largest of all diamonds yet known, from Borneo, weighs 367 carats (2½ oz.). Kohinoor (mount of light) has been famed for long centuries. It is today among the British crown jewels. It weighs 106 carats (not quite 1 oz.). Orlow, the diamond on the point of the sceptre of the former Russian emperors, weighs 195 carats (about 1½ oz.).[1] But *here* is a wall of precious stone some 6,000 miles long and 250 feet high, all of crystal! Truly all things earthly pale before the heavenly, and become simply nothing. They sink into insignificance. In fact, not only the sufferings of this world but also its glories are not worthy even to be compared with the glory

[1] Its greatest diameter is less than 1½ inches, and its greatest height is not even 1 inch.

which shall be revealed to usward (Rom. 8: 18).   Therefore says
the Lord: "Thou miserable, storm-tossed, uncomforted!   See,
I will set thy stones in antimony and lay thy foundations with
sapphires, and I will make thy pinnacles of rubies and thy doors
of carbuncle and all thy borders of precious stones" (Isa. 54: 11,
12).

IV. THE GATES OF PEARL

"And it had twelve gates, and at the gates twelve angels, and
names written thereon, which are the names of the twelve tribes
of the children of Israel . . . and the twelve gates were twelve
pearls; each one of the several gates was of one pearl" (Rev. 21:
12, 21).   They are:

1. Gates which are open—for the cross has unlocked them
(John 1: 51; Acts 7: 55; Isa. 26: 2; 60: 11; Psa. 100: 4).   The
pearl is itself an emblem of redemption.   It originates through
specially strong secretion of mother of pearl by the pearl shell-
fish as a reaction against injury from without, as by the inrush
of inanimate objects, conferva (threads of seaweed), water-mites
and the like.   It is thus the answer of a wounded life to injury
from without.   So also the opening of the pearly gates of heaven
is the answer of the fatally wounded life of the Redeemer to the
sin at Golgotha, even the murder of Himself, the Son of God.

2. Gates towards all quarters of heaven—for salvation is for
all (Rev. 21: 13; Isa. 45: 22, comp. 43: 5-7; Ezek. 48: 30-35).
Toward each of the four quarters of the earth are three gates:
for the Divine glory (3) is appointed for the whole world (4).

3. Gates with the mild radiance of pearls, not with the
flashing gleam of the diamond—for they are gates of grace (Rev.
21: 21; Matt. 11: 28-30; Eph. 2: 5, 7, 8).

4. Each gate of one glorious pearl—for they lead to glory
(Rev. 21: 21; comp. Isa. 60: 18).

5. Gates for the people of God only—for their number is
twelvefold (Isa. 33: 24; Rev. 21: 13, 27), which is the number of
the people of God. comp. pp. 194.

6. Gates under the holy guard of angels—for the angel of the
Lord guards them (Rev. 21: 12; Psa. 34: 7; Isa. 62: 6).   These
angel guards at the open gates of pearl stand in blessed contrast
to the cherubic guards at the closed gate of Paradise (Gen. 3: 24).

7. Gates with the names of the people of Israel—for salvation
comes from the Jews, as Jesus Christ Himself said (John 4: 22,
comp. Rom. 11: 18; Heb. 11: 10).   Abraham is the father of all
believers.   Only he who has entered by the Messianic door has
entrance to the gate of pearl.   The nations will benefit by the
heavenly city through submission to the converted, renewed,
and glorified Israel on the new earth.   Jesus, the Son of David

(John 4: 9; Matt: 1: 1) says: "I am the door: if any one enters through me, he shall be saved." Only he who has entered through the "narrow gate" (Matt. 7: 13, 14), secures "wide" entrance into the kingdom of heaven. Only he who has found "the pearl of great price" (Matt. 13: 46), only to him opens the door of pearl above.

V. The Inhabitants of the City

Who dwell in the city?

1. *God and the Lamb.* "The throne of God and the Lamb is in it" (Rev. 22: 1, 3). "Behold, the tabernacle of God is with men!" (21: 3).

2. *Myriads of angels.* "Ye are come unto mount Zion and to the city of the living God, the heavenly Jerusalem, and myriads of angels, the general festal assembly"[1] (Heb. 12: 22, 23; Rev. 21: 10–12).

3. *The redeemed of Israel.* The names of the twelve tribes of Israel stand on the doors (Rev. 21: 12). In the new Jerusalem dwell the "remnant" of Israel of the time of the new covenant (Rom. 11: 4, 5; Rev 7: 3–8), as also the believers of the preceding Old Testament time, who "without us shall not be made perfect" (Heb. 11: 40; Gal. 3: 9, 14). It is the city which Abraham awaited, of which God is architect and builder (Heb. 11: 10), and for the sake of which the "perfected righteous" (Heb. 12: 23) —that is, the Old Testament saints—were prepared to be only guests and strangers on earth (Heb. 11: 13). "Wherefore God is not ashamed of them, to be called their God, for He hath prepared for them a city" (Heb. 11: 16).

4. *Those out of the peoples of the world* who through the gospel are called into the church. The new Jerusalem is the mother of us all (Gal. 4: 26). We also have come unto the heavenly Jerusalem (Heb. 12: 22, 23). For us also it is the city which we seek, the future city (Heb. 13: 14). Also upon the overcomers from among the nations the name of the eternal city of God shall one day be written (Rev. 3: 12).

VI. Life in the City

Now are they all there, the redeemed of all times, the prophets and apostles, the martyrs and witnesses, the far off and the near, all who on their different ways inquired after Him and in their several places bowed to His truth. There they are now as palm-bearers and harpists (Rev. 7: 9; 15: 2), as psalm-singers and priests unto God (Rev. 15: 3; 5: 10), crowned with golden crowns (Rev. 4: 4), adorned with white robes (Rev. 7: 9), clothed with the wedding garment of righteousness (Rev. 19: 8). There

[1] The Greek *paneguris*, meaning festal assembly, is more than *ecclesia*, assembly, church.

they stand now before the throne of the Lamb, as His servants who serve Him, as His holy ones who see Him, as His priests who worship Him and sing eternal praise to Him (Rev. 22: 3, 4; Matt. 5: 8). And He Himself is there, the sun of the whole scene (Rev. 21: 23), the centre of the universe, the heaven of heaven. Truly, "If the Lord the prisoners of Zion will redeem, then shall we be as those who dream; then shall our mouth be full of laughter and our tongue be full of praise" (Psa. 126: 1, 2). Then shall we see them, the golden streets, the bejewelled foundations, the gates of pearl, the golden radiance of the city, the crystal river of life (Rev. 22: 1). Then shall we see them, the myriads of angels (Heb. 12: 22; Rev. 21: 12), the saints gone on before, the perfected righteous (Heb. 12: 23), all who had washed their robes, and whitened them in the blood of the Lamb (Rev. 7: 14). There shall we see *Him,* the King in His beauty (Isa. 33: 17), the Lamb that was slain, the Victor of Golgotha (Rev. 5: 5–10).

This is Jerusalem. She is built as a city where they come together. It is the goal of redemption, the longed-for of man-kind, the seen from afar, the light-flooded pilgrim goal of the world. It is the inheritance preserved in heaven for the holy (I Pet. 1: 4; Col. 1: 5; Matt. 5: 12), Paradise lost, refound, glorified.

And these are the blessings which the redeemed enjoy:

1. *A holy walk in the sunshine of God.* "Gold" is, so to speak, crystallized sunlight, the visible image of the sun. The "street" is the picture of the "walk," the life-movement and activity. The "golden streets" signify therefore the movements of the holy life in sunny clearness, the God-moved spiritual life in the light of eternity, the holy walk in the sunlight of perfection.

2. *Harmonious variety.* Each one shines, yet each differently. Each of the twelve foundations is adorned with a different jewel (21: 19, 20). The twelve gates of pearl are inscribed with twelve different names (21: 12). The perfected kingdom of God is the glorifying of all Old Testament and New Testament variety. This is shown by the various names of Israel on the gates of pearl, and the various names of the apostles on the jewels of the jasper foundations. Not dissolution but redemption, not elimination but setting in service, not abolition but transfiguration of the human personality in God's goal in glorifying. Holiness is at the same time strongly marked personality. Therefore the picture of a "city" of God; for in the ideal sense a "city" is not an indistinguishable mass of people but a fellowship of members, an harmonious organism, a multiplicity in unity, a conjoining of numerous individual powers into so much greater total energy.

At the same time the names of the twelve tribes of Israel signify the variety of glory of the inner life of the redeemed.

3. *Happy harmony*.   Yet in spite of all variety there rules wondrous unity.   Therefore the city of God is called also the city of peace, Jerusalem, for in heaven is the perfected fellowship of the holy.   That ancient oriental prince, in the period before Abraham, who called his settlement Urusalim,[1] Castle of Peace, City of Peace, stood, without knowing it, under Divine over-ruling.   For from then on Jerusalem, simply because of its name, was through centuries long, a prophecy of the city of peace in heaven, the common life of the glorified in holy harmony.[2]

Shall we know each other again?   Without a doubt!   We know each other here, and certainly we shall not be more foolish in heaven than we are now.   Did not the rich man, even in his torment, recognize Abraham, whom he had not before known, and likewise Lazarus (Luke 16: 23)?   Did not Peter on the mount of transfiguration recognize Moses and Elijah, whom likewise he had never before seen (Matt. 17: 3, 4)?   NO; in heaven we shall assuredly not be wandering hieroglyphs, but one will recognize the other, yes, look into the very depths of his soul; indeed, in a sense, only there will he, for the very first time, really see him.   For on earth no man has ever truly "seen" his fellow-man.   What we now so term takes place only through the clay covering of the body, the fivefold door of eyes, voice, action, countenance, and bodily form.   But there it will be a perception from spirit to spirit, that is, by intuition; no more evasion, no hide-and-seek of the thoughts, no untransparency, but all things perfectly clear as transparent gold, a lightning perception of crystal-clear personalities.

What joy to cultivate fellowship with all the saints who had gone on before, with Abraham and Moses, with Elijah and Isaiah, with John and Peter, with Augustine and Luther; with all the great and the small in the annals of the kingdom of God; with all we knew, who loved us and whom we loved; with all whose

[1] This is the name of the city in the Canaanitic–Egyptian "Tel-el-Amarna Letters," about 1300 B.C.

[2] Comp. the Messianic typical significance of the name in Heb, 7: 2.   The history of Jerusalem in reference to the history of salvation runs through seven periods:

(*a*) The heavenly Jerusalem: the original.

(*b*) The ancient Semitic Jerusalem: 2300–2000 B.C.   As its Semitic name shows Jerusalem was founded by Shemites *before* the Hamitic Canaanites (according to Gen. 10: 6, Canaan was a son of Ham) took possession of the land (Gen. 10: 15–19), therefore between the Flood and Abraham.

(*c*) The Jerusalem of the Hamitic Canaanites; 2000–1000 B.C., ending with the driving of the Hamitic Jebusites out of the citadel of Zion by David: II Sam. 5: 6–9: Gen. 10: 16.

(*d*) The Israelite theocracy in Jerusalem: 1000 B.C. to A.D. 70.

(*e*) Jerusalem controlled by the nations.   A.D. 70 to the Millennial kingdom (Luke 21: 24).   In this period Jerusalem conquered more than twenty times, and so today covered here and there with 90 feet of rubble.

(*f*) The Messianic Jerusalem, in the Millennial kingdom.

(*g*) The "new," eternal, heavenly Jerusalem: on the new earth.

names are written in heaven (Phil. 4: 3; Luke 10: 20). Yes, what an intense joy to greet them all, and in one united chorus to praise the Redeemer!

"Yet each his own sweet harp will bring,
And his own special song will sing."

And the centre of the whole will be the Lord Himself.

4. *Holy Worship.* Here especially are four heavenly rays which constitute the glory of the heavenly saints:

in relation to the majesty of God—
holy worship (Rev. 7: 9, 10; 15: 2–4):
in relation to His nature—
conformity to the image of His Son (Rev. 22: 4; Rom. 8: 29);
in relation to His life—
creaturely sonship[1] (Rom. 8: 23):
in relation to His kingdom—
reigning with Christ (Rev. 22: 5).

But what is common to all, the heart of it all, is that they *see His face.* "Blessed are the pure in heart; for they shall see God" (Matt. 5: 8; Rev. 22: 4; I John 3: 2). "Thine eyes shall see the King in his beauty" (Isa. 33: 17). To see Jesus, our Saviour and Deliverer, to see Him, the Lamb of God, with the wound marks of His love (Rev. 5: 6)—that will be the all-inclusive happiness, the bliss of all bliss, the heaven of all heavens!

VII. The Size of the City

"In My Father's house are many dwellings" (John 14: 2). In heaven there is room for all. This is expressed figuratively by the gigantic measurements of the new Jerusalem—1,500 miles long, 1,500 miles broad, 1,500 miles high, that is, say, 3,000 millions of cubic miles in the whole. All the buildings in the world, all houses and halls, all cities and villages, everything which the 2,000 millions of men today inhabit, taken together do not make 300 cubic miles. Thus there is room in the heavenly Jerusalem for hundreds of thousands of generations, and yet, according to Biblical chronology, only 200 generations have passed since Adam.

But the numbers are not to be taken literally. What matters is the colossal vastness and the symbolic meaning of the sacred number twelve. Even while holding firmly the *embodiment* of spirit, it must be said that the figurative mirror of the eternal is by no means the same as the essence and content of the eternal. John himself testifies that the measure which the angel has is a human measure (Rev. 21: 17), that is, that the angel employed

[1] [Such sonship as created beings can receive, in distinction from the eternal sonship of the "only begotten Son."]

N

human measures and forms, so as to bring the infinite to the consciousness of the finite spirit. He spoke to him in pictures of human conception, but the eternal itself is inconceivable, beyond our perception, super-earthly, super-worldly, simply "the other." The reality of its substance is therefore far from denoting the verbal literality of its measurements. The form in which its spirit embodiment is presented is figurative, the spirit embodiment itself is actual.[1] The revelation therefore does not claim to give a description but only a hint of the eternal; what matters is not the form but that which forms it; the meaning is the ultimate, not its symbol. [Thus the tabernacle made by Moses was not a copy of the actual true sanctuary in the heavens but of a pattern of the latter: the original was the important matter, rather than the copy (Exod. 25: 40; Heb. 8: 5).]

The ruling basic number is twelve: twelve foundations, twelve precious stones, twelve names of the apostles, twelve gates, twelve angels, twelve inscriptions on the gates, 12 times 12 the height of the wall, 12,000 furlongs the extent of the city on all sides.

But why this precise number everywhere? Three is the number of God; four is the number of the world.[2] Three plus four (3 + 4) is the number of the *covenant* between God and the world, therefore seven is the number of salvation's history.[3]

Three times four (3 × 4) is the number of the world so far as it is made fruitful by God, so far as it is His vineyard and tilled land, His seed and His harvest; the earthly (4) multiplied by the heavenly (3), the creation developed and blessed by the Creator. This means that 12 is the number of the people of God, and therefore the number of the communion of saints. Therefore 12 tribes, 12 princes (Num. 1: 44), 12 stars (Rev. 12: 1), 12 loaves of shewbread, 12 apostles, 12 thrones (Matt. 19: 28).

---

[1] Therefore the changes in the self-revelation of the unchangeable. Thus the angel of Jehovah appears now as flame (Exod. 3: 2), now as voice (I Sam. 3: 2–9), now with a form of light, now as an ordinary man (Gen. 18. 1–8), and similarly angels in general (Dan. 10: 4–6; comp. Heb. 13: 2). So also the cherubim appear now with four wings (Ezek. 1: 6), now with six wings (Rev. 4: 8), now with four faces (Ezek. 1: 6, 10), now with one face (Rev. 4: 7). Far from seeing here any "contradictions," we rather perceive in this a proof that the form of prophetic revelation and presentation is symbolic, and also of the susceptibility of heavenly material to change of form, that is, of the freedom of the spirit in its spirit body.

[2] Four "building stones" of the universe (number, time, space, material), 4 quarters of the heavens, 4 seasons of the year, 4 dimensions (according to the old conception—length, breadth, depth, height: Eph. 3: 18), 4 elements (according to the old conception—fire, water, earth, air: Nah. 1: 3–6), 4 world empires (the 4 beasts of Daniel; the life of the world in its estrangement from God: Dan. 7), 4 cherubim (the 4 living creatures of Ezekiel—the life of the world in the service of God: Ezek. 1: 10; Rev. 4), 4 Gospels (the message of salvation for the whole world).

[3] Therefore 7 days of creation (including the sabbath), 7 chief festivals in Israel (Lev. 23), 7 days of the week, 7 churches (Rev. 2 and 3), 7 seals, 7 trumpets, 7 bowls of wrath, 7 thunders, 7 stars.

Therefore the heavenly Jerusalem is ruled by the number 12, because it is the dwelling place of the redeemed church.

But yet more. In the number 12,000 which the book of the Revelation gives as the measure of the Heavenly City, twelve is further multiplied by a thousand, that is, by the result of multiplying the number ten three times by itself ($12 \times 10 \times 10 \times 10$). So the number 12,000, according to the Biblical symbolic language, presents itself as the result of multiplying the number of the people of God (12) by the number of completion and conclusion(10),[1] and this three times (three being the Divine number). By this it indicates that in the heavenly Jerusalem the *people of God*, the church, will have reached its God-appointed goal in full glory and perfection, it will be the eternally glorified church.

And that the City is represented as a cube, being in all its dimensions (Eph. 3: 18) ruled by the same number 12,000 (Rev. 21: 16), expresses likewise the idea of perfection: it is proportionate on all sides, symmetrical in all its parts, one harmonious whole, the eternal glory.

[1] Ten is the last of the numerals, therefore the number of conclusion, of completed unfolding, the end of development. Noah is the tenth from Adam, Abraham the tenth from Noah; the fourth antichristian empire ends as a ten-horned kingdom (Dan. 7: 24); 3 and 7 are numbers of God, 4 and 10 numbers of the world.

CHAPTER III

THE PERFECTED TEMPLE OF GOD

Behold the tabernacle of God is with men (Rev. 21: 3).

GLORY is the radiance of holiness. Holiness is the essential basis of all glory. The All-glorious must therefore be at the same time the All-holy.

1. *The cubical form.* For this reason in former days in the tabernacle and temple the perfection of the All-glorious was symbolized by the cubical form of the All-holiest (Exod. 36: 15–30); for the cube is the figure of perfection (See p. 195.) And since the new Jerusalem is also presented as a cube (Rev. 21: 16; comp. Ezek. 48: 16), it is thereby taught that it is the perfect, heavenly All-holiest.

2. *The absence of a temple.* Under the old covenant there was a temple *in* the city; in the perfect condition the city itself will be the temple. The presence of a temple in the former time was based always upon a distinction between temple and non-temple; between priestly and non-priestly ground, between all-holy and not-all-holy (comp. Ezek. 42: 20). A temple was a section, a part cut out,[1] a limited area, a projection of the eternal world into the earthly, and this in a but shadowy and typical manner (Col. 2: 17; Heb. 10: 1). But here *all* is the All-holy. Here is the purest and most spiritual worship. Here the tabernacle of God is with men (Rev. 21: 3; John 4: 24). Therefore can there be here no separate temple area: "I saw no temple therein" (Rev. 21: 22). A temple in the new city would be a piece of the old world in the midst of the new, an indication of imperfection amidst perfection, a principle of the world of shadows amidst the world of the essential. Therefore the disappearance of the temple is a sign of the perfecting of the idea of a temple. This is further proved by:

3. *The foundation of precious stones.* On the breast-plate of the high priest under the old covenant the twelve tribes of Israel were represented by twelve different jewels (Exod. 28: 17–21, 29). Also the twelve foundation stones of the heavenly city are adorned with twelve radiant jewels; which means that the heavenly Jerusalem rests, as did the earthly, on the ground of a high priesthood. But it has not only an Aaronic basis, but also that of Melchizedek (Heb. 7); it is supported by the person and the

---

[1] According to its derivation the very word "temple" comes from the Greek *temno*, I cut.

work of the eternal High Priest.   From all of which it follows
that the new Jerusalem is the perfected temple of God.

Therefore also there is

4. *No longer an ark of the covenant,* for the throne of God itself
is in the city (Jer. 3: 16, 17; Rev. 22: 1, 3).   Therefore, too,

5. *There is no more sunlight,* for in the Holiest of all there never
was created light.   Only in the holy place was there light, that
is, from the seven-branched lampstand.   The Holiest of all was
dark (I Kings 8: 12; comp. Exod. 20: 21).   For God "dwells in
a light which no one can approach" (I Tim. 6: 16).   His invisibility could be expressed figuratively only by the absence of every
creaturely light, that is, the absolute Light only by symbolical
darkness.   But in the new Jerusalem His face will be seen
(Rev. 22: 4; Matt. 5: 8; I John 3: 2).   Therefore *this* Holiest
of all is no longer dark, but filled with radiant brilliance (Rev.
21: 11).   "The Lord, God, will shine upon them" (Rev. 22: 5).
"The city needs no sun or moon to shine in it; for the glory of
God illumines it, and its light is the Lamb" (Rev. 21: 22; 22: 5).
Therefore

6. *God's name is on the foreheads of the glorified,* for each one is
consecrated to God, as was the high priest (Rev. 22: 4; Exod.
28: 36; Zech. 14: 20, 21).   Therefore

7. *The radiant jasper-shekinah,*[1] for the glory of God illumin-
ates the entire heavenly temple (Rev. 21: 11; Isa. 4: 5; Exod. 40:
34–38).

But with the idea of the temple is connected the thought of
Paradise.   The Holiest of all, paradise, and heaven belong
together.

In the temple is the shewbread, the emblem of life—[2]
in Paradise, the tree of life.

In the temple is the lampstand, the emblem of knowledge—
in Paradise, the tree of knowledge.

In the temple are the flowers,[3] the emblem of beauty—
in Paradise, the flowering magnificence.

[1] "Shekinah" (from the Hebrew *shachan,* to settle, dwell, remain) was the
word used by the Rabbis of the shining cloud of the glory of God (comp. Exod.
14: 19; 40: 34; I Kings 8: 10).

[2] Compare John 6: 48–51; and the pot of manna in the ark of the covenant
(Heb. 9: 4; Rev. 2: 17).

[3] So especially the cups, flowers, and almond blossoms on the tree of light
of the seven-branched lampstand (Exod. 25: 31–34; lit.).   Further the golden rims
(or wreaths or garlands) around the table of shewbread, incense altar, and ark of the
covenant (Exod. 25: 24, 25; 30: 3, 4; 25: 11); and also the pomegranates on the
robe of the high priest (Exod. 28: 33, 34).   Comp. also in the ark of the covenant,
Aaron's rod that had budded (Heb. 9: 4).   Life in the sanctuary of God is "bloom-
ing" life (Psa. 92: 13, 14).

The temple was closed, the emblem of separation[1]—
before Paradise stood the cherubim (Gen. 3: 24).

But in Christ all is perfected and made new.   He is the great
Preparer of the way and Opener of the door.   In Him Paradise
and the All-holy are thrown open.

Now everything is accomplished.   Heaven is open.   But
heaven is Jerusalem, Jerusalem is the All-holy, and the All-holy
is the heavenly, glorified Paradise.

---

[1] The Holy place could be entered only by priests and the high priest, the
Holiest of all by the last only and by him but once a year (Heb. 9: 6–8).

CHAPTER IV

THE GLORIFIED PARADISE

"He who overcomes, to him will I give to eat of the tree of life, which is in the Paradise of God" (Rev. 2: 7).

THE end of history and the beginning of history belong together. The last leaf of the Bible corresponds with the first. Holy Scripture begins with Paradise (Gen. 1: 2); with Paradise it ends (Rev. 22).

But the conclusion is greater than the beginning. The Omega is more powerful than the Alpha. The future Paradise is not only the lost and regained, but above all the heavenly and eternally glorified Paradise.

In the lost Paradise there was danger: "On the day on which you eat thereof you will die the death" (Gen. 2: 17); in the glorified Paradise full security reigns. "There shall be no more curse" (Rev. 22: 3).

In the lost Paradise the *serpent* said: "You will become as God" (Gen. 3: 5); in the glorified Paradise the *Scripture itself* says: "His name (that is, His nature) shall be on their foreheads" (Rev. 22: 4).

In the lost Paradise stood a tree of knowledge (Gen. 2: 9); in the glorified one it is no longer required (Rev. 22: 1–5); for the perfected behold with direct vision the face of God (Rev. 22: 4).

The lost Paradise had an end through the defeat of man (Gen. 3: 24); the glorified Paradise abides eternally for the overcomers (Rev. 2: 7). "They shall reign for ever and ever" (Rev. 22: 5).

There one tree of life (Gen. 2: 9); here whole avenues of trees of life (Rev. 22: 2; 2: 7).[1]

[1] "The leaves of the tree serve for healing the nations." It would be wrong to draw from these words the inference that on the new earth the healing process for mankind will still continue, so that for those who before the great white throne might be still not completely justified there would yet remain a hope that, as nations on the new earth, they may at last partake of full salvation. This would mean that even *after* the great white throne there would still be a salvation for the judged, until at last all, without exception, would experience full redemption. Upon this Dr. F. Düsterdieck remarks: "The expression is just as little to be pressed to mean that a *then still* present sickness of the nations is supposed, as we are permitted to draw the inference from Rev. 21: 4 that the tears which God will wipe away from the blessed are signs of *then still* present pain. It much rather means that just as the tears which they had shed on account of *earthly* suffering will be wiped away in the eternal life, so the healing leaves of the tree of life serve for the healing of the sickness from which the nations *had* suffered during their *earthly* life, but shall never suffer again in the new earth."

There a river of water out of Eden (Gen. 2: 10–14); here a river of life from the throne of God (Rev. 22: 1; comp. Ezek. 47).

There lordship over the earth alone (Gen. 1: 28–30; 2: 19, 20); here lordship over the universe (I Cor. 6: 2, 3).

There a created sun; here the eternal, the Creator, God Himself the sun (Rev. 22: 5).

Thus everything in every respect is a "new creation":

on us   — a new name (Rev. 2: 17);
in us   — a new song (Rev. 5: 9; 14: 3);
around us — a new Jerusalem (Rev. 3: 12; 21: 2);
under us — a new earth (Rev. 21: 1);
over us   — a new heaven (Rev. 21: 1);
before us — always new revelations of the never-ending
                 love of God (Rev. 3: 12)[1]

Truly, "He who sits on the throne said: 'Behold, I make *all things* new" (Rev. 21: 5).

We behold with worship this age-long plan of God.   The record of salvation in the Bible has conducted us from the gate of eternity *before* all time to the gate of eternity *after* this time. "The final end is the glorified and eternally new beginning." The goal is exactly as the commencement (Psa. 90: 2), GOD HIMSELF.

"THAT GOD MAY BE ALL IN ALL"
(I COR. 15: 28).

But He Himself, the King of the ages (I Tim. 1: 17, lit.), will then bring forth ages upon ages out of His inexhaustible, infinite fulness (Rev. 22: 5; Eph. 2: 7, lit.).   In heavenly Jubilees will His redeemed creatures praise Him, and through the spheres and worlds of the new creation will ring and resound the triumphant, exultant song:

"UNTO HIM THAT SITTETH UPON THE THRONE, AND UNTO THE LAMB, BE THE BLESSING, AND THE HONOUR, AND THE GLORY, AND THE DOMINION,

"FROM ETERNITY TO ETERNITY! Amen" (Rev. 5: 13, 14).

---

[1] This is intimated by the "new name" of the Redeemer in the perfected condition (Rev. 3: 12).   The name signifies the nature; and that in the glorified state the Lord will reveal Himself by a new name means that in the future He will give quite new revelations of His glory never before seen, so as by kindness to display in the coming ages the exceeding riches of His grace (Eph. 2: 7).

HOMILETIC INFORMATION

(List of the Ninety outlines for Biblical Addresses included in the Text.)

Introductory Remarks

Our age needs the proclamation of the counsels of God unto salvation. Amidst all the conflict and controversy concerning the essence of the gospel *positive* presentation of the Divine message is the most effective, victorious weapon. God's mighty plan of salvation must be more and more clearly understood, and in public preaching be more and more energetically declared. To this end the outline addresses scattered throughout this book may render some service. To brethren engaged in the work of the Lord they may be a help in their work and may incite to further meditation.

In addition, the very numerous (about 3,700) Scripture references are calculated to help those who will use what is here offered in preparation for preaching the word, and especially in private Bible *study*. Not seldom they are at the same time an expansion of the line of thought.

The outlines are in part very short, offering only certain main points, and purposely leaving the proper working out to the mind of the reader (e.g. pages 84, 85). But sometimes whole chapters may likewise be used as outlines of Biblical addresses or lectures. In such case there is more detail and explanation.

Not all chapters are outlines. The book is not in the first instance for the preparation of addresses, but an attempt to give an outline picture of the New Testament historical revelation.

In the following Homiletic Index the short outlines are shown with one page number, the more detailed with more than one page number. In every case—particularly with the short outlines—it is recommended to observe the whole context.

INDEX